The publisher and the University of California Press Foundation gratefully acknowledge the generous support of the Constance and William Withey Endowment Fund in History and Music.

Tasting Qualities

ATELIER: ETHNOGRAPHIC INQUIRY IN THE
TWENTY-FIRST CENTURY

Kevin Lewis O'Neill, Series Editor

Tasting Qualities

THE PAST AND FUTURE OF TEA

Sarah Besky

UNIVERSITY OF CALIFORNIA PRESS

University of California Press
Oakland, California

© 2020 by Sarah Besky

Library of Congress Cataloging-in-Publication Data

Names: Besky, Sarah, author.
Title: Tasting qualities : the past and future of tea / Sarah Besky.
Other titles: Atelier (Oakland, Calif.) ; 5.
Description: Oakland, California : University of California Press, [2020] |
    Series: Atelier: ethnographic inquiry in the twenty-first century; 5 |
    Includes bibliographical references and index.
Identifiers: LCCN 2019042808 (print) | LCCN 2019042809 (ebook) |
    ISBN 9780520303249 (cloth) | ISBN 9780520303256 (paperback) | ISBN
    9780520972704 (ebook)
Subjects: LCSH: Tea trade—India—Quality control.
Classification: LCC HD9198.I42 B47 2020 (print) | LCC HD9198.I42 (ebook) |
    DDC 338.1/73720954—dc23

LC record available at https://lccn.loc.gov/2019042808
LC ebook record available at https://lccn.loc.gov/2019042809

Manufactured in the United States of America

25 24 23 22 21 20 19 20
10 9 8 7 6 5 4 3 2 1

CONTENTS

ILLUSTRATIONS

TABLE

FIGURES

ACKNOWLEDGMENTS

This project has been a very long time in the making. I started research for it in 2008, with the support of an American Institute of Indian Studies Junior Fellowship. I went to the tea auctions of Kolkata to try to understand how international agricultural certifications like organic, fair trade, biodynamic, and Rainforest Alliance affected the way that tea was valued. The short answer was that these certifications didn't really shape valuation practice at all. I then spent months observing tasting and auctioning for many kinds of tea, which in summer 2008 fundamentally changed with the introduction of computerized auctioning. Ethnographic narratives from this pivotal moment in the Indian tea industry became the nucleus of this book. I owe a great debt of gratitude to the many tea brokers, buyers, and blenders in Kolkata and Siliguri who allowed me to follow them as they tasted tea, sit in on auctions, and ask them about their work. I also would like to extend a very special thanks to the Asian and African Studies Reading Room staff at the British Library, as well as the staff of the Indian Tea Association (ITA) Calcutta, the National Library in Kolkata, the London Metropolitan Archives, and the Cambridge South Asia archive.

This project was made possible with the financial support of Fulbright Hays, the American Council of Learned Societies, the Andrew Mellon Foundation, the University of Wisconsin–Madison, the Michigan Society of Fellows, and the Center for Contemporary South Asia at Brown University. A Hunt Fellowship from the Wenner-Gren Foundation funded a teaching leave so that I could complete the final stages of writing.

Since this project entailed more than ten years of research and writing, there are many people to thank for helping make it possible. In addition to the support of my colleagues at the University of Wisconsin and Brown

University, this project incubated during my time in the Society of Fellows at Michigan. The comradery and intellectual support I found there helped usher this book into being. My thanks to all the fellows, with special thanks to Donald Lopez and Linda Turner.

Colleagues at the following institutions graciously listened to and provided valuable feedback on sections or chapters of this book: Brown University; Stanford Graduate School of Business; University of Toronto; Emory University; the Holtz Center and the Center for Culture, History, and Environment at University of Wisconsin–Madison; Brandeis University; Rice University; University of Washington–Seattle; University of Chicago; MIT's Sloan School of Management; Dartmouth College; University of Freiburg; Southern Methodist University; School for Advanced Research in Santa Fe; Heidelberg University; University of Zürich; University of Edinburgh; University of Cologne; North Carolina State University; University of California, Santa Cruz; and University of Michigan.

I owe a great debt to Dwai Banerjee, Ashley Carse, Poulomi Saha, and Aarti Sethi for providing their warm and generous feedback on an early draft of the manuscript. In addition, conversations with friends and colleagues over the past several years have stretched and strengthened this book: Nikhil Anand, Alex Blanchette, Jane Collins, Jason Cons, Nick D'Avella, Elizabeth Ferry, Shaila Seshia Galvin, Radhika Govindrajan, Jill Harrison, Karen Hébert, Mythri Jegathesan, Stuart Kirsch, Phillip Lutgendorf, Nayanika Mathur, Townsend Middleton, Daniel Münster, Paul Nadasdy, Kirin Narayan, Jonathan Padwe, Bhrigupati Singh, and Claire Wendland. Over the past few years, I presented sections of this book at several conferences, and I was privileged to receive feedback from several colleagues. For supportive and helpful discussion comments, I want to thank Jessica Cattelino, Michael Fischer, Matthew Hull, Martha Lampland, Anne Meneley, Aradhana Sharma, Amy Trubek, Paige West, and Andrew Willford. Thank you to my two stellar undergraduate research assistants, Divya Mehta and Arundhati Ponnapa, who collected some of the media materials on which I draw in chapter 5.

Portions of chapters 1, 2, and 6 were published in "The Future of Price: Communicative Infrastructures and the Financialization of Indian Tea," *Cultural Anthropology* 31, no. 1 (2016): 4–29; and "Tea as 'Hero Crop'? Embodied Algorithms and Industrial Reform in India," *Science as Culture* 26, no. 1 (2017): 11–31. Parts of chapter 5 appear in "Exhaustion and Endurance in Sick Landscapes," in the volume *How Nature Works: Rethinking Labor on a Troubled Planet,* coedited by Alex Blanchette and me (School for Advanced

Research Press, 2019). Short pieces also appear on the *Cultural Anthropology* website: "Sickness" (2018), as part of the series Naturalization of Work edited by Alex Blanchette and me; and "Monoculture" (2017), as part of the series Lexicon for the Anthropocene yet Unseen edited by Cymene Howe and Anand Pandian.

It has been a pleasure to work with the University of California Press again. A huge thank you to Kate Marshall for her support and editorial eye, as well as to Enrique Ochoa-Kaup, Tom Sullivan, Cindy Fulton, and the marketing and publication teams. Working with the Atelier series has been a truly rewarding experience. Thanks to Kevin O'Neill for the invitation to participate in the series and to the entire Atelier community, especially my cohort members Nomi Stone and Christien Tompkins, for their early readings of the manuscript. I am particularly grateful to Daniel Reichman, Marina Welker, and the anonymous peer reviewers for UC Press.

And thank you to Alex for more than I can enumerate here, including spending precious winter breaks in Siliguri, listening, ever so patiently, to every idea that made it into these pages and the many others that did not, and for being a steadfast companion in this and all things. Without your support, along with the support of Kitty, Sidney, Floyd, and the most recent addition to our menagerie, Momo, this book would not be possible.

Introduction

THE PRODUCTION OF QUALITY

WHAT MAKES A GOOD CUP OF TEA? Ask consumers in different tea-loving places, from London to Lucknow to Louisville, and you'll likely get different answers. Some like it hot. Some like it iced. Some prefer a splash of milk; others take it with a heap of sugar. While the way to prepare a proper cup of tea may vary from place to place, most tea drinkers will agree on where to start: with a simple bag of black tea.

Even to the most devoted consumers, the black tea bag can seem banal. Tetley. Lipton. PG Tips. Yorkshire Gold. The off-brand tea bag in your hotel room. There's nothing fancy here. No single-origin stories, no pricey packaging. The attraction of the black tea bag is its reliability, its sameness. A "nice cup of tea" is comforting because, like a favorite chair or a memorable song, it calls the consumer back into the realm of the familiar and the routine.

It is not only the taste but also the rhythm of making a cup of tea that is so familiar: filling the kettle, reaching for your favorite mug, ripping open the tea bag, waiting for the kettle to hiss or ding, pouring the hot water into your mug (being careful to not submerge the paper flag), then dunking the bag up and down a few times. As you dunk, the color dissipates in wisps and swirls into the water. As the deep reddish-brown hues slowly bleed out, you resume your day. Cups of tea can punctuate a leisurely morning or a busy afternoon.

When tea drinkers reach for a bag of black tea, they are reaching for something dependable and standardized, not something unique and distinguished. This book tells the story behind that dependability and standardization. The sameness and reliability by which tea drinkers judge a good cup of tea is the result of a hidden, complex process that traverses the history of European colonialism, postcolonial economic debates, and the development of modern industrial food science. Above all, this book tells a story about quality: the "nice" in that "nice cup of tea."

In a way, tea consumers today think as much as they ever have about quality. If they have switched to a fair trade or organic black blend, they presumably have the quality of the tea-producing environment or the life of the tea plantation worker in mind. But they also might justify spending a few extra cents on this specially labeled box because what is inside is just as good as, or maybe even a little bit better than, what is inside the conventional box.

The discussion of quality in this book is, in a word, *qualitative.* This does not mean that I am only interested in people's opinions about the flavors, look, and smells of mass-market black tea. Indeed, the main focus of this book is not tea consumption per se. What counts as quality tea is not just a matter of consumer preference or even of environmental and labor conditions at the point of production. Though what goes on at kitchen tables and on tea plantations is certainly important to the story of quality, this book also attends to the spaces in between: those of brokerage, blending, auctioning, and food chemistry. Even the cheapest, most ordinary-looking tea arrives in its cup in that reliable form thanks to a set of linguistic, technological, and aesthetic techniques not just for judging quality—as if quality were always just waiting there to be perceived—but for producing it.

No single corporation or institution fully controls this set of techniques. Over the history of the modern tea industry, these techniques have been debated, distributed, and refined by professional tea tasters, auctioneers, blenders, and scientists. What these people all have in common is that they occupy intermediary positions in the system that circulates tea from farm to cup. These intermediary figures and the spaces in which they work are the subjects of this book. The work of these figures helps make the black tea bag reach consumers in the form they come to expect, time after time. Focused on the production of black tea from India from the late nineteenth century to the present, I trace debates among these figures about what quality is, how quality can be promoted and maintained, and how qualities can be made to seem distinguishable from one another yet remain economically commensurable.

In contemporary capitalism, the relationship between quality and the market is often reduced to numbers. A quality product may be that which yields a high price or that which has more numerous traits that, according to market research, a given consumer demographic considers desirable.[1] In the interdisciplinary field of food studies, a "quality turn" has been under way for over twenty years. Many studies of quality in food focus on the growing market for artisanal, luxury, or organic products.[2] "Price differentials" between these kinds of products and "conventional" goods are made meaningful to consumers by expert-driven systems of evaluation.[3] Yet what the sociologists Michel Callon, Cecile Méadel, and Volonoa Rabeharisoa call the "economy of qualities" is not limited to luxury goods. In fact, I argue, if we look instead at a seemingly undifferentiated, readily available, mass-market product like the black tea bag, it becomes possible to understand better how quality is produced.[4] Callon and colleagues suggest that the "qualification" of goods, by which they mean the identification of their distinguishing characteristics, is essential to the functioning of modern markets.[5] As Karen Hébert notes, this process of qualification, or "making things singular," follows many of the same logics that make things interchangeable and fungible.[6] A product like, say, PG Tips tea bags, is paradoxically both "singular" on the market and "comparable" to other tea bags available, even at the same price point.[7]

The techniques that produce quality are not entirely unique to the tea industry, but the story of tea shows that the "economy of qualities," far from being a new phenomenon, was central to the process by which colonial plantation production in India was transformed into a postcolonial capitalist enterprise. The qualification of reliable, cheap things is the outcome of historical and contemporary modes of economic inequality, racial and gendered differentiation, and environmental transformation.[8] Black tea comes primarily from former British and Dutch colonies, from East Africa to Southeast Asia.[9] In these places, tea is plucked and pruned by hand on plantations, vertically integrated production systems in which factories, fields, and laborers' homes are all located in one place and are often controlled by owners in faraway urban centers. From plantations, tea is crated and shipped, ready for sale, to auction centers in former colonial port cities like Kolkata, Colombo, and Mombasa, where it is tasted, priced, and sold.[10]

Mass-market black teas are blends of many different tastes, origins, and grades of tea, selected to match distinct flavor profiles. A bag of Tetley, PG Tips, or almost any tea consumers might encounter around the world is often a blend of twenty to thirty different kinds of tea, which traders refer to as "invoices." Large and small companies alike buy invoices from different tea-growing regions to make their blends. Some invoices may be recently harvested, while others may have sat in a warehouse for months before blending. Some invoices are chosen for their flavor (whether malty or floral), others for their appearance (whether "wiry" dry leaves or "bright" steeped leaves), and others for cost, with an eye to ensuring that the price of a particular blend stays within a desired range. Reach for another box of the same brand a week or a month later, and it will likely be composed of a completely different set of twenty-something teas and a totally different combination of regions, grades, ages, and flavors. The teas inside will be different, but the taste will be familiar. In fact, the tea in your preferred tea bag tastes the same *because* the teas inside are totally different. Tea seems to be infinitely reproducible, despite the fact that what tea *is* is highly variable. So while we might think of the ordinary black tea bag as a static, simple thing, getting the Tetley tea bag you drink today to taste the same as the Tetley tea bag you drank last month—and getting the tea in that Tetley bag to react in the same way to everything from the hardness of water to the fat content of milk to consumer preferences in places as different as London, Louisville, and Lucknow—is actually a complex and fraught undertaking.[11]

It is tempting to think of the plantation as the starting point for the production of quality, and of the auction or retail sale as the mechanism by which quality is transposed to consumers. In this view, quality matters because suppliers must meet the demands of consumers. (An alternative view is that suppliers define quality and manufacture demand through marketing.) My research leads me to join other scholars of capitalist markets in seeing such stories of "supply and demand" as deceptively simplistic.[12] The plantation and the auction are just two nodes in a much larger array of sites that also includes laboratories, agricultural experimental stations, and bureaucratic offices, as well as spaces of consumption. While the plantation shapes the quality of black tea in the sense that colonial imagery of plantation landscapes and workers still dominates advertising and packaging, the reverse is also the case.[13] Black tea—its sensory qualities, its "niceness," the images and memories it conjures, and normalized expectations about all of these things—also works to keep the plantation together. Efforts to standardize and objectify quality were central to the British colonial project that gave birth to the mass-market black tea that tea drinkers across the world know and consume. The resulting linguistic and technoscientific conventions for describing tea's qualities help maintain the colonially derived plantation form. Following feminist scholars of science and technology, I suggest that such conventions help materialize abstract notions about gender, culture, and ethnicity, fixing them in place.[14] Quality is the momentary outcome of what the feminist historian of science Michelle Murphy calls "spatial arrangements of relationships that draw humans, things, words and nonhumans into patterned conjunctures."[15]

In this book, I discuss several such spatial arrangements, including the tea tasting room, the auction hall, the plantation, and the laboratory. In these sites, I ask both *what* quality is and *where* it is, geographically and historically, but I also ask what quality *does*—what claims about it are made, by whom, and with what consequences. Quality is not an end in itself—a final destination for economic, colonial, or postcolonial projects—but an opening for those projects. To tell the story of quality is to explore historically particular ways of relating to the material world through knowledge (both linguistic and embodied) and work (both productive and reproductive). Before a more in-depth discussion of what quality entails, I want to step back and provide a broader view of the Indian tea industry.

THE PAST AND FUTURE OF INDIAN TEA

Tea auctioning began in London under the auspices of the East India Company in the late 1600s. In these auctions, traders bought tea acquired from China. With the expansion of colonial control in India and the development of tea plantations there, beginning in Assam in the 1830s and moving to what is now West Bengal by the 1850s, the tea auction infrastructure expanded to include Calcutta, where the first sales were held in 1861.[16] The environmental and social upheavals of plantation expansion under the British Empire ran parallel to the development of the new sciences of food chemistry and agronomy, the government regulation of an expanding global agribusiness, and the emergence of consumer consciousness about the taste, health effects, and safety of everyday foods and beverages.[17]

Tea remains central to debates that are ongoing in India today about the country's agricultural and economic future. Tea is part of the Indian national imaginary. The humble, affordable cup of *chai* is a central feature in both private and public spaces—from homes to hotels—across the subcontinent.[18] Tea unites Indians of all classes and regions. It is drunk in dusty bazaars out of clay cups, in shiny office buildings, and in newfangled urban corporate café chains aimed at the upper middle class. India's current right-wing leader, Narendra Modi, explicitly portrays himself as the son of a railway station *chai-walla* (tea seller).

The tea that Modi and his father sold on a railway platform in rural India and the tea offered by high-end urban retailers all originates on plantations. The plantation is far from an anachronism or relic of a bygone era. It is both a crucible of the modern food system and an enduring driver of it.[19] The tea plantation was a site at which scientific and economic experts first experimented with quality, devising methods for what they called the "improvement" of India's landscapes, people, and tea itself.[20] Within a few decades of carving out plantations in Assam from native forest, planters began to shift from hand-processing tea (the method used in China) to machine processing. They constructed on-plantation mechanized factories, working toward a faster, more efficient, and vertically integrated system for converting highly perishable green leaf tea into a fermented, dried, and transportable form.[21]

The plantation system allowed planters to monocrop tea, with a vast workforce that constantly pruned tea plants (which frequently grew into trees in China) into flat-topped bushes. Tightly pruned bushes grow into each other, creating a nearly solid green shelf. Today, tea workers, most of them women, must pull themselves through tightly packed hedges to pluck from their flat, manicured tops. Tattered pieces of tarpaulin protect their legs and torsos from scratches and punctures. They return to the same bushes nearly weekly for ten to eleven months a year to find the freshest sprigs of tea—the iconic "two leaves and a bud." In the short dormant season, these women prune those same bushes to incite more sprigs to grow next season. On innumerable advertisements and packages, images of two leaves and a bud and of stooped, comely Indian tea workers create the illusion of an entirely natural production system.

But black tea as we have come to know it is far from natural. Black tea's very existence in India and in the cups of consumers in the metropole is the result of a distinct industrial ecology, an ecology that contains and constrains the botanical variability of the tea bush into a standardized form. I have spent much of the past decade living and working on the plantations of Darjeeling, in the Himalayan foothills of West Bengal, where some of the world's most expensive tea is produced. In 2015, I began research in the adjacent region of the Dooars, at the base of the foothills and just a few hours' drive from Darjeeling. Plantations in the Dooars produce India's cheapest black teas, sold largely on the domestic market. In both Darjeeling and the Dooars, plantations operate much as they did during the colonial period, even though British companies have given way to Indian ones. As I have shown in my previous research, the plantation remains so ingrained in the tea industry that even ethical sourcing schemes like fair trade and organic certification, which are intended to ensure quality for both consumers and producers, can neither avoid it nor effectively challenge it.[22] *All* plantations still rely on a vast workforce of ethnically marginalized laborers who depend on the plantation not just for their daily wage, but for food, housing, and healthcare. While many stories about contemporary capitalism highlight the paradox that low-paid workers cannot consume what they produce, nearly all tea plantation workers are tea drinkers. Tea punctuates the plantation working day and the home lives of laborers, and quality matters to low-paid tea workers, albeit in a way that is quite distinct from how it matters to tea brokers, not to mention consumers in the Global North.

Factories and monocropped fields were not the only "improvements" European planters made to tea production. Tucked between sections of tea are the villages where plantation laborers live. In order to meet the demands of year-round production, planters need workers with the skill to properly maintain tea bushes to live on plantations year-round and season after season.[23] Today, small two- to three-room houses are mandated for all workers by Indian plantation labor law. What all of this means is that workers on tea plantations do not freely come and go from the land. They do not sell their labor by the season like fruit pickers in California and the Pacific Northwest. For Indian tea workers, the plantation is home, yet they do not own the land under their houses or have any claim to the land under tea. Importantly, rights to that home are conferred more often than not by women's labor, since women make up the majority of the plantation workforce. Neither these women nor their ancestors had any say in the decision to plant tea there—or, as I explain later, the decision to keep it there after Indian independence in 1947.

On Indian plantations, there are two different factory-finishing processes. "Orthodox" tea is the tea that most Euro-American consumers would recognize. Orthodox production yields long cylindrical twists of tea that resemble the botanical material from which they are derived. CTC (cut-tear-curl) finishing involves tearing the leaves and rolling them into tiny balls, which, once fired, are visually reminiscent of instant coffee. (Figures 1 and 2.) CTC production uses machinery that can produce greater quantities of black tea over a shorter time than the orthodox method, at a lower cost of production. CTC and orthodox black tea (as well as green and oolong teas) come from two plant varieties: *Camellia sinensis* and *Camellia sinensis* var. *assamica,* known respectively in India as the China *jaat* (type) and the Assam *jaat*. The China jaat has smaller leaves, which yield light, flavorful teas like those produced in Darjeeling. The Assam jaat has broader leaves, which produce a maltier, darker cup. In everyday agricultural practice, however, these are largely ideal types. What workers pluck on Indian plantations today are

FIGURE 1. Orthodox tea. Photo by author.

clonal varieties of both jaats.[24] It was not until after the widespread adoption of CTC manufacture in the 1950s that tea became an object of mass consumption in India. When people think of black tea as India's "national beverage," it is CTC, boiled with milk, sugar, and spices, to which they are referring.[25]

After it is processed and packaged on plantations, railways, constructed during the colonial period, bring crates of processed tea to brokerage houses in urban centers, where professional tea brokers make judgments about quality, giving feedback to plantation companies not only on the color, smell, and taste of the leaves but also on the management of the field and factory laborers who pluck and process them. By the late nineteenth century, this all-male class of tea brokers had become the main arbiters of quality in the tea

FIGURE 2. CTC tea. Photo by author.

industry. They controlled—and to a large extent, continue to control—the tasting, pricing, and auctioning infrastructure that converts individual invoices of tea into the standardized blends consumers recognize today. At auction, buyers bid not on generic lots of a single commodity but on a wide array of qualities expressed in catalog descriptions, an esoteric language, and a range of numbers indexing everything from weight to age to location.

Tea brokers and traders, still overwhelmingly men, are central figures in this book. Much of my research took place in the auction halls and brokerage offices of Kolkata and Siliguri, a city in the northern reaches of West Bengal. In these sites, I followed tea brokers as they tasted tea, and I observed the lively public sales at which they auctioned tea to buyers. In addition, I spent time in the Kolkata archives of the Indian Tea Association (ITA), the guildlike organization that represents tea plantation managers and owners; in the National Library in Kolkata; and in the British Library in London, to which the ITA's London branch donated its materials after the office downsized in the 1970s. Focused on the years between the founding of the ITA in 1886 and the passage of the Foreign Exchange Regulation Act of 1973, which officially ended British capital's control over the tea industry and other enterprises in India, my archival research traced the ITA's central role in the development of standardized aesthetic and scientific methods for discerning quality. In the quest to improve Indian tea, the expertise of professional tea brokers was both juxtaposed to and blended with that of scientific experts—chemists, agronomists, and botanists—engaged by the colonial and post-colonial tea industries.

Throughout the British colonial period, the ITA governed the production of tea on plantations and its movement by rail into Calcutta and by ship out of the city's port. After India gained independence in 1947, the Government of India's Tea Board took over many of these responsibilities and created new forms of oversight. An abiding concern of both the ITA during colonial occupation and of the Tea Board of the newly independent nation-state was how to establish Indian tea as both commensurable to tea grown in East Africa, Southeast Asia, and East Asia and appreciably unique. This tension between commensurability and uniqueness continues into the present.[26] Today, Tea Board of India bureaucrats and private tea brokerage firms grapple with the question of how colonially rooted products like tea come to have a place on the global market. Regulatory efforts by the Tea Board to reform the tea industry have been hampered, as much as anything, by the entrenchment of quality itself.

BODIES, MATERIALS, AND MARKETS

Understanding quality—in this case, what makes a cup of tea not just come to be, but come to be *good* (or bad, or tasty, or bitter, or soothing, or even just "nice")—requires attending to several dimensions. Though the framework I describe below is somewhat specific to tea, my approach to quality is applicable well beyond the world of tea and even beyond the world of food. Quality matters in a variety of contexts, from the construction and maintenance of water systems to the production and consumption of pharmaceuticals or cigarettes to sperm banking to precious metals and minerals to development metrics and global health indicators.[27]

First, understanding quality requires attending to the embodied legacies of empire, or the power relations that allow a thing, whether cheap or precious, to come into contact in reliable ways with human and other bodies, whether through consumption, labor, or scientific research. Consider a 2017 essay in *Al Jazeera* by Hamid Dabashi, titled "How British Colonialism Ruined a Perfect Cup of Tea."[28] The essay explores what Dabashi sees as the mass illusion among the British that the tea they rely on and consume in mass quantities actually tastes good. He juxtaposes his unpleasant encounters with the milky brown substance the English call "tea" to his own memory of encountering the "perfect cup" as a child in Iran. For Dabashi, those childhood encounters with tea provided a sense of connection to his mother, his local shopkeeper, and Iranian notions of collective belonging, the sense of we-ness and energetic force that Émile Durkheim, appropriating a term from Oceanic languages, called "mana."[29] As Dabashi explains:

> The entire joy of drinking tea, as any Turk, Russian, Iranian, or Central Asian teahouse master will tell you, is the exquisite delicacy of negotiating a peaceful, cooperative, and delightful coexistence between the bitterness of tea and the sweetness of sugar, diplomatically negotiated inside your mouth. Can you even imagine Donald Trump, Benjamin Netanyahu, or Theresa May trying to grasp that sublime sense of peaceful coexistence?[30]

Dabashi is arguing against a certain strain of cultural history that sees food as a mere object on which consumers (usually, wealthy, white consumers) imprint the value judgments that come to be known as "qualitative." In these kinds of histories, value judgments often trickle down from the circles of wealth and power into mass consumer society.

Dabashi's critique of this conventional kind of historiography and his postcolonial theory of tea bring attention to the social life not just *of* things, but *in* things.[31] How do ineffable and unquantifiable characteristics like taste become normalized as goods that express a collective identity or sense of togetherness—for better or for worse? Answering this question requires us to center taste, rather than bureaucracy or religion or caste, in the analysis of empire and its consequences. This approach grounds the sensorium of everyday life in a long history of exploitation and extraction, as well as resistance to these experiences.

Something as seemingly mundane as the taste of tea brings attention to what William Mazzarella terms a "memetic archive" that is opened up through acts of consumption.[32] In his essay, Dabashi is defending an idea of "good tea" against British butchering, but at the same time he is recognizing that in drinking tea, he unavoidably becomes who he is in relationship to figures like Trump, Netanyahu, and May. Tea possesses panacea-like effects in mainstream (white) British culture, where it is a means for calming the nerves, for dealing with tragedy, or for facing a day of office drudgery. Dabashi, by contrast, interprets the British willingness to drink a milky, brown, unappetizing version of his grandmother's tea as "redemptive suffering," a penance for the terror wrought by slavery, empire, and environmental destruction.[33] For Dabashi, colonial violence is archived—and archived over and over again—through the mimesis of tea consumption, in the taste and smell of what the British euphemize as "a nice cuppa."

Second, understanding quality requires thinking about materials as more than passive objects. Dabashi's memories about how "the bitterness of tea and the sweetness of sugar [are] diplomatically negotiated inside your mouth" point us to the idea that substances like tea (and sugar and milk, for that matter) play an active role in their own qualification.[34] This is a point that has been made recently by anthropologists studying "specialty" or "alternative" food production in the United States and Europe. For example, Heather Paxson illustrates how the "goodness" of artisanal raw milk cheese depends on a pragmatic (if not also diplomatic) negotiation between cheesemakers, the tools they use to make cheese, and the microbial cultures that impart flavor to cheese.[35] Cheesemakers recognize microbes as active, if also somewhat unruly, collaborators in the crafting of "good" cheese. Elsewhere, Brad Weiss has explored how these material aspects of quality are historically informed, arguing that "heritage" breeds of pigs—whether they are alive in their pens or butchered and served up on white dinnerware—embody the sensory qualities that artisanal pork connoisseurs in the United States desire. For Weiss, the good taste of artisanal pork is far from natural. Eaters and cooks alike must learn to appreciate what heritage breeds bring to the table.[36]

Third, understanding quality requires thinking about markets. In capitalist markets, quality indexes that which we come to expect sensorially—consistent flavors and smells—as well as that which we come to expect materially—consistent physical properties such as weight or biochemical contents. If the taste of your Tetley tea is "off" for some reason—if it does not seem the same as it always does—this may reflect "poor quality." *Quality* is the term we use to capture what foods or other commodities are supposed to taste, smell, look, or feel like.

Quality in market terms can also be about how products take on value as commodities and the role of experts in keeping that value consistent, or, put another way, making that value *appear* consistent and commensurable with that of other things. When it comes to food and drink, we generally think that this work involves translation back and forth between the rational domain of price and the sensory domain of taste. Price and taste are, in turn, shaped by the historical forces of colonial and postcolonial development, science, and financial markets. Rather than attempt to discern where quality is quantitative and rational and where it is sensory and subjective, however, I join other theorists in approaching quality in the market as processual and pragmatic. Along with scholars who have examined capitalism through the lens of science and technology studies, I see the production of quality as one element in the making of markets themselves. Markets are not pregiven; rather, they are engendered through the operation of what Callon dubs "market devices," sociotechnical tools that shape and reshape markets. These devices include financial instruments (derivatives, futures, stock tickers), but as I suggested earlier, they also include techniques of "qualification."[37] Like other market devices, these are experimental rather than instrumental.

EXPERIMENTS WITH QUALITY

Anthropologists of capitalism have frequently approached the question of quality by "following" notions of taste, ethics, or aesthetics as they circulate through "commodity chains," the pathways traveled by goods, from production to brokerage to consumption. Anthropologists in the 1970s and 1980s began to map the dynamic linkages between production and consumption, inspired in large part by Sidney Mintz's classic study of sugar, which showed how taste for sugar among the English working class was forged through the elaboration of the Caribbean slave plantation.[38] Subsequent approaches added a close-up ethnographic dimension to Mintz's historical approach, tracing the "careers" of goods that included secondhand clothing, high art, and curios.[39] By doing what George Marcus calls "following the thing" and "following the idea," scholars were able to explain how quality morphs as things circulate across spaces and contexts.[40] As Theodore Bestor puts it, at each link in a given commodity chain, "objects acquire or shed meanings, identities and implied qualities that render them worthy of use and exchange. Without this culturally constructed valuation, goods have no value as a commodity in the sense of objects of *either* social or economic advantage."[41]

It is difficult to follow a thing as materially multiple, yet seemingly standardized, as a mass-market black tea bag. Because almost all of them are blended, tea bags manage to be consistent, even though one is never exactly the same as the next. But the difficulty is not due to blending alone. A tea bush will react differently to different soils or temperatures, just as processed black tea will react differently to boiled water, sugar, or milk. In order to follow not only the tea bag but also how and why it steeps the way it steeps and feels the way it feels—to understand steeping as a social process that puts bodies, materials, and markets into a qualitative relation—it is essential to understand how these reactions reverberate across the entire commodity chain.[42] To do this, I draw inspiration not only from anthropological commodity chain studies but also from the work of Michelle Murphy, who describes how PCBs, methyl mercury, and other chemical by-products of heavy industry seep and sediment into soils and human, plant, and nonhuman bodies.[43] Their effects may take decades to manifest themselves, and—like the moral, political, and cultural values traced by anthropologists of commodity chains—those effects move in an unpredictable, often nonlinear fashion. Knowledge about these effects is made in piecemeal ways. Experts specialize in particular aspects of production, circulation, or evaluation. No one actor—no one form of expertise—maintains the system. Importantly, as Murphy points out, these effects are *felt* as much as they are seen; and they are felt unevenly across disparate locations.[44]

While chemical effluents and tea can seem quite distant from one another, I find Murphy's observations about historical and material seepage and reverberation useful for understanding quality. In fact, a great deal of time and money has been invested over the past century in understanding tea's chemical makeup. Exotic-sounding substances like theine, tannins, polyphenols, theaflavins, and thearubigins—substances that are also sensed as much as they are seen and whose material effects manifest over decades of colonial and postcolonial plantation production—are key players in this story about Indian tea. A caffeine jitter in Johannesburg is linked to the work of tea plantation laborers from East Africa to Sri Lanka who bring tea into being, while these laborers live in villages and landscapes that are themselves saturated with agricultural chemicals. Sensation and affect matter not just when it comes to consumption, but throughout the production and circulation of everyday things.

With these ideas in mind, my historical and ethnographic work documents what Callon, Méadel, and Rabeharisoa call "real life experiments," or "trials."[45] For them, qualification, the process of identifying the distinguishing properties of goods, requires standardized experimental systems. In a marriage of marketing and science that Steven Shapin calls the "aesthetic-industrial complex," firms since at least the 1940s have used devices like flavor wheels and hedonic indexes to "account for taste" and thereby make consumers active participants in defining the very qualities of the products they consume.[46] This approach to quality is experimental because both the products being evaluated and the devices used in that evaluation are constantly being updated and revised.[47] Such experimentation is essential to the operation of markets, even if it also "blur[s] habitual distinctions between production, distribution and consumption."[48]

From the inception of the tea industry in India, quality has consistently been the subject of experimentation. Indeed, experimentation happens long before a blended tea bag makes its way into a consumer's cup. Experiments with quality have shaped, and continue to shape, the work of tea brokerage firms, scientific laboratories, regulatory offices, economic consulting firms, and even plantation management. Actors in these interstitial spaces between production and consumption have deployed a range of devices, including words, economic policies, land tenure arrangements, factory machinery, and even their own bodies, to coax bitterness, sweetness, floralness, astringency, and other components of tea into a knowable and exchangeable form.

I use "experimental" as an analytical term, then, but I also use it because, at various points in tea's history, people inside India's tea industry have explicitly described their work with tea as experimental. Though a colonial economic and social order certainly set the basic terms for experimentation with the quality of tea, no such order is ever fully fixed or immutable. Quality is a moving target. A working experimental system never really reaches a finality or end.[49] Rather than something that is won and lost, accumulated or dissipated, quality remains an open question.

TASTING QUALITIES

This book contains a lot of historical material, but it is not organized chronologically. Since quality is immanent in the operations of the tea industry, I have chosen to begin in a particular site of experimentation, the tea brokerage firm, and move outward in space and time to other sites, including the plantation, the laboratory, the auction, and the many different contexts in which tea is consumed. Above all, as I noted earlier, the narrative is organized as an examination of what quality is and what it does, in addition to where it is. Quality is never sitting in one place or lodged in a discrete set of attributes. It has always been actively composed, often by divergent means. The effect of this is that quality does many different things simultaneously and that what quality was in the colonial past has serious implications for what it might be in the future.

In chapter 1, I describe how professional tea brokers learn to taste and value tea. A tea broker's body is not a proxy for a potential consumer. Instead, his body is an instrument for evaluating production and consumption at the same time. The question of whose bodies count as properly qualified to evaluate tea is a highly gendered one. The techniques of brokerage were developed by British experts, and for decades brokerage was exclusively the province of white men. Since Indian independence in 1947, however, the ranks of professional brokers have been taken over by middle-class Indian men. Just as taste helps reinforce the ethnic distinctions between pluckers, factory workers, and managers that regulate the life of the plantation, it also helps constantly reinvent middle-class Indian identity. Middle-class Indian masculinity, too, emerges through engagement with material goods, as well as through the long legacy of sexualized imperial labor regimes. Indian tea brokers are not simply mimicking or fulfilling a British archetype. Rather, middle-class identity and masculinity are constantly coming into being and being rearticulated through the embodied processes of tasting and trade.

Once tasted, individual invoices of tea must be sold, one by one, in live "open outcry auctions" (so called because buyers bid by crying out offers to an auctioneer). These auctions are the subject of chapter 2. In the case of the brokerage firms I studied, the person auctioning was the very same person who, days before, had tasted and evaluated those thousands of invoices. Brokerage thus requires a deep knowledge not only of how to taste tea but also of how to cut a deal and of how to talk and comport one's body while doing both. While chapter 1 explores techniques for discerning quality through brokers' direct interaction with tea leaves in the tasting room, chapter 2 examines how quality emerges through their interactions with the numbers that constitute auction catalogs. These numbers include age, weight, number of packages, warehouse location, and other important details about each invoice. The one number not printed in the auction catalog is the estimated monetary value of the invoice. Prices emerge through a complex communicative infrastructure, for which the catalog serves as a schematic map. Chapter 2 shows how numbers other than prices mediate the interaction between the bodies of traders and tea itself.

After tea is bought at auction, the majority of it is rendered into standard blends. Chapter 3 recounts the relatively recent history of blended tea, and it uses the story of blending to provide a genealogy of quality. It tells the story of how the ITA and the British government worked to make blended black tea, or "Empire Tea," the tea of choice across Britain, Europe, and the United States. Amid this market expansion, tea became a vehicle for early twentieth-century British consumers and physicians to imagine the consequences of the extension and intensification of plantation-based agriculture in South Asia. They linked the sensations induced by blended tea, felt from taste buds to intestinal tracts, to conditions in the landscapes of production. This imaginative connection centered on the substance and the idea of tannins, a chemical compound that gives tea its characteristic bitterness and color. In response to generalized fears about the physical effects of mass tea consumption, tea industry scientists put tannins under experimental scrutiny and reinterpreted them as beneficial to consumers' bodies.

Chapter 4 describes further attempts to understand the relationship between tea's chemical constituents and its quality. From the 1930s through the 1960s, the ITA developed two wedded experimental projects, one in London and the other in Northeast India. In London, a thirty-year research program enlisted biochemists to identify the chemical makeup of different teas on the market. The program sought to identify the discrete chemicals that matched up to brokers' evaluations. After independence in 1947, Indian government officials became increasingly unsatisfied with the attention paid by tea scientists to the chemistry of quality. By the late 1960s, the objectives of Indian tea science had shifted, from tracing the chemical *constituency* of quality tea to pushing technological innovations for increasing the *yield* of tea, particularly through cloning and the improvement of tea processing machinery. But this story is not simply one of a decolonizing state claiming sovereignty over science. In the years following Indian independence, tea moved in accretive and messy ways from a crop of empire to a crop of national development and patrimony. New and unexpected entities resulted from the tense comingling of colonial chemical experimentation and development-oriented agronomic and mechanical experimentation. These included an entirely new method for producing mass-market black tea: CTC. The turn from quality to yield occurred precisely at the moment in India's history when agricultural outputs were becoming a proxy for economic development and, by extension, quality of life.

The book's last two chapters ask how quality has both enabled and hindered experimental attempts to change how tea is produced in India. Chapter 5 focuses on a series of efforts to reform the plantation system in the Dooars, where partly as a result of the Indian government's modernizing emphasis on yield and partly because of geographic conditions plantations have long been dedicated to the production of cheap black tea. Chapter 5 uses the one-rupee packet of CTC tea, a ubiquitous item in shops across India, to tell the story of how the problem of quality meets awkwardly with the market objective of cheapness and accessibility. I show how the *taste* of tea—even cheap CTC tea—is changing as the result of reform-oriented shifts in agricultural production. In the Dooars, the Tea Board of India has begun promoting smallholder tea as an even cheaper, higher yielding alternative to plantation-grown tea. Drawing on ethnographic research with brokers and blenders in Siliguri, where most CTC tea from the Dooars goes to auction, I argue that cheapness is a quality unto itself. Here at the bottom end of the tea market, taste still matters. Efforts to move the market beyond its colonial past by the aggressive expansion of smallholder tea production are not just visible in changing landscapes. According to many experts I interviewed, the taste of CTC has been compromised by agrarian reforms. This change in taste has brought attention to economic, health, and social precarity on both plantations and small farms.

Reform efforts are not just focused on plantations. The Tea Board of India has also set its sights on another colonial holdover: the auction. Today, most mass-market foods, including coffee, sugar, milk, and meat, are sold through speculative financial instruments called futures contracts. Tea, sold in live auctions, is an exception. Chapter 6 shows how, beginning in 2009, the Tea Board mandated that all Indian tea circulating through auctions do so via an online system. For the Tea Board, the embodied technique of tea brokers was at odds with the free market. For tea brokers, the efficient circulation of tea could not occur without their expertise. In what amounted to a real-time economic experiment, the "natural" ability of the broker was set in opposition to the "natural" circuitry of the market. Against the backdrop of calls for "direct trade" and the removal of intermediaries in commodity chains of all kinds, chapter 6 explores the rollout of new valuation technologies in India, and it also explores the implications of this rollout for the ethics of commodity circulation and the role of states in a liberalizing global economy.

Moving between historical and ethnographic registers, as well as between auctions, archives, plantations, and the offices of private and public operators in the industry, affords a nonlinear view of capitalist value. This book shows how quality, as a domain that links bodies, materials, and markets, emerges in a sometimes collaborative, sometime contentious engagement between different experimental systems. In my analysis of everyday practices of tasting and auctioning, historical attempts to scientifically standardize those practices, and plantation and auction reform efforts, questions about the historical relationship between bodies and materials meet lingering anxieties about India's economic future.

ONE

The Work of Taste

BUREAUCRATIC AND COMMERCIAL INFRASTRUCTURES converge in a bustling district near the center of Kolkata. The area is known today as BBD Bagh, named after Benoy, Badal, and Dinesh, three freedom fighters who shot N. S. Simpson, British imperial inspector of prisons, in 1930. The central landmark is Lal Dighi (Red Pond), a small, square body of water. Lal Dighi is commonly thought to predate the British East India Company's arrival in the region in 1690 and the Company's subsequent conversion of the Hooghly River's banks into its center of operations in India. Working outward from Lal Dighi, the East India Company built an urban landscape for converting India's material resources into commercial value.[1]

From the monumental commercial structures surrounding Lal Dighi, cash crops, including most prominently jute, indigo, and opium, were evaluated, auctioned, and later shipped around the world via boats docked along the Hooghly. Tea was a latecomer to this portfolio of crops. It was not until the East India Company was replaced by the British imperial administration in the 1850s that Indian-grown tea became a major commercial enterprise.

Although the East India Company—a prototype for the global corporations like Tata and Hindustan Unilever that now dominate much of India's tea industry—officially ceded control of Kolkata more than 150 years ago, administrative and business functions still mix in the architecture and social life of BBD Bagh. On the northern edge of the square sits the Writers' Building, so named because it originally housed the writers for the East India Company.[2] The Writers' Building became the seat of the viceroy of India, and until 2013 it housed the offices of the Government of West Bengal.[3]

Next door to the Writers' Building is Saint Andrew's Church, one of many churches built in Calcutta so that East India Company officials might uphold their religious as well as mercantile duties. Across the street and over the tram lines, R. N. Mukherjee Road runs diagonally to the south.[4] Halfway down this one-block street, adjacent to the Old Mission Church and across from a trio of popular tea stalls pouring cup after tiny earthenware cup of milky, sugary tea, sits Nilhat House. Nihat House is home to the longest-running tea auction in the world.

Even though the space is now dedicated almost exclusively to tea, the name "Nilhat" refers to its previous life as the site of Calcutta's indigo auctions. (In Bengali, *nil* means "blue," and *haat* means "market.") Today, Nilhat House is a towering modernist structure, though its blue and white paint scheme references its past life. The building was inaugurated in 1961 by Prime Minister Jawaharlal Nehru, and it remains a place where the legacies of India's colonial, mercantile past blend uncomfortably with both Nehru's postindependence turn to nationalist development and more recent visions of a global, corporation-driven future. Brokers from a number of firms come to the auctions at Nilhat House every week to sell tea to a host of buyers, from the largest globally oriented corporations like Hindustan Unilever and Tata to small family-run businesses in Kolkata. It is here at Nilhat House that our story about quality begins.

A tall concrete and steel gate separates Nilhat House from the bustling sidewalk. The gate also serves as a durable surface on which food vendors can tether tarpaulins to shelter themselves from rains and blistering sun. BBD Bagh is a well-known location for street food in a city that is itself a gastronomic destination. The sidewalks of R. N. Mukherjee Road support an array of culinary craftspeople. Diesel fumes mix with the sour, spicy aromas of tantalizing treats—*kati* rolls, *puchka, momo*—served from pull carts and covered *dhaba*s that open and close on a rolling basis, ensuring that no passerby goes hungry or thirsty from the break of dawn until well into the evening.

Inside the Nilhat House compound, closely cut topiaries and freshly swept asphalt contrast with the sidewalk's effervescence. Chauffeured cars carry graying, besuited tea brokers up to the gate. With a honk, the sea of sidewalk social life parts and then reconstitutes in each car's wake. Big corporate buyers also arrive here, sometimes in chauffeured cars but more often by foot from their offices in BBD Bagh, tattered faux leather briefcases in hand. Younger brokers and freshly recruited apprentices walk in from the metro or bus stops a couple of blocks away. Brokers and buyers alike stop for a cup of tea or a little snack at one of the stalls outside the gate. They take the last drags of their cigarettes and then toss both the butts and their single-use *bhar* (unglazed clay teacups) against the walls as they head through the gates. Bhar are a fixture around Kolkata, used most frequently for tea and yogurt. Plastic has replaced clay in most tea stalls around the country, but here in Kolkata these cups, crafted locally from clay sourced from the Ganges, are said to highlight the taste of tea.

Uniformed guards funnel foot traffic up the polished marble steps into the building. Inside, entrants are greeted by another private security detail. After the 2009 terrorist attacks in Mumbai, the state government deemed the tea auctions—regularly scheduled gatherings of notable men—a potential target.

At Nilhat House, tea is not sold as a raw commodity like, for example, green unroasted coffee beans. Since freshly plucked tea leaves are highly perishable, tea must leave plantations fully processed. Each tea plantation contains a factory in which workers wither, ferment, roll, dry, and sort teas to give them particular flavors. A multiplicity of botanical material—the result of regional, geographic, climatic, and clonal variety—yields a multiplicity of qualities. Each variation in altitude, humidity, and plant selection necessitates tweaks in the factory finishing process. This variability leads to volatility, both in price and in taste.

In order to sell their teas, plantations contract with one of a handful of Kolkata-based brokerage houses. Shipments of finished tea, or invoices, first arrive at the brokerage firms' secure warehouses on the banks of the Hooghly. Invoices are marked with plantation name, grade, and date of production. From these warehouses, brokers send out fifty-gram samples of each invoice to buyers registered with the Calcutta Tea Traders Association (CTTA), an organization of buyers, brokers, and sellers. Brokerage firms also ensure that samples are dispatched to their own tasting rooms.

THE TASTING ROOM

J. Thomas and Company is the oldest and largest brokerage house in India and has been operating on the site of what is now Nilhat House since the late 1800s.[5] J. Thomas's tasting room is on the fifth floor. There, every day, tasting room workers prepare trays of teas for brokers to taste (figure 3). One of these workers moves down the long tables weighing out tea samples. He is remarkably accurate, needing to adjust the weight of the tea by only a tiny pinch or so. After weighing, he dumps this tea into white ceramic mugs lined up and down the tables. Then he puts the small sample bag behind the mug. A

FIGURE 3. Setting up a tasting at J. Thomas. Photo by author.

coworker follows him, filling the mugs with hot water from a large electric kettle. A third follows behind, placing a lid on top of each mug with a *clink*.

Their movements create a din of crunching leaves, clanging crockery, and crinkling plastic. White enamel-coated, English-made Albert Bishop regulator clocks tick in the background. After five minutes, one of the workers moves back down the line, straining the liquid from each mug into a tea-stained cup by tipping it on its side and slowly twisting the lid, allowing the steeped tea to pour out. Then he flips the mug upside down and taps it so that the wet tea leaves collect onto the lid. He presses or pinches the leaves so that they stay in place. Finally, he places the upturned lid, topped with a pyramid of aromatic freshly steeped tea leaves, onto the rim of the empty mug. The resulting trio—a cup of tea liquor, a pile of steeped leaf, and a bag of dry leaf—sit together on the tray. At the end of

FIGURE 4. Line of CTC teas ready for tasting at J. Thomas. Photo by author.

this process, dozens and sometimes hundreds of invoices have been arranged on wooden trays in sets of thirteen cups. Throughout the day, workers in the tasting room repeat these actions, cup after cup, tray after tray, table after table (figure 4).

Like other components of quality, taste is constantly varying. Even with the regimentation and steady rhythms that govern the fifth floor of Nilhat House, tea does not taste the same on a Monday as it does on a Friday. The invoices are of course changing throughout the week, but the water used to steep the tea sits in storage tanks all weekend, which affects the taste of all the tea on Monday morning. If tasted again later in the week, it will be different. The first duty of the broker is to put the unruly variability of regions, sizes, styles, and grades into a discernible order. Each broker focuses on a particular category. Some focus on malty Assam teas, others on muscatel

Darjeelings, and others on tannic CTC teas.[6] Regardless of specialty, the tasting process is the same.

Mr. Dey, a broker who has worked for J. Thomas for thirty years, barrels past the tasting room guard and through the swinging door marked "No Admission." He grabs a tea-speckled white monogrammed apron from a row of pegs hanging by the door, flips his tie over his shoulder, and drapes the apron around his neck. Working his way down a line of cups, Mr. Dey first lifts the lid filled with steeped tea to his face, burying his nose in the damp aromatic leaves to breathe in the delicate essences. He palpates this wet leaf, moving it around the upturned lid to assess the evenness of the color. Then he slams the saucer down, reaches for the cup filled with lukewarm tea, takes three aerated sips—*Slurp Slurp Slurp*—and spits the tea out in a thin arching stream into a dented waist-high aluminum bucket. In tea brokerage, the taster allows the tea to enter his mouth, but he does not swallow it. Instead, he inhales air through the liquid so that it can hit all points of his palate.

As he works his way down the line, Mr. Dey carries two pieces of thick cardstock, printed with the J. Thomas logo. In addition to tasting the tea and examining the steeped leaves, he picks up the sample packet of dry tea and pours its contents onto one of the cards. He fans the tea with his fingers and sifts it back and forth. He bends his cupped hands and pours the tea from one piece of cardstock to the other, looking for any stems and unevenly sorted leaves in the finished tea. Such extraneous materials are a detriment.

Mr. Dey then turns to his assistant. Drawing from a controlled list of English adjectives *stemy, hiscuity, cheesy, knobbly*—he describes the trio before him: liquor, steeped leaf, and dry leaf. The sights and smells of all three components are part of the evaluation. Mr. Dey kicks his spit bucket down the line and repeats the procedure with the next cup.

As I follow him through the tasting room, Mr. Dey reminds me that tea is unlike coffee or wine, which are annual vintages. In tea, vintages do not correspond to years. Instead, each plantation, or often section of a plantation, on a given day, constitutes a kind of vintage. Each tea, from day to day and season to season, might be fired at different temperatures or fermented for different amounts of time. Quality also depends on the time of harvest, what people in the tea business refer to as "flushes," or seasons: first flush (mid-March to mid-April), second flush (mid-April to May), monsoon flush (June to August), and autumnal flush (September to November). As if the taster's task were not already complicated enough, as I mentioned in the introduction, there are two factory finishing processes, orthodox and CTC. Before tea reaches brokers, plantation companies assign a range of grades to both CTC and orthodox tea in an attempt to order this variability (see table 1 on p. 40). Each plantation with which a brokerage firm has a contract may be sending multiple invoices produced on the same day. This variability ensures that each invoice, each week, tastes differently.

Using his specialized vocabulary, Mr. Dey translates the sensation of each tea—its taste, touch, and smell—as well as his recollections about color, aroma, and texture to compare this week's invoice to an invoice from the same plantation from last week or the week before. He works cup by cup, grade by grade, plantation by plantation.[7] A tasting room clerk follows him, pushing a large easel on which he records Mr. Dey's dictated evaluations, known to brokers as "quality comments."

TASTING BODIES

Printed on the top of each sheet of the J. Thomas cardstock used by Mr. Dey and his colleagues to sort dried tea leaves are the words, "It pays to make good teas." This phrasing is instructive. Brokers do not see themselves as just "qualifying" tea by separating the "good" from the average or subpar. They explicitly understand their work as one of actively bringing good teas into being. For them, qualification "pays"—it is remunerative to them, to sellers, and to buyers—because it is part of the production process. In this way, the process of tea tasting in brokerage houses exemplifies what Deborah Heath and Anne Meneley describe as "the historical dialectic between techne (knowledge as embodied art, craft, or skill), on the one hand, and episteme (knowledge as systematic classification or regimes of taste, value, and expertise), on the other hand."[8] In many ways, brokers are aesthetic experts, not unlike storytellers or visual artists. On the techne side of the dialectic, they must hone an embodied ability to craft subjective experiences of taste into words and numbers. On the epistemic side, brokers are guardians of a system of classification and valuation. They are part of a commodity infrastructure that spans from remote tea plantations to antique coal-fired processing factories to secure riverside warehouses to bronze scales, stained ceramic cups, and white aprons. These devices are tools for harmonizing the cyclical brewing and steeping process, monitored in Nilhat House by the regulator clocks and executed by the tasting room workers, with annual cycles of growing and harvesting (figure 5). The task of differentiating between grades, tastes,

FIGURE 5. Between tastings. Photo by author.

regions, and factory processes is one of several "real-life experiments" aimed at producing quality in the market.[9]

Making quality tea means at the same time making, and reproducing, quality bodies. Shapin, drawing on the work of the sociologist Antoine Hennion, notes that an outsize amount of theoretical attention has been paid to "the social uses of taste, . . . taste as a social marker[,] . . . explanations of changing tastes, [and] . . . fashion as a social phenomenon."[10] Embodiment is important in this line of analysis, where "taste" connotes both a sensory experience and a metaphorical referent for what the social theorist Pierre Bourdieu terms "distinction."[11] Some*thing* can taste good, and some*one* can have good taste.

The tasting procedures of brokers like Mr. Dey date to the British colonial period. The implements, the words, and even the clocks on the walls are reminders of this legacy. Among Mr. Dey and his colleagues, the fact that British merchants devised this entire evaluation system is well known and even celebrated. An article in the Indian newspaper *The Hindu* refers to tea brokerage as "the gentleman's trade," replete with "the romance of colonial hangover."[12] Tasting is a technique that reproduces a particular kind of body—that of an expert (male) broker. In Kolkata, that body exudes the values that attend middle-class Indian masculinity.

Mr. Dey is considered to be good at his job in part because he possesses that particular kind of "good taste" in manner, dress, and words. This is what Bourdieu might call the *habitus* of the successful broker, a set of bodily and personal dispositions that are determined in large part by his place in a capitalist, colonially derived social structure.[13] College-educated, born into a prominent family, and a member of several social and sporting clubs, Mr. Dey is a connoisseur of tea as well as Scotch whiskey (he prefers Laphroaig). Company profiles of tea brokers tend to list their interests in cricket, football, and badminton, as well as theater and travel. While some younger brokers avoid alcohol, cigarettes, garlic, and onions for fear that they might damage their palates, Mr. Dey remains a committed gourmand. He has no doubt about his abilities.

On one of my first days at work in Nilhat House in 2009, I joined Mr. Dey in the office of Mr. Chetal, another senior broker with decades of experience at J. Thomas. I asked them how they became tea brokers. They looked at me as if I had asked them how to make a bowl of cereal. They stressed that their path to tea brokerage was anything but "interesting." They answered nearly in unison, "When we finished our studies, we just applied to the companies." They were talking about an array of companies. Tea, tobacco, textiles, and advertising were the big growth industries at that time, now nearly forty years ago. Mr. Dey and Mr. Chetal both remembered that they were, as they put it, "picked up" by tea but that they had friends who were picked up by other industries.

In his foundational study of taste, Bourdieu asked where seemingly natural embodied know-how—about dress, food, art, and music—comes from. For Bourdieu, how foods or drinks are supposed to taste is bound up with class-based norms about how someone is supposed to act or how someone is supposed to dress. Darjeeling tea, for example, is supposed to be drunk without milk or sugar. Its taste is supposed to be light-bodied with a muscatel flavor. Thanks to colonially and economically embedded ideas about how people are supposed to behave and how things are supposed to taste, Mr. Dey's abilities and the tea before him come to appear natural. These normative assumptions about masculinity, class, and success are immaterial legacies, somatic and linguistic remains of the Bengali elite's entanglement with British economic and political elites in the commercial spaces of old Calcutta. Mr. Dey and Mr. Chetal seemed to be indicating that they had been "picked up" because they had a kind of inborn know-how. "Again, it's not really that interesting," Mr. Chetal insisted.

Bourdieu's ideas suggest a plausible connection between quality and markets, but following Heath, Meneley, and other scholars, I want to propose a slightly different answer to the question of why things like tea come to appear naturally possessed of qualities such as taste and texture, as well as why certain individuals come to appear naturally endowed with the ability to identify those qualities. One thing that gets left out of analyses of taste that focus on human habitus is the lively material force of nonhuman objects. Theory in feminist science and technology studies emphasizes that techniques of evaluation are never independent of the objects being evaluated.[14] Quality can only can be determined insofar as tea is *actively* affecting the body of the taster. Tasting is a thus process of what Karen Barad calls "intra-action." In intra-action, body and matter are difficult to separate analytically.[15] Masculinity still matters here, but from the perspective Barad outlines, economic and racial differences circulate with and are rearticulated through intimate sensory engagement with tea.

As Shapin argues, drawing again on the work of Hennion, to understand tasting as technique rather than just an expression of social distinction, it is necessary to attend to "tasters' efforts momentarily to make themselves objects rather than subjects, to arrange 'a stronger presence of the tasted object', to attend to and respond to what the tasted object reveals, what it is saying."[16] The feminist anthropologist and philosopher Annemarie Mol adds, "The 'body' able to sense, to appreciate, and to be pleased, is not singular and isolated, but linked with others and the world. . . . [T]he tasting body is socially embedded. . . . [I]t does not just learn from others, but also from what it eats and drinks."[17] Tasting—or arranging a stronger presence of the things we taste—can make the historical, political, and geographic differences engendered by colonialism and capitalism appear natural, but as Mol suggests in her discussion of tasting fair trade chocolate, it might equally "infuse" the body with values of ethicality, fairness, or justice.[18] But this infusion goes both ways. Tasting can also confer qualities on the thing being tasted. When tea exits the tasting room, no matter where it goes, that embodied encounter, that maleness, that colonial legacy, is embedded in it.

The head is the locus of Bourdieu's notion of taste. It is where the materiality of the thing meets the materiality of the body.[19] Eyes, noses, and tongues sense teas. Those same heads render sensory experience into words and numbers. But the tea that brokers evaluate in their daily tastings is the product of other kinds of work, namely, that of plucking, pruning, and machine processing that takes place on plantations. Taste thus emerges not just at the point where tea meets the heads of brokers but also where it meets the feet, hands, hair, arms, and legs of tea workers hundreds and sometimes thousands of miles away. In other words, the work of producing commodities through machinery, soils, plants, and the other trappings of commodity chains is that of training and disciplining bodies across space and time, in a nonlinear fashion.[20]

When brokers evaluate tea, they are not just thinking in one direction, about an imagined buyer or consumer. They are also deeply concerned with what goes on in plantation fields and factories. The brokers here are Janus-faced "buffers" between different groups of people and different material things.[21] The importance of this buffering can be read in the cups of the tasting room. Steep after steep of black tea stains the white ceramic vessels. One day, one of the office clerks saw me looking at the empty cups and, unprompted, said, "You may think it's dirty, but it's not. In a clear white cup, you don't experience the *deepness*." Tea does not taste the same in a squeaky-clean cup. The patina left by previous cups serves as a kind of visual reminder of the past and future of these practices. For brokers, "deepness" is both spatial and temporal.

In my interviews with Mr. Dey and Mr. Chetal, both men seemed far more interested in talking about the on-the-job training that took place at Nilhat House than talking about what they had done before they came to J. Thomas. As Mr. Chetal put it, "You train and train under your seniors, and one day you realize that you are training yourself through your own processes of experimentation." It is at the point that you embrace this experimental approach, they agreed, that you actually become a tea broker. In tea, training includes how to make a cup of tea—taking into account weight, "cuppage," timing, and water temperature—but it also includes orientation to the dynamics of geography, seasonal variations, factory finishing, and shipping. This knowledge is hard to transmit between people by writing or speech alone. For this reason, according to the brokers, the "right kind" of person has to be invited to train.

On a busy day during the height of the summer's monsoon flush in 2016, I entered the tasting room of J. Thomas. Samples of tea were lined up in little plastic bags down the windowsill and across the front table, waiting to be steeped. Mr. Dey swept through the door of the tasting room, and a line of apprentice executives (also referred to as "juniors," "junior brokers," or

FIGURE 6. An apprentice and a senior broker tasting. Photo by author.

"management trainees") filed in behind him (figure 6). The apprentices grabbed aprons and tried awkwardly to loop them over their necks as they followed him at full speed to the back corner of the tasting room. I had been talking casually to one apprentice, Sarath, when he suddenly cut himself off midsentence. "I have to go taste with my senior," he interjected, and fell in line with the others.

Summer 2016 had seen the intake of a fresh crop of young apprentice brokers. After Sarath ran off to taste with his senior, I turned to two very new recruits, Vivek and Benoy. Vivek had only been with J. Thomas for a couple of days at that point. Benoy had been working there for a few months. Benoy grew up in Kolkata, went to school in Pune, and then received a master's degree in international finance at Durham University in England. Vivek was working in a hotel in New Delhi while completing a degree in hospitality management before he started at the company. Vivek told me that one of the other new apprentices, Kunal, also came to J. Thomas after working in hotels.

Vivek seemed particularly interested in showing me and anyone else who would listen that he possessed "good taste" in the Bourdieuian sense. Vivek told the company in his job interview that he wanted to do for Assam and Darjeeling something akin to what others had done for Scotch whiskey. As his senior broker, Mr. Hazarika, told me proudly, "He was in hoteling and was a food management guy—he knew his alcohol. He will have to make us cocktails sometime."

At one point, Vivek took it upon himself to follow up on his mission to Scotch-ify Indian tea. He began to tell me—in a litany of details—about Scotland, tartan, shortbread, bagpipes, and all, naming geographic points of interest and linking regions to different tastes and qualities. His eyes widened when I told him that I had visited Scotland several times. "Wait! Let me guess what kind of Scotch you like." He deliberated for a second. "Speyside." Since I had actually heard of this before, I said that yes, it was my favorite. He told me that Speyside Scotch was not very smoky, unlike Balvenie and Lagavulin, which he preferred.

Vivek certainly knew the right words, but technique was another matter. Mr. Hazarika, who was the senior broker in charge of CTC, called for Vivek, Benoy, and me to come with him to taste. We each rolled a spit bucket with us and fell in line. You can spot novice brokers by their spitting technique. Mr. Hazarika danced between leaf and cup—touching the infused leaf and pressing his index finger into it before deftly spitting the aerated tea into the bucket like a water fountain. The apprentices and I had to dip our heads closer to the spit bucket so as not to make a mess.

Mr. Hazarika turned to tell us that there were several old teas in this sale. "See how they are pinkish?," he asked, pointing to the cups of liquor. "They taste like plastic, don't they? Why do they taste like this?" He picked up one of the cups and told me to taste it. While I was slurping, he answered his own question: "It is because they have been sitting in their packing material for too long, and they've gotten a little damp." We were tasting an invoice from April, so at this point, in mid-July, it was already quite old. CTC, and all tea really, "is a game against moisture," Mr. Hazarika explained. The type of container in which tea has been shipped, the time spent in storage, and the journey time from the mountain regions of Darjeeling or the flooded plains of Bengal or Assam all must be factored into any judgment of its quality.[22]

Mr. Hazarika called out numbers across the table of samples to the clerk, who recorded them as he pushed his writing easel down the line. "And again. . . . And again." The clerk called out a grade—"BPS"—and the taster replied with a price and a quick justification for that price. "Dull Cup." Slurp, slurp, slurp. Spit. "Green." Another price.

An alarm on the wall dinged, indicating to the tasting room staff that it was time to decant additional trays of tea. Boxes of Amul Taaza milk sat on the counter waiting to be added to the liquor for tasting. The broker slurped another cup. "Bright infusion. 180." He turned to one apprentice and pointed out that this tea was also old, and that "it has no keep. . . . It is going to go flat in a few months' time. You may be able to sell it to smaller packeters, but people who would want to export won't be interested. Exporters might sit on a tea for seven to eight months before blending it or shipping it—maybe as much as twelve months. They need a tea that can keep." You can discern "keep," Mr. Hazarika summarized before moving on to the next cup, from the brightness of the infusion.

Bright. Keep. Dull. Pink. Green. The words made less and less sense. Another senior broker, Mr. Agarwal, who also specialized in CTC, joined us and pulled me back to the tray that we had just tasted. He narrated the tray for me, highlighting the different yellow and brownish liquors. It was my assumption that brown was good, yellow was not so good, and pink was bad. But he pointed out that it was not about goods and bads. Brown and yellowish teas each have a different market. And pink tea, of course, has a market too, "the price-conscious market," Mr. Agarwal said, smirking.

I fell back in line with Mr. Hazarika and his apprentices. "Thinner cup," Mr. Hazarika told the clerk. "Dull infusion. Keep it at 50."

TEAWORDS

Teas are not just valued for the way they taste when brewed. No single sensation connotes quality.[23] Words like *bright* or *stewy* are partial attempts to describe the human experience of look, smell, feel, and taste. As Mr. Pal, a broker specializing in orthodox tea, once told me, "[Tea is] an *agri*-product, so this is a *natural* variability." Brokers claimed to be able to corral tea's "nature" into a few clipped words. Mr. Pal picked up a lid with leaves piled on top of it. "See the color of this?," He asked. "See how it is brighter than this one?" He picked up the lid of a tea farther down the line. "This is brightness." *Bright* can describe both steeped leaves and liquor. *Brightness* is a good quality for tea to have.

Next, Mr. Pal pointed out black flecks in another infusion. Some of the leaves were black, but not all of them. He explained that this tea was fired in the plantation factory at too high a temperature and thus did not have enough moisture left in it. The dry leaves had soaked up too much moisture during transport, and the end result was *blackness*. A *blackish* tea would have no shelf life.

"It's common sense," Mr. Pal said. For trained brokers like him, these words had come to seem like natural descriptors of tea's quality. I tried to scribble down everything Mr. Pal was saying as fast as I could. "Put your notebook away," he reprimanded. "The words are not important. They will not help you. You have to learn to taste first. Go study the words at home. It's like doing homework. You don't read while you are at lecture. You read before. Then you need to taste a lot of teas. *A lot.*"

The CTTA regularly publishes a glossary of nearly 150 words to describe tea. This glossary, which was indeed studied by apprentice brokers between tastings, was first devised in the early 1930s by C. R. Harler, the chemist and meteorologist at Tocklai, the Indian Tea Association's scientific headquarters, located in Assam. In 1932, Harler published an article titled "Tea Tasters' Terms" in the ITA's *Quarterly Journal.* There, he described what he saw as a pressing need to determine quality scientifically and objectively. At the time, "there was no common language, even among Brokers, to describe the characteristics of tea."[24] Aware of tea's variability, Harler noted that "a complete analysis [of made tea] would also indicate ultimate differences between teas from various districts, and useful conclusions might be drawn regarding methods in different areas."[25] Harler longed for definitive statements of quality—for words that captured those "ultimate differences" among teas. He wrote, "With the help of the tea taster, much empirical knowledge relating to the effect of factory methods on the finished product has been gained." The utility of a glossary for tea tasting, he argued, would be to express "the effect of leaf and factory conditions on the tea made, and . . . the influence of various conditions in withering, rolling, fermentation, and firing on the finished commodity."[26]

Harler's article included a "Glossary of Tea Tasters' Terms," comprising what he determined to be the "commoner" words in circulation. His glossary sought to use only ordinary words—words that, he surmised, would be of most use to planters who wanted to improve the market value of their tea.

The glossary was met with considerable debate across the industry. Harler's standardized lexicon was, according to one ITA assessment, "controversial but in some cases completely inaccurate."[27] The ITA may have been skeptical of Harler's proposal (and, in fact, he left Tocklai shortly after writing his article), but he had touched a nerve.[28] There was a growing dissatisfaction among tea planters in India with brokers' comments about the quality of their tea. It became clear to ITA officials in London and Calcutta that a standard glossary would help planters and brokers understand each other.

With the assistance of the London-based Tea Brokers' Association, the ITA set out to revise Harler's list of terms. The ITA published a revised glossary in 1938, and it was adopted after several revisions by British brokers' associations, planters, and scientists at Tocklai. Word by word, representatives from different corners of the industry in Britain and India added to, subtracted from, and refined the glossary of terms that would be used to describe dry leaves, steeped leaves, and liquor.

Eventually, the CTTA published its own version of the glossary, republishing it in 1975, 1986, and 2008 with few changes.[29] The Tea Research Association (TRA), the quasi-public scientific agency that assists tea planters with agronomic and technical issues, has been publishing and revising its own (slightly longer) glossary since 1953. As a result of these efforts to establish a lexicon for describing tea, brokers' descriptions are now more uniform. The words aid in the effort to understand what has been produced in the past and to improve future production.

On the surface, the language used to describe tea, whether in 1938 or today, seems similar to that used to describe fine wine, in that there is a relatively small pool of familiar terms that occur over and over again. As in the world of wine, a familiarity with the tea lexicon—and the ability to deploy it authoritatively—is as important a marker of specialized knowledge as the dress, accent, and hobbies of upper-middle-class men.[30] But tea's language is somewhat distinct from the language of wine, in that it does not travel outside the space of brokerage.[31] Even occasional wine drinkers might feel comfortable describing a California Chardonnay as "oaky," but as the chairman of J. Thomas told me, "The language of tea is an intra-trade language. Tea is unlike wine, whose language is applied toward the consumer. [Wine] terms are evocative, finely tuned, and pleasing. They generate emotion." You could read the tea glossary in any number of forms—on posters lining the walls of the apprentices' cramped offices, in the pages of the CTTA *Tea Digest,* or in publications released by Tocklai—but to be able to use the glossary and communicate your evaluations with others, you had to "train yourself" by tasting tea.[32]

To help me understand, the chairman asked, "If I said 'stewy' to you, what would you think? It has the characteristics of stew, right? Thick, cloudy. But no, that's not what it means at all! The meaning is much more exact. It refers to the exhaust temperature. It means that it was fermented at too high a temperature, that it overfermented; it therefore has become *soft*." The words tasters used, while indicative of the sensory attributes of tea, were also indexes of particular moments in the production process. Teas were nearly always described using multiple terms from the glossary. The broker's hypothetical *stewy* tea was also *soft*. A soft tea lacked *briskness* (a quality of the liquor being live, like "fresh spring water") and *brightness* (a liquor and leaf that lacked harmful bacteria and whose colorful pop would be visible even when it was mixed with milk).[33]

In tea's intraindustry lexicon, then, a word like *stewy* is pragmatic as much as it is emotional. Each word in the lexicon "focuses the attention" of brokers and plantation managers (and, as I show below, of plantation laborers).[34] The words in this lexicon are all historically particular forms of what linguistic anthropologists call "qualia," "experiences of sensuous qualities ... and feelings."[35] When sensations and experiences become recognized as qualia, they can become endowed with cultural, social, and economic value.[36] Much like the cultural "keywords" (including "nature" and "culture") explored in Raymond Williams's classic Marxist analysis of the English language, these "teawords" signified and reified the embodied experiences of a historically particular group of powerful, white, male aesthetic experts, that is, colonial-era tea brokers.[37] These British men's decades-old responses to the sensuous qualities of Indian tea, routed through the technoscientific and institutional circuits of Tocklai and the London and Calcutta headquarters of the ITA, are indirectly recalled in those posters and intraindustry publications.

But teawords are not just hegemonic linguistic ruins of empire. They are continually redeployed in the contemporary Indian tea industry as "market devices," "material and discursive assemblages that intervene in the construction of markets."[38] The glossary of teawords acts as what Shapin terms an "intersubjectivity engine," which "allow[s] people to coordinate their subjective experiences and to agree about the language to be used in sharing those subjective experiences with others."[39] This sharing, however, is always uneven. It is the circulation of teawords within the closed communicative circuit between tea brokerage houses, tea plantations, and tea research stations that continually maintains the unequal material and social conditions of tea's production. The result is not only the rendering of taste into the numerical register of price but also the recapitulation and reinforcement of colonially derived forms of bodily discipline. The training of bodies—of brokers and of distant field and factory laborers—to respond to tea's material qualities in a coherent if differentiated way is a prerequisite to setting prices, to making sales, and even to marketing the beverage to consumers who more than likely will never hear of such a thing as a *stewy* tea.

MUSTERING TASTE, VALUING BODIES

Brokers have two objectives when they taste. First, they taste so that they can give advice to plantations on how to improve their manufacturing processes. Second, they taste so that they can put a monetary value on each invoice up for auction. Brokers divide this work into two different tastings: muster tastings and valuation tastings.

A muster tasting happens within days of a brokerage firm receiving an invoice from a plantation. Though plantation managers give each invoice a grade (see table 1), these grades are never taken at face value. Here is how Mr. Dutta, the senior broker "looking after" J. Thomas's Darjeeling catalog evaluated a few trays of tea in a muster tasting at the end of the second flush in 2009:

> [*Slurps. Picks up the bag of dry leaf and reads it, then examines the leaf. Slurps again.*] Tippy clonals still have fair *make*. More emphasis on sorting would be of benefit.... [*Smells leaves. Slurps one cup, then the next.*] *Mixed*. Fannings are acceptable.... Clonal has *brightness* and *character*, but *quality* is not there. 300. [*Slurps another cup.*] And again.... A little short in appearance and also not entirely *clean. Bloom* is lacking.

Mr. Dutta next poured the dry leaf onto a piece of cardstock. He shook it back and forth, giving it a few flicks with the back of his fingertips, before bending the cardstock in his hand and funneling the tea back into the bag. In the process, bits of tea escaped onto the floor, crunching beneath his feet as we moved down the table. "Special Chinas have fair *make,* although a little *uneven.*" "TGBOP?," the clerk prompted.

> Contains *broken* as well as *flaky* leaf. [*Slurps another.*] Brokens are *mushy*. [*Slurps. Shrugs while spitting.*] Fannings *neat*, suitable. [*Slurps another.*]

Suitably sorted and clonal has a good show of *tip*. Good flavor and *brightness . . .* 350. [*Slurps another.*] Clonal sample hardly has any *tip*. . . . Fannings acceptable sizes. . . . Earlier invoices have some *brightness* and *character*, but teas from 18 [the invoice number ending in 18] onwards show a decline . . . 350 . . . and again . . . and again.

The numbers at the muster tasting are messages to plantations about the prospective price of each invoice. When Mr. Dutta says "350," he is naming that prospective price in rupees per kilogram, and he is promising that J. Thomas will pay the plantation 50 percent of that price before auction. After auction, J. Thomas will pay the difference between that initial payment (in this case Rs. 175 per kg) and the sale price. When Mr. Dutta says "again," he is indicating that the invoice he is tasting should be given a prospective price identical to the previous one.

Mr. Dutta moved on to a new tray, and a different plantation's tea.

[*Slurps a couple of teas in a row.*] Leaf grades need more *style*. Slight improvement on later dates, but teas need to be more *even*. . . . [*Slurps.*] Second flush needs to be *heavier*. On the *blackish* side . . . 300. [*Slurps another.*] Short in appearance and contains brokens as well as *flaky* leaf. Not free from *stalk*. . . . [*Slurps another.*] Touch of *briskness*, but *character* needs to be more prominent. [*Slurps another.*] Brokens and fannings suitably sorted but teas are a little *plain* . . . 280.

Mr. Dutta pointed to one of the teas on this last tray. "See the difference?," he asked his apprentice, who had been following him down the line.

The apprentice nodded. Then Mr. Dutta directed his quality comments to the clerk: "Grades become *smaller* and *uneven*, need to possess more *style*. . . . The liquors of 98, 99 have a little *brightness* and *character*, but the remaining cups are a little *colory*. . . . [*Slurps and spits.*] 300. . . . [*Slurps and spits.*] 550."

If they get a burnt sensation, brokers dictate in their quality comments that the tea has been fired at too high a temperature. If they see thick stalks amid the steeped tea, they report that the tea has been "clumsily" or "coarsely" plucked or not sorted properly. Quality comments, rendered in teawords, have direct implications for the management of the laboring bodies who pick, prune, and process leaves. Muster tasting is a process by which metropolitan male experts evaluate tea harvested by ethnically marked women in fields on the edges of India, from Assam to Kerala.

On tea plantations, women workers manually comb tea bushes for tender shoots of tea, breaking them off between their thumbs and index fingers and

TABLE 1 Grades of Tea, CTTA (2008)

ORTHODOX TEA

Whole Leaf

FP: Flowery Pekoe
FTGFOP: Fine Tippy Golden Flowery Orange Pekoe (also FTGFOP1 and STGFOP/
SFTGFOP) ["S" means Super or Supreme]
TGFOP1: Tippy Golden Flowery Orange Pekoe 1
TGFOP: Tippy Golden Flowery Orange Pekoe
GFOP: Golden Flowery Orange Pekoe
FOP: Flowery Orange Pekoe
OP: Orange Pekoe

Broken

BOP 1: Broken Orange Pekoe One
GFBOP: Golden Flowery Broken Orange Pekoe
BPS: Broken Pekoe Souchong
GBOP: Golden Broken Orange Pekoe
FBOP: Flowery Broken Orange Pekoe
BOP: Broken Orange Pekoe

CTC TEA

Broken

PEK: Pekoe
BP: Broken Pekoe
BOP: Broken Orange Pekoe
BPS: Broken Pekoe Souchong
BP1: Broken Pekoe 1
FP: Flowery Pekoe

Fannings

OF: Orange Fannings
PF: Pekoe Fannings
PF1: Pekoe Fannings 1
BOPF: Broken Orange Pekoe Fannings

NOTE: Most brokers with whom I worked would say that there is no clear hierarchy of grades. These are thus given in the order that the CTTA presents them.

tossing fistfuls into conical straw baskets strung from their foreheads. Indian labor law mandates that workers be issued plastic aprons and rubber boots to protect them from the sharp, protruding branches of the tea bushes, as well as from leeches and snakebites. In the off-season, women flog these same bushes with small sickles to ensure that the tender shoots return with the next rains.

Blistered, cut, and blackened by dirt, sap, and chlorophyll, women tea workers' bodies are monitored and protected by national labor codes as well as international trade standards. Women on India's numerous organic-certified plantations, for example, are prohibited from wearing gloves. Regulators fear that cotton or other fabric might adulterate the tea. Indeed, it is the image of a woman's bare fingers, pinching two leaves and a bud, that often accompanies tea advertisements and adorns packaging. Value in the consumer market is attached to a symbolic association between women and tea, but the tasting process reveals that this association is more than symbolic. In its taste, smell, and appearance, tea contains messages about the material conditions of field labor, and when brokers relay those messages back to plantation management, everything from work hours to wages to protective equipment are up for reevaluation. Through the tasting process, the noses and tongues of male brokers at Nilhat House are thus materially and semiotically linked to the hands of women tea workers in plantation fields.

Ideas about people and their proclivities for agricultural labor were integrated into colonial algorithms for the efficient production of tea. From its inception, the plantation system depended on the careful and repeated evaluation of racially marked bodies.[40] Though British tea-growing regions were inhabited by indigenous populations, the British recruited or indentured "coolies" from regions and ethnic groups they determined most suited for the construction and maintenance of plantation infrastructure.[41]

Since the colonial era, the job of tea planters in India has been to maximize quality according to algorithms designed to control the costs of production. The quality comments from muster tastings are intended to help optimize the relationship between raw material, machinery, and labor. In their calculations of the costs of production and the monetary return on each invoice of tea, planters must consider the comments of brokers in Kolkata alongside an array of other technical questions, from the proportion of burned coal to made tea to the cost of rubber boots to the price of rice and flour rations to the cost of nurseries and primary schooling for the children of workers who live on the plantation.[42] In the muster tasting, or more precisely, in the dried, steeped, and strained tea under review, the spatialities and temporalities of field, factory, and tasting room become entangled. As Barad argues, following Leela Fernandes, gender and ethnicity are not merely cultural add-ons to economic structures; they are co-constituted by political economic systems and the hardware (from rubber boots to sickles to coal-fired machinery to tasting procedures) that supports then.[43] The embodied work of plantation laborers and tea brokers reverberate through tea itself.

If the muster tasting is a technique for disciplining the bodies of faraway workers, it is also one of several moments in which brokers, as Mr. Chetal put it, "train themselves." Much of this training happens in the Juniors' Room, two small, crowded interconnected offices on the fourth floor of Nilhat House. The suite is filled with old wooden desks and leather swivel chairs, all facing toward the center. Taped to the walls are maps of tea-growing regions and J. Thomas–issued posters explaining the tea tasting process and the glossary of teawords. On one of his first days as an apprentice, in June 2016, Vivek sat at his desk with a binder of printouts open in front of him, complaining that it was really difficult to remember the names of all the plantations. "The Darjeeling ones kind of make sense," he said, "but the other ones are difficult." One of the three women apprentices, Radhi, could relate. She had only been working at J. Thomas for a month and a half and was "still trying to keep them straight."

During my research in 2009 and 2010, I never saw another woman in the tasting room. When I returned in 2016, there were four women executives. Women had not been officially barred from the profession. One of the most notable women tea brokers worked in the 1980s with one of the firms in Kolkata, but she left the business to open a now-popular tea shop in South Kolkata.

Much as I had quizzed Mr. Dey and Mr. Chetal, I asked Radhi how she got into tea. She recalled a familiar if slightly more formalized recruitment process. While she was still a student at St. Xavier's, a posh coeducational English-language college in Kolkata, J. Thomas alerted the school that it would be hiring new executives. One hundred eighty students from St. Xavier's tried to get a "placement." J. Thomas anticipates these kinds of numbers and regularly recruits from St. Xavier's (the alma mater of a slew of prominent Indian scholars, businesspeople, bureaucrats, and public figures), as well as from a few other select English-medium institutions in Kolkata. To negotiate the scale of applications, the firm holds group discussions, or what Radhi and her peers called GDs, with ten students and three senior employees from J. Thomas. As Radhi explained, group discussions are not political or about anything for which one might need prior or specialized knowledge. The topic of Radhi's GD was, "Where there is a will there is a way." I asked her what that meant. "It was just a group discussion," she said. I must have looked a little baffled, because she continued, "We just talked about what that meant. It wasn't really that big of a deal, and with that many people, you couldn't say that much anyway.... You know, we just talked about perseverance."

After the GD, a select number of students are invited for personal interviews, or PIs. After that, there is a written test and another PI. "It took *so* long," Radhi said. It was during the process of waiting that Radhi actually met one of the other women, Puthi, with whom she now shared this half of the Juniors' Room. They were put in touch by mutual friends as everyone else they knew was slowly rejected in the consecutive rounds of screening. Radhi and Puthi were the only two people recruited from St. Xavier's that year.

I asked Magha, the third woman on this side of the Juniors' Room, if she "applied" to work at J. Thomas. "No. How would I know to apply?," she scoffed. Magha was enrolled in St. Xavier's for her master's degree in marketing when she "got picked up" the year before Radhi and Puthi. "I hardly knew anything about tea. I had no idea that the industry was so big," she explained. She took a long drag of her cigarette and blew it straight into the middle of the room. "I thought I knew about tea. I knew about the gardens, but not that there were fourteen-hundred-odd of them."

Normally quiet, Puthi echoed, "Who would have known?"

"What about J. Thomas? Had you ever heard of them?," I asked.

"No way. I was just going to school over there," Magha said. She pointed back in the direction of Park Street and St. Xavier's, a couple of metro stops away. "I never knew *this* was here, or that tea was brokered. I didn't know anything about tea other that it is something that I liked to drink."

It was only because the company was recruiting through St. Xavier's—and it turned out that they were explicitly trying to recruit women—that Magha, Radhi, and Puthi came to work at J. Thomas.

Vivek never had a GD. GDs, he explained, are only used when there are many applicants from one institution. He applied directly to the company by sending his résumé.

"So you knew about J. Thomas, then?," I asked.

"Of course," he said. He came to Kolkata for an initial PI. Then he came back for another PI and the written test. Vivek did his second PI and his written test on the same day as Kunal.

I asked about the written test. Kunal explained, "It's an IQ test. Riddles and things like that. Normal IQ stuff."

The written test, like the GD, is not something for which you can study. It does not test specific knowledge about tea or anything else. All five of the apprentices started trying to remember the questions.

"There was the one about a painting hanging on a wall . . . ," Radhi said.

"Ohh. Ohhh! The widow question . . . ," Vivek exclaimed.

"Oh right, right," said Kunal, standing up, trying to viscerally jog his memory. "Something like, 'In Scotland, can you marry the wife of a widower?'" There was a collective pause.

"What did you answer for that?," Vivek asked Kunal, clearly unsure of his own answer.

"It doesn't matter that it's in Scotland. You can't marry the wife of a widower because the wife is dead," Kunal said. Then he turned to me. "See. They're simple, but you just keep thinking about them."

In an interview with Mr. Agarwal, a senior broker who also participated in a round of GDs at St. Xavier's, I asked what made a good tea broker. What were they looking for among the students vying for these positions? He answered that they were looking for people who "could use their brains."

"We are not looking for the smartest guy, but someone who can apply their knowledge." The ideal apprentice should not be "book smart." Instead, Mr. Agarwal and other senior brokers looked for someone who played sports.

"Any sport in particular?," I asked.

It did not much matter, he explained, as long as they were *team* sports. Formal team sports are more common at expensive English-language residential schools like St. Xavier's and the primary schools that feed them. The kinds of questions asked in GDs and PIs, and even in the written test, attempted to identify in the applicants an ability to work collaboratively, to follow rules, but also to respond, like a well-trained athlete, to subtle environmental cues.[44] In addition to people with the cultural capital that came from expensive private schooling, what J. Thomas was looking for was the kind of person who would be able to experiment on himself (or herself).

In the middle of our discussion of the recruitment process, Mr. Agarwal came into the Juniors' Room and barked orders to the apprentices to start contacting sellers. They all scattered, punching in numbers on their mobile phones.

Vivek was not working with any accounts yet, so when Mr. Agarwal called everyone to order, he sat down at his desk and began to study the names of CTC tea grades he had written out on a piece of notebook paper.

"I joined late," Vivek told me. He needed to catch up. He would start his formal training next week. I asked what this would entail. He thought that he would start by going to the warehouses on the banks of the Hooghly where J. Thomas stored tea in advance of auction. Then he would move to the accounts and computer department, across the hall from the Juniors' Room. There were a couple of computers in this department, but perhaps more striking were the towering stacks of paper piled high on antique wooden desks and shelves upon shelves of files recording the valuations and sales of tea going back further than the executives even knew. "At least a hundred years," Vivek guessed confidently.

Vivek looked across the Juniors' Room from his desk in the corner, watching his fellow executives take long draws on cigarettes as they tapped on their computer keyboards or walked in and out of the office, papers and mobile phones in hand. He leaned over the desk and whispered to me, "Those cigarettes will destroy their palates."

TASTING PRICE

In the muster tasting, brokers communicate not just notes on the qualities of production and manufacture but also a prospective price. These prospective prices travel back to plantations along with quality comments, but they are not the prices that will be circulated to buyers prior to auction. These "valuation prices" are determined in the second tasting that brokers perform: the valuation tasting. While the muster tasting happens almost as soon as brokers receive an invoice, in the valuation tasting, brokers are seeing teas for a second time, just a few days before the auction sale.

For a valuation tasting of early monsoon CTC teas in 2010, the tasting room staff at J. Thomas busily laid out 300 samples for Mr. Chetal. After steeping and straining the teas, a worker walked through and dropped a teaspoonful of milk into each cup. (CTC brokers do their valuation tastings with milk, since CTC is nearly always consumed with milk.) The steeping time is tightly regulated, but after steeping, the cups can just sit there, sometimes for hours, jiggling under the blowing of the air-conditioning. Brokers do not taste hot teas. They insist on waiting for them to cool down so that they can be evaluated with more accuracy. As a result, CTCs awaiting tasting develop a thin layer of congealed milky film on top.

Mr. Chetal picked up a cup. [*Slurps.*] "A little *blacker*. Try 146." He then turned to the clerk and asked, "OF [Orange Fannings] value?" The clerk responded, "142."

Whereas samples of tea in the muster tasting are referred to as invoices, in the valuation tasting, they become "lots." While "invoice" indicates a

FIGURE 7. Orthodox tea tasting. Photo by author.

movement from producer to broker, "lot" indicates a movement from broker to buyer. As if to mark this subtle change of status, in the valuation tasting, small aluminum tins, adorned with lot numbers marked in green paint, replace the plastic bags that held the dry leaf in the muster tasting (figure 7). Mr. Chetal dumped the contents of the aluminum tin onto his cardstock and sifted it around. "A little *black*, 144. Good sizes."

"OF?," he asked the clerk.

The clerk responded with a last-sold-at price of 144.

"*Grainy,* leave it at 144," Mr. Chetal said.

"Lot 19?" the clerk prompted.

"*Grainier, blacker.* Drop 2."

"Lot 20?

"Again. *Red* cup."

"Lot 21. Last sold 122."

"*Browner.*" Mr. Chetal went all the way back to Lot 6 and compared it to Lot 21. "Take 4 rupees off that [off of Lot 6]." He crunched the kernels of CTC under his feet as he moved back and forth down the line of teas. Again, he took two different samples of dry leaf on his cardstock—one in each hand. He looked at them and then reversed them, putting one hand under the other to give him a different perspective. He switched back, looked, then brought the opposite hand under the other. He switched back one final time before calling out two valuation prices for the two lots.

"From Central Dooars, last sold 138." [*Slurps.*] "This is a much better tea. This will be 142."

On another lot, he noted that the quality had declined. [*Slurps.*] He examined the color of the liquor, holding the cup up against another. "*Pink* cup." He dropped the price from last week's sale. [*Slurps the next cup.*] "What's the lowest BPS [Broken Pekoe Souchong]?," Mr. Chetal asked the clerk. He took this cup of tea back down the line, slurped, and spit one and then the other. "Drop by 1." [*Slurps another.*] "Hmm. That is a nice tea." "Value?," he asked the clerk.

"144."

"Why not? 144," he responded. [*Slurps another.*] He stopped for a moment. [*Slurps the next one and spits.*] "A little *duller*" [*Slurps.*] "*Harsh, smoky* . . . 140 . . . 138."

"BOP?"

[*Slurps*] "A little thin. *Blacker, chemical. Dry.* Drop it to 120."

"BOP Supreme?"

"Leave it at 126. Good cup."

"BP Supreme?"

"*Small.*"

"Valued at 180."

"Try 180. [*Slurps another cup.*] Some discolored particles. Drop it to 112. . . . This looks like another tea . . . " He trailed off, cup in hand, and walked down the line to find it. Fluorescent lights reflected off the surface of the milky tea as he passed. [*Slurps.*] "Hmm. Still not as good as the first one. Try 160." He looked at another tea, tasted it, and shook his head: "Terrible. 104 . . . [*Slurps another.*] I did a BP Supreme like that . . . " Mr. Chetal paused, as if trying to jog his memory.

The clerk called out a lot number to remind Mr. Chetal of the other BP Supreme's location. Mr. Chetal went down and compared it to the cup he just tasted. "Hmm. 128. That's a better tea." He picked the steeped leaves of the next cup and pushed on them with his index finger. He picked up the liquor and slurped. *"Blacker.* Tastes very *smoky."*

Dry leaves, steeped leaves, brewed liquor. Although this was CTC, the cheapest product available at auction, Mr. Chetal examined each of these elements in each lot in a manner identical to that which would be applied to fine orthodox teas. *"Thin.* 126." He tasted another. "Hmm." He pondered, while the tea was still in his mouth. With tea still in his mouth, he lifted his hand and flipped his fingers upward, implying that the clerk should bring the price up. Then he spit.

"Slatey. Flaky. Burnt." He dropped the price of another lot by five rupees. He pushed around the steeped leaf of yet another, picked up the cup and slurped, then asked the clerk, "Standard is how much?" He walked back down the table to a sample that was not accompanied by a number. This sample was a standard from the previous sale, to which these teas could be (but did not need to be) compared (not all brokers taste using standards). He tasted the standard and looked at the cup, comparing it to the cup that he was tasting. "Make this one 124."

He picked up another cup. Then he picked up the cup of the next lot. He compared the look of the liquors. Then he switched them from left to right, right to left, slurped and spit one, then the next. "Less *bloom.* BPS large. A little *soft.* Drop this to 148. [*Slurps the second one again and looks at the leaf]* Fiber. 150 . . . "

There is a lot of walking back and forth in the valuation tasting. Valuation involves comparison, across the broker's palate and among lots. "Making good teas," as J. Thomas's motto has it, and making such teas "pay," requires suturing language to price. A broker will often only alter the valuation price of a new lot from the last sold price by one or two rupees. Price differentials might be small, but small differences in valuation price can be very significant given the quantities of CTC that will be up at auction. Brokers stake their reputations on their ability to determine the right price for each particular lot. If the quality comments at the muster tasting must be clear enough to successfully travel back to plantations, the prices given at the valuation tasting must seem "natural" enough to successfully travel into the marketplace. But encounters between the orderliness and certainty of numbers and the effusiveness of sensation are anything but predictable, as I show in the next chapter.

The Auction and the Archive

IN SUMMER 2016, VIVEK, RADHI, or one of the other apprentices was often asked to escort me down to the second floor of Nilhat House for lunch in J. Thomas's dining room. The dining room is located behind an unmarked mahogany door. Inside are two large wooden tables set with placemats and water glasses. One of the tables is for the staff and junior executives, and the other is for the senior brokers. Every day, a full kitchen staff serves a three-course meal: soup, an Indian or Continental entrée (vegetarian or nonvegetarian), and a dessert (jellied fruits topped with whipped cream served in a frilly glass-stemmed bowl was particularly popular). The walls are adorned with wood paneling and larger-than-life portraits of European men, all previous chairmen of J. Thomas. The dim light of the ornate Victorian fixtures, which seem anachronistic in the context of the otherwise modernist lines of the exterior of Nilhat House, cast shadows across the hunched diners. Junior executives talk in whispers, especially when there is an important senior broker at the other table. A soft din coming from behind the swinging door of the kitchen drowns out some of the hushed conversation.

One day when I was coming out of the dining room, I was intercepted by Mr. Agarwal, who informed me abruptly that I had been granted access to the J. Thomas boardroom, located opposite the dining room. I had asked to see the boardroom several times since I started doing research at Nilhat House in 2009, but by this point, seven years later, I had given up on ever getting the chance. Pictures of the boardroom were featured in most newspaper stories about the tea auctions, and it also contained J. Thomas's archive. I was being granted access today—right now. Mr. Agarwal told me that he was unsure if access would be granted again.

He unlocked another large mahogany door, framed by two indoor ferns, telling me as he did so that since he was very busy and had many clients to call, he would only stay for a moment. The boardroom foyer, which was also accessible by a small hidden elevator, reminded me of the lobbies of the Raj-era fetish hotels (often called heritage hotels) in central Kolkata and in Indian hill stations. Its large brass fixtures shone brightly, and its marble floors seemed to have little wear. As in the dining room, the walls of the foyer were adorned with eye-level portraits of previous chairmen. While the portraits on the walls of the dining room portrayed chairmen of the firm from before independence, the foyer portraits featured three generations of Thomases—the firm's namesakes—as well as the chairmen who had served after independence. Near the end of the line of portraits, the faces started to include Indian men, dressed in conservative suits and ties.

Although I had been asking to see the boardroom because I had been told by brokers that it contained some semblance of a paper archive—in particular, old auction catalogs—the decorations and the portraits on the wall formed another kind of archive. They traced J. Thomas not just back to the Raj, but to the earliest days of the global tea trade.

The first European tea auction is popularly thought to have taken place in March 1679 at the headquarters of the East India Company on Leadenhall Street in central London. At this auction, and throughout the 1700s and early 1800s, the Company sold tea that had been purchased by traders in China. An array of products sourced from Colombo to Canton, including opium, indigo, and spices, were offered at quarterly Company auctions in March, June, September, and December. The number of brokers who attended the East India Company's early tea auctions was relatively small. These brokers purchased tea on behalf of wholesale dealers, who sold them to individual grocers.[1]

An anonymous tea dealer, writing in the early 1800s, described the Company auctions this way:

> The sale generally occupies about ten days, during which time noise and confusion reign. To the uninitiated a Tea sale appears to be a mere arena, in which the comparative strength of lungs of a portion of his Majesty's subjects are to be tried. No one could for an instant suspect the real nature of the business for which the assemblage was congregated; in point of gesture and contention, the Chamber of Deputies in Paris can only be placed in comparison; and I think a candid Frenchman must own (however mortifying the admission) that the Tea Brokers *"have it."*[2]

The conduct of brokers, even in the early days, seemed both bombastic and oozing with a kind of enigmatic cultural capital.

The wall of portraits in the foyer of the J. Thomas boardroom archived a lineage of men in Calcutta who also "had it." From the foyer, Mr. Agarwal led me into a small sitting room, which doubled as a kind of miniature museum of British masculinity and colonial commerce. Its overstuffed chairs and antique tables were surrounded by memorabilia and decorative tea accouterments. The wall decorations included a plaque from J. Thomas's original building, also located at this site on Mission Row. Tucked between teacups and saucers and Victorian-era bric-a-brac were a smattering of awards highlighting 150 years of company wins and notable finishes in badminton, polo, and cricket competitions. Between a pewter tankard commemorating fourth place in the 1993 Merchants Cup polo match and a brass plaque memorializing a well-fought win in the 1938 Calcutta Open Limited Challenge Cup (held at the Calcutta Club) sat a trophy celebrating record-high prices for tea sold at auction. A portrait of the firm members in 1883, posed seated outside of the building at Mission Row, looked out over the sitting room. This image hung opposite a cluster of photos showing the inauguration of Nilhat House in 1961 by Jawaharlal Nehru.

Past the sitting room was the boardroom itself. To the right was a small writing desk that held some antique office implements, including an old manual calendar, the kind you turn every day to display the date and day of the week. The calendar had been set to today's date, even though the rest of the room seemed locked fifty years in the past. At the far end of the room, on a smaller table, sat a headless antique Buddha statue with no caption or provenance. The centerpiece of the boardroom was a long table, surrounded by ten matching chairs. Mr. Agarwal called my attention to the head of the table.

"Look," he said, "all of the former chairmen have carved their initials into it." The table had been refinished so many times that I couldn't feel the indentations made by the older names. A couple of new sets of initials were scratched into the near end, closest to the sitting room door.

Finally, Mr. Agarwal brought me over to a set of floor-to-ceiling glass-front cabinets, which ran down an entire wall of the boardroom. The cabinets were filled with the books that constituted the J. Thomas paper archive. These included a 1929 copy of the *Encyclopedia Britannica* and decades of annual issues of the *Tea Report* and the *Jute Report*. From season to season and year to year, these reports documented an array of statistics on the production costs and sale prices of these key colonial crops. The shelves also contained several volumes of the *Garden-wise Report,* an annual circular sent to stockholders about the conditions of tea plantation production. The *Garden-wise Report* included statistics, as well as assurances about both the tractability of the Indian labor force and the health and well-being of the European staff.

These trade journals all date to the end of the second Opium War (1856–60), when the British monopoly on the trade in Chinese tea dissolved. In the years leading up to the first Opium War (1839–42), East India Company agents explored the potential for tea cultivation in Assam, which had come under colonial control following a decade of British military incursions in the region. In the mid-nineteenth century, the East India Company, a commercial project that extended its reach through government support, gave way to the British Empire, a governmental project that extended its reach through trade and agriculture. At this point, back in London, Company auctions became "public auctions." The London tea auction venue shifted as well, from East India House on Leadenhall Street to the newly built London Commercial Sale Rooms on Mincing Lane, in what is now London's financial district.[3]

Tea plantation, retail, and brokerage interests grew around Mincing Lane, which became the global center of the tea trade. Private tea brokerage firms took the place of Company agents as brokers and auctioneers, and the field of buyers grew. Brokers sold tea on behalf of plantation companies to buyers who blended these teas for large and small retailers. This blended tea circled back around the world, neatly packaged and specially calibrated to the tastes, as well as the water chemistry and milk sources (e.g. cow, buffalo, goat), of particular markets. The London tea auctions became a weekly event. Throughout the mid- to late 1800s, more and more tea was shipped to London for sale. First came tea from India, then Ceylon, the Dutch East Indies, and, by the turn of the twentieth century, East Africa.

The first lots of India-produced tea were sent to the London auction for sale in 1838. Over the next fifteen years, tea production grew steadily in Assam and later across regions of India and colonial Ceylon, where labor and land were cheap, plentiful, and exploitable.[4] In Northeast India, "wasteland rules" permitted the accession of lands traditionally occupied by small farmers and swidden agriculturalists, whom the British deemed insufficiently industrious and whose bodies and temperaments they considered a poor fit for plantation work.[5] Recruitment schemes sent indentured laborers to Assam from central India to work on the plantations. After the annexation of the Dooars from Bhutan in 1865, plantations came to blanket much of

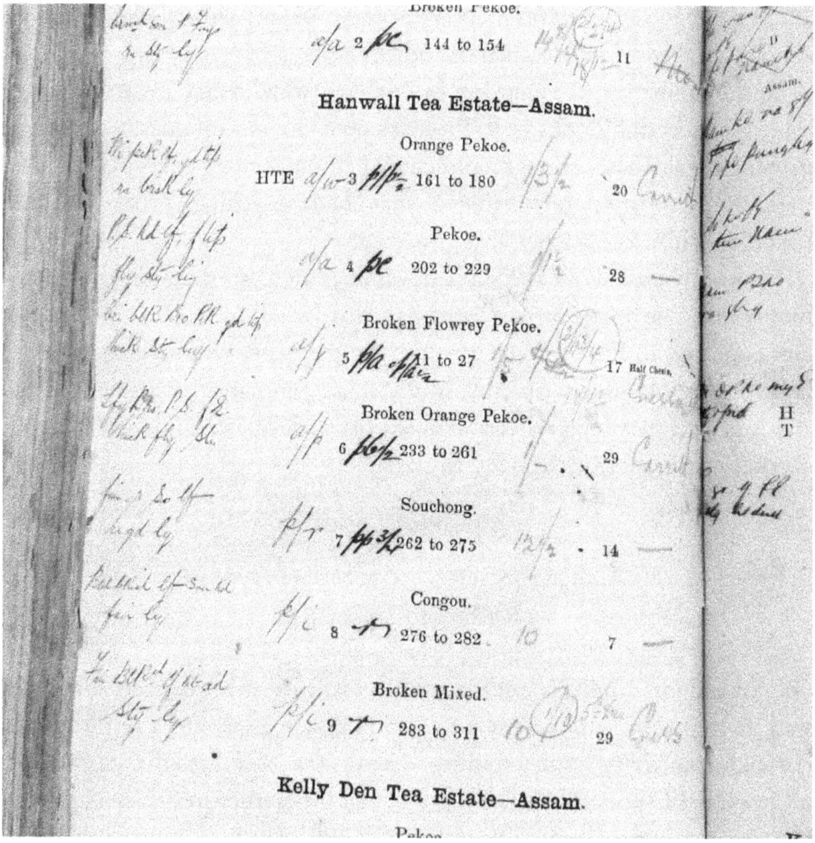
Broken Pekoe.
2 144 to 154 11

Hanwall Tea Estate—Assam.

Orange Pekoe.
HTE 3 161 to 180 20

Pekoe.
4 202 to 229 28

Broken Flowrey Pekoe.
5 11 to 27 17 Half Chests.

Broken Orange Pekoe.
6 233 to 261 29

Souchong.
7 262 to 275 14

Congou.
8 276 to 282 7

Broken Mixed.
9 283 to 311 29

Kelly Den Tea Estate—Assam.

FIGURE 8. Tea auction catalog, Calcutta, July 9, 1873. Photo by author.

Bengal and the Northeast.[6] By the 1880s, Indian and Ceylon teas had supplanted Chinese tea in popularity.[7]

Every week, suit clad buyers and brokers would pack into the auction rooms at Mincing Lane. Brokers sat at the front of the room on a raised lectern, and buyers fanned out around them, tucked into wooden seats. The scene was a theatrical one. Buyers bid on thousands of lots each week while representatives of plantation companies looked on to see how their teas fared. Rival brokers observed the excitement generated by their competitors' catalogs. Sales lasted all day. Indian teas took up two days (Mondays and Wednesdays); Ceylon teas (Tuesdays) and Java and Sumatra teas (Thursdays) took up one day each. China teas were offered on Thursdays as well, but increasingly these were distributed through private sales.[8] Lots were not announced one by one. Instead, buyers and brokers followed along with an auction catalog, which detailed the order of lots.

In the cabinets in the boardroom, Mr. Agarwal directed me to a stack of four tightly bound books of J. Thomas's own auction catalogs, grouped by date (figure 8). These catalogs represented J. Thomas's early years of operation in the 1860s. At this point, he told me that I had everything I needed and that I should let him know when I was finished.

I carefully pulled out the stack of catalogs and laid them on the boardroom table. The brittle brown paper flaked as I read them. Most of the catalogs appeared to have belonged to the same broker, who made shorthand notes in the margins with tiny, immaculate penmanship. These catalogs archived a century-long transition in the tea trade by which the main site of auctioning moved from London to India.

CATALOGS AND COMMUNICATIVE INFRASTRUCTURE

The tea auction catalog is not just a historical tool; it is a conceptual one as well. It is both a material remainder of a past regime and a testament to the enduring fixity of the trading system. The liquidity of commodities is always made possible by the fixity of the infrastructures through which they flow.[9] It is easy to presume that that infrastructure always comprises hardware like factory machinery, warehouses, and railway lines. The catalog draws our attention to an equally important *communicative* infrastructure. Communicative infrastructure is a kind of fixed capital, just as essential to the continued circulation of tea as more familiar kinds of infrastructure. As forms of capital that are relatively fixed in place, infrastructures "create the grounds on which other objects operate."[10] Communicative infrastructures are the grounds of social exchange, including its grammars, its scripts, and even its wardrobe.[11] It is only through fixed ways of communicating about tea in the auction that individual, singular lots can be circulated and, ultimately, blended. The quality of communicative infrastructure is essential to the making of quality tea. Just as the method of tasting entails experimentation on the body, within a limited set of parameters, the method of auction sale entails experimentation with words and numbers and narratives. Like forms of sensory valuation, the forms of communication recorded in the catalogs serve to keep the tea economy embedded in the fabric of contemporary Indian life.[12]

The infrastructure of auctioning and commerce in colonial Calcutta was originally built not for tea but for opium and indigo.[13] Throughout the 1700s, East India Company occupation of the subcontinent enabled the extension of the cultivation of these two crops.[14] As demand for and production of opium rose during the eighteenth and nineteenth centuries, so too did the demand for indigo-based dyes. By the mid-nineteenth century, thousands of chests of indigo were brokered in Calcutta each year by one of several firms in the city and sold in public auctions.

The auctioneers MacKenzie Lyall, whose headquarters were on Mission Row in the 1860s, sold opium, in addition to porcelain, furniture, land, houses, and livestock.[15] MacKenzie Lyall also operated the first tea auction in Calcutta, on December 27, 1861.[16] The sale was of two hundred fifty chests of tea produced by the East India Tea Company and one hundred chests produced by the Bengal Tea Company. Both companies sent Pekoe, Souchong, and Congou grades to auction.

Though MacKenzie Lyall hosted the sale, the auction was facilitated by a brokerage firm, R. Thomas & Company, an early incarnation of the contemporary J. Thomas & Company.[17] Intermittent auctions offering tea from across the Northeast and Bengal took place over the next few years. R. Thomas and another brokerage firm, Moran & Company (antecedent of the contemporary brokerage firm Carritt Moran), added more tea contracts to their existing portfolios in indigo. The auction catalogs in the J. Thomas boardroom showed that by 1864 these brokerage firms were hosting their own auctions, not contracting with independent houses like MacKenzie Lyall. Within the first ten years of the first tea auctioning in Calcutta, trade increased one-hundred-fold.[18]

R. Thomas's auctions were held at New Mart, on the site of Nilhat House. Moran & Company held its auctions one block away, on Mangoe Lane at the "Old Mint Mart." Shortly after this, all of Calcutta's brokerage firms began to hold consolidated auctions at Mission Row, offering their teas one after another and gathering buyers in one location.[19] As demand for Indian tea increased among European blenders, the last two decades of the nineteenth century saw the doubling of acreage under tea in Assam and North Bengal and a parallel rise in the amount of tea on offer at auction in Calcutta.[20] The auction catalogs, too, had grown in length.

After Indian independence in 1947, London's position as the major auction center slowly waned, as governments in India and Sri Lanka sought to take bureaucratic control of their industries. The new incarnation of Nilhat

House, along with new auction centers set up in South India at Cochin, Coimbatore, and Coonoor and in West Bengal and the Northeast at Siliguri and Guwahati, absorbed more of the trading demand.

In 1998 the London auction finally closed. News coverage of the closure glinted with Raj-era nostalgia. "It's the end of an era for the tea trade and the City of London," John Leeder, commodities director for R. Twining & Co., told the *New York Times* at the last auction.[21] Calling it a "sad day," Tim Clifton, chair of the Tea Brokers Association of London, located the auction closure among other assaults on "traditional" forms in the tea industry by "modern" methods and materials, such as the replacement of softwood tea chests with plastic sacks and of leather-bound ledgers with email.[22]

Throughout most of the time of my fieldwork, tea was traded, as it was in London in the 1680s and Calcutta in the 1860s, in live outcry auctions, in which an auctioneer with a gavel sat before a room of potential buyers who would bid by calling out prices, making eye contact, or raising their hands. Other well-known food commodities such as coffee, pork bellies, and frozen concentrated orange juice are not sold in this way; instead, for decades, other major mass-market goods have been traded in futures contracts. On futures markets, traders might be interested in different commodities on different days. In the work of these traders, commodities are generic. Coffee, for example, can be divided into broad categories (arabica and robusta, for example), but a commodities trader has little connection either to the actual sites where the coffee beans are grown or to the people who do the growing. The generic nature of these categories allows financial speculation. In many global food commodities markets, buyers are actually investing in the production of a food crop rather than buying that crop outright. Futures traders agree to pay a set price for a quantity of a given good, which will be delivered to the market in the future. At every point in the circulation of these commodities, producers, sellers, buyers, and investors assume that products grown in different places can be treated as generic and interchangeable.[23]

Tea is different. There is no speculative market in futures contracts for tea, even though brokerage firms like J. Thomas have longed played a role as financiers, paying advances to plantation companies for the tea they sell at auction. One purpose of this book is to explain why this is so: why an outcry auction located in Kolkata remained such a vital part of the global tea market well into the twenty-first century.

Both futures markets and outcry auctions are economic practices designed to ensure liquidity, that is, to keep commodities moving. In outcry auctions, however, the imperative is not to keep tea *in general* moving from field to market. Rather, it is to ensure that *specific teas* find a price. In this sense, tea is what economists call a "lumpy" commodity, and the brokers at Nilhat House are, in Bestor's words, "in business for the lumps."[24] The auction catalog, the form of which has remained much the same since the start of the auction system in Calcutta, structures the auction in such a way that buyers and brokers must consider the qualities of each specific lot on its own terms.

A London-based tea broker described the tea auctions in London as a "little piece of theater."[25] Though plastic and email have also worked their way into Nilhat House, the trade there could still be described in this way. Trading practices, as well as the ties, trophies, and three-course lunches of Nilhat House, are part of the "mimetic archive" of mass-market black tea.[26] Tea trading remains a bodily and linguistic performance. If tea auctions are kinds of theater, then the auction catalogs I reviewed from the early decades of the trade are archives of past performances.

But auction catalogs are also devices for structuring and scripting future performances. Every week, J. Thomas and every other brokerage firm in Kolkata produces a new auction catalog. The weekly catalogs, together with forms of etiquette and dress, form a communicative infrastructure that buyers and brokers see as essential to getting tea to market. The success of the auction depends on the presence of brokers who can perform taste—who belong to the right clubs and who can translate sensory experience into the right vocabulary and with the right panache. It also depends on brokers who can cooperate. Brokers must work with each other to see that as many lots as possible find a buyer. A set of well-established conventions makes this combination of etiquette and economic compromise possible. For buyers and brokers, the ability to experiment within this rather strict communicative infrastructure is essential to finding quality prices for each lot of tea.

CATALOGS AND CHRONICITY

After tasting teas for valuation, brokers from J. Thomas and a number of other firms in Kolkata go to the auction rooms on the ground floor of Nilhat House to sell their teas. During my fieldwork in 2009 and 2010, sales ran on Mondays and Tuesdays and on Wednesdays at the height of the monsoon rains or at the end of the season when plantations are trying to get rid of tea they could not sell earlier in the year. To participate in the auction at Nilhat

House during most of the period of my fieldwork (and for decades leading up to it), a company had to be based in Kolkata, and it had to be registered with the CTTA.[27] For this reason, companies from outside India who wanted to purchase Indian tea had to contract with one of the registered firms based in Kolkata.

Nilhat House contains two auction rooms, connected by a large, light-filled atrium with floor-to-ceiling windows overlooking the manicured grounds. On days when there is a sale, the atrium is abuzz as people stream into the building. The atrium, which has a baby-blue marble floor set against dark wood paneling, doubles as a smoking lounge. Buyers finish their cigarettes before going into one of the auction rooms, where smoking is now prohibited.

There are four auction categories: Darjeeling, orthodox, CTC, and CTC dust. At 8:30 on Monday mornings, the Darjeeling auction starts in the smaller of the two auction rooms. At the same time, the CTC auction begins in the larger hall on the other side of the atrium. When the Darjeeling sale finishes, the small room transitions to auctioning orthodox tea. And after the CTC auction ends, the CTC dust sale starts.

Before each outcry auction, brokerage houses send out small samples of each lot of tea on offer to buyers, along with a circular that lists all the valuation prices determined in the valuation tastings. The auction catalogs, distributed separately from the price circulars, outline the grade, age, warehouse location, and number of packages of each lot of tea sold by a firm in a given week. Lots are organized by plantation, and each plantation's lots are listed from the fullest leaf grade to the smallest leaf grade. Studying the catalog in advance of the sale and following along during the auction itself allows buyers to direct their attention to the catalog according to their needs and to locate the precise lots they want to buy.

Since several firms sell their catalogs of tea in the same weekly sales, the auction is tightly scheduled. Firms rotate their auction time slots so that no one firm is always starting or ending at the same time each week. While there is no predictable competitive advantage to the timing of a firm's sales, depending on the season or stock, it might be disadvantageous to go last, since many smaller buyers may have already bought much of what they need by the end of the day's sales.

This is one reason that auction catalogs are so vital to the process. Indeed, the numbers in the catalog are arguably more important than the valuation prices in the separate circular. Temporally, they structure the interactions between brokers and buyers. They serve as a kind of script for the auction. The auctioneer will sell the lots in the precise order in which they are listed in the catalog, so a buyer might wait until the end of the day to bid on a particularly desirable lot.

To be effective participants in the tea auction, buyers must master the skills of tasting tea. Buyers must also learn to master an equally esoteric set of linguistic and bodily norms. Within these norms, there is some room for experimentation and improvisation. When I attended the auctions, I liked to try to sit near a buyer called "Shiva." Buyers are known in the auction room by the names of their companies, but "Shiva" was not just the name of this buyer's company. It was part of his entire professional persona. He had a cartoon of the Hindu deity Shiva set as the background on his smartphone, and dancing religious icons scrolled across its screen when it was locked. Between bids, he shoveled paan from an extra-large bag into the corner of his mouth using a little spoon designed for the purpose. Many buyers carried personalized tools of the trade: mobile phones, paan, pencils, all manner of folders—some fancy and leather, some mangled plastic—to hold the auction catalogs.

Buyers do not work in isolation. They constantly shift between the two auction rooms to see how their colleagues are faring. Friends and colleagues sit next to each other, spreading their catalogs out in front of them like bingo cards. They hover over one another, read off of each other's papers, and copy information into the margins of their catalogs. There are small stylistic variations, but for the most part, everyone's marginalia take the same form. Before coming into the auction that morning, buyers have copied all of the valuation prices (or at least the valuation prices for any lots they might be interested in) from circulars sent to them by the brokerage firm into the right-hand margins of their catalogs. As the auction proceeds, buyers note which company bought each lot of tea, also in the right-hand margins. A long slash ("/") through the lot in the catalog means that the buyer himself has purchased the tea. A long dash ("—") in the left-hand margin means that the lot went unsold. It is important to note unsold lots because they will return to the catalog three weeks later. Catalogs thus serve as the archive for buyers and brokers alike.

Over the course of the year, the size of brokers' catalogs will increase as the weather gets warmer and rainier and plantations across India produce more tea. In this way, the catalogs reflect the relative saturation, as well as the seasonality, of the market. In the catalog, as in the tasting room, tea is never generic. It is always associated with a specific space of production. In Kolkata's auctions, this is always a plantation. Buyers see it as essential to know not only what tea they are buying but also which plantation that tea has come from, which warehouse is holding it, and how long ago it was plucked, fired, and packeted. Even though it contains no actual prices, then, the catalog gives price its chronicity.

THE BIDDING

J. Thomas's auction of the 2009 Darjeeling first flush began on a Monday morning in April. Mr. Dey arrived a few minutes early and looked on as the brokers from another firm finished their sales. When the previous auction was over, he stepped behind a large wooden three-tiered lectern, and two other tie-clad brokers from the firm took their places on either side of him. At Nilhat House, the broker sitting in the middle and serving as auctioneer is the mouth and eyes of the auction. The second and third brokers, usually a junior broker and a more senior broker, note all of the selling prices, the names of the bidders, and the names of the eventual buyers in the margins of their own copies of the catalog.

Buyers shuffled into rows of desks before Mr. Dey and the two other brokers on the stage. Lot by lot, according to the order in the catalog, Mr. Dey attempted to fetch something close to the valuation price he had set upstairs a few days earlier. Brokers like Mr. Dey see the valuation price as a reflection of each tea's quality, but their judgments are not the end of the story.

A relatively small number of mass-market buyers prefer the lighter-colored, lighter-tasting first flush Darjeeling teas. There would be more buyers here in November and December, when the autumn harvest teas, as well as previously unsold "old tea," go up for sale. Those later season teas tend to be a bit cheaper. At the end of the year, many plantations send teas to auction that they were not able to sell directly. Many of the buyers present in the room on that April day were looking to add small amounts of expensive, lighter-colored Darjeeling to otherwise cheaper, darker teas in order to give their blends some visual appeal.

The first lot of fresh first flush tea in J. Thomas's 2009 catalog opened at Rs. 12,000 per kilogram. The next several lots each yielded thousands of rupees per kilogram as well. The buyers in the room, having read carefully through the catalog, knew that these lots came from "quality gardens." There was some interest, but Mr. Dey still needed to do some coaxing.

"Lot 9. Starting off at 700."

Placing a bid can be loud—a yell of "Hup!" or "Hip!" or of a number—but often, especially in these early season Darjeeling auctions, bidding is subtle. It is done with a slight nod of the head or the tip of a pencil. When the price is climbing, particularly when two buyers are interested, the bidding lasts until someone pushes a hand away, indicating that the other bidder can take it. Active bidding can be maintained just by remaining in eye contact with the auctioneer. When a buyer breaks eye contact, they are no longer interested.

For Lot 9, the bids went steadily up to 955, then 1055.

"Lot 10. Let's start at 700." The bids climbed, stalling at 830.

"Lot 11, any interest? Any bids? Why not 800 on this one?" Mr. Dey saw a nod in the crowd. "50 also bid." He saw another nod. "900, Rahul." Like all auctioneers, Mr. Dey referred to bidders not by their given names but by company names. In this case, "Rahul" was a small Calcutta-based tea company.

The price for Lot 11 went up in 10-rupee increments before the tea sold at 940, to Rahul.

"Lot 12."

"700."

"900."

"905 to Ganji," Mr. Dey called out and slammed the gavel. Mr. Dey and other auctioneers used the gavel in a particular way, gripping its bulbous heavy end rather than its handle to control its sound. And Mr. Dey did not need to use the clichéd language "Going, going, gone" to announce the end of the bidding. Instead, he used his eyes to scan the room for continued contact, in the form of a gaze, a raised hand, or a tipped pencil.

"Lot 13. Any interest on the—"

A buyer shouted out a low bid.

"Thank you for your bid, Teesta, but not at those prices."

"1,100."

"Again, not at those prices. I am looking for 2,000!"

"1,200."

"1,800, sir. Ok?," Mr. Dey offered.

"1,500."

"1,770," Mr. Dey relented, and the price went up steadily from there.

"1,960 bid. On Lot 13." Mr. Dey waited for any other movement. Then he slammed his gavel.

"Lot 14. Any start? Any bid?"

"1,100."

"1,500, again, I can start." A buyer nodded in agreement, and the bids climbed to 1,950, then 1,960, and topped off at 2,010.

"And the China. Lot 15. Any bids on these?"

"What is the bid, sir?," a trader called out for clarification.

"500 is bid. 600 I will sell." A nod in agreement from a buyer. The price climbed from 600 to 770.

"Lot 16."

"550."

"600 from Teesta. 605 Tata." Sold at 700.

"Lot 17? Any interest?"

"600."

"No, sir, not at those prices. This one at 700, sir." The buyer remained still. "Fine, let's start it. 600." Lot 17 ended up going above 700. "700, Papu . . . 705 Teesta." Sold.

Although they were careful to refer to one another by their company names or "sir" during the auction, buyers and brokers knew one another well. The community of tea trading is a small one, relationships are typically collegial, and the trading decorum is reserved. The auctions at Nilhat House, then, are quite unlike the combative trading pits of the commodities auctions in Chicago, where many commodity futures are bought and sold.[28] Brokers and buyers are collectively motivated to see sales come to a satisfying end.

"Lot 18. FTGFOP1. Any interest on this tea? On the FP1?" Mr. Dey heard a low bid. "No good at those prices. Anyone want in at 500?"

"400."

"Be realistic, *sir,* that is what I can do."

"450."

"500."

"500 to Tea Promoters . . . 15 to Tata." Bidding steadily climbed. "580 bid?" Gavel slammed.

"And the brokens, Lot 19? Any bid?"

"170."

"200."

"230 is bid. Let's start it, sir." Sold to Bata for 355. Gavel.

At the crying of "Lot 20," everyone flipped the page of their catalog in unison. "Any interest on 20?"

"200."

"At 260 I can, sir." No response. "Again at 40 I will start." No bids. The lot went unsold. Lot 21 was absent; it had already been sold in a private sale.

Mr. Dey's bodily comportment and language are as important in the auction room as they are in the tasting room. He coaxes buyers to bid on certain lots and doles out friendly chastisement when their bids are too low. He controls chatting in the room. He even scolds buyers for standing up in the middle of the bidding.

"Lot 30 on the fannings. Anyone?"

"30."

"Again, 80 I will sell." Some low bids were called out. "Fresh tea can't sell at that price." The buyers responded with more numbers, more yelling. "195 . . . 200." Gavel. Sold.

At auction, the distinction between "fresh tea" and "old tea" is important. All teas offered at auction sit in secured, CTTA-registered warehouses until they are ready for sale. After sales, buyers can rent space to keep their tea in these warehouses or they can transfer it to their own warehouses. If a lot goes unsold, it remains in the registered warehouse.[29] "Old tea" may have sat in warehouses in Kolkata because it was previously brought up for auction but not sold. If this is the case, it returns for sale three weeks later. Buyers who carefully read the catalog can track the journeys of "fresh teas" from plantations to warehouses, as well as the virtual journeys of "old teas" from warehouse to auction room and back. In this way, the small additional clarifying words used by auctioneers (exceptions made for *this* tea, as opposed to another) are always statements not just about the leaves themselves, but about the network of plantations, factories, packages, and warehouses in which they are held.

QUALITY SALES, QUALITY GARDENS

By the time the auction for the second flush of Darjeeling teas started several weeks later, the room had gotten more packed. The collective energy also seemed higher. Many buyers were pleased to see that the J. Thomas catalog had grown in size in the time since the first flush, which had been relatively sparse. The last few years had seen shorter and less productive first flushes, largely because of changing climate patterns. Darjeeling, in the Himalayas, had been particularly affected.

I was sitting next to Suvo, a trader from Orchid Tea, a company that owns plantations in Darjeeling and Assam and buys tea at auction. He assured me that despite the concerns about changing seasonal patterns, the market for Darjeeling tea was good. "And Tata and Levers come to sweep up the lower-grade teas for their blended teas," he explained. He pointed over to the other side of the room where buyers from these mega corporations were seated (people in the industry refer to Hindustan Unilever simply as "Levers").

Just as he said this, Mr. Dey tried to get Tata's buyer to bid Rs. 160 per kilogram on a lot, but the Tata buyer was not interested in this one. He flipped the back of his hands toward the podium.

Then teas from the famed Castleton Tea Estate came up for auction. There was noticeable excitement. A buyer on the other side of the room whooped out a bid. Prices for these lots climbed quickly, Suvo explained, because "Castleton is a marker." He meant that Castleton had broad name recognition as a "quality garden." Castleton Tea Estate is located on the main road to Darjeeling town. Plentiful roadside signage advertising the plantation made it memorable to the many buyers and potential consumers who spent holidays in Darjeeling, a popular destination for middle-class tourists from Kolkata.

Suvo was fairly chatty on this day. After a while, he wasn't even bothering to write in his catalog. He had brought along someone else from his company, who had taken over most of the play-by-play documentation. Since they have already studied the catalog in advance of the auction, most buyers have some downtime between lots, but I guessed aloud that Suvo, more than most, seemed to be enjoying being a spectator. He assured me that this was not the case. He had come today with the objective of buying tea grown on his own company's plantations.

I was confused. Why would Suvo be purchasing tea that his company already owned? Suvo explained that the company, which also blended and procured tea for other companies as a proxy buyer, was low in its second flush inventory. Even though the company had already commissioned J. Thomas to auction its tea, it had its own orders to fill. The only way to maintain control of the tea was to have Suvo buy it back at auction.

This was not an anomaly. According to a government regulation called the Tea Marketing and Control Order, plantations must sell a minimum amount of the tea they produce at auction.[30] These minimum levels vary based on how much a plantation produces, whether it "packets" its own tea, and whether it exports the tea outside India. Though there are some loopholes in this rule, today about half of the tea across the four auction categories eventually comes to auction. The rest is sold directly to buyers in private sales. The auction serves an important role in the tea industry, Suvo explained. For small gardens or plantations that need the money, brokerage firms work as financiers. A plantation manager can send lots of teas to a broker in Kolkata three to four weeks before they would be sold. Brokers receive the teas, warehouse them, taste them, give them a prospective price in the muster tasting, and send the plantation 50 percent what they think the lot will fetch at auction. Many plantations depend on this advance to finance their day-to-day operations.

The auction also helps producers deal with the mind-boggling variability of tea, variability caused by weather and climate, the location of plantations, and the vicissitudes of the plucking and factory processes. As Suvo explained:

> So say I am used to making a certain amount of tea out of a given section at a certain time of year, and all of a sudden, this year, the production goes up 20 percent. I can't stop production at where it was last year. What to do with all of this other tea? I can't go around to all of the Indian buyers or all of the buyers in Kolkata, trying to secure direct sales.

The auction is the solution to this hypothetical overproduction problem. The auction ensures liquidity. Buyers who bid on this tea could read the numbers in the catalog, filter them through their own knowledge of Suvo's hypothetical plantation, and calculate their own prospective asking prices. "It is an old system," Suvo admitted, "but it is an important one."

Plantation owners I interviewed in Darjeeling and the Dooars generally all had the same reason for sending their teas to auction. One early monsoon night, over fish cutlets and tea in the garden of the Calcutta Club, I asked one Darjeeling plantation owner how he decided which tea to sell directly through private sales and which to sell at auction.

"That's easy," he answered. "I sell at auction what I can't sell directly." He tried to make direct sales within a week or so of production, but after that he sent the tea to the auction. Because his was a "quality garden," he added, he sent a lot more tea to auction during the monsoon than during the first and second flushes. A quality garden should be able to find private buyers for its sought-after first and second flushes. During the late season autumn flush, private sales pick up again but not to the same degree as the early season first and second flushes. All told, this plantation owner sent about 50 percent of his teas to auction. Despite the regulations of the Tea Marketing and Control Order, which technically require all plantations to send some teas to auction, he confided that he knew of many plantation companies that "send practically zero to the auction." Other plantations simply dump all of the teas that they cannot sell during the year into the auction at the end of the year, which accounts in part for the increased volume of tea sold through the auction at that time of year. With some disdain, he explained that those plantations that flaunted the rules were also the ones that "had the ear of the Tea Board," the government regulatory board that makes all of the rules.

Auction bidding, then, requires a deep knowledge about the strategies used by plantation companies to bring teas to market. Even on a particular plantation, over a given season, as Suvo's story shows, the plantation management's judgments about the quality and desirability of its own outputs vary. Companies thus have the ability—to a limited extent—to manipulate the communicative infrastructure of auctioning and play it off against that of private, direct sales. While direct sales might seem like the venue where specificity and specialization matter most, thanks to the combination of regulatory control by the Tea Board, the unpredictability of a changing climate, and shifts in the inventories held by large buyers like Tata and Hindustan Unilever, specificity matters at the outcry auction as well. The status of the quality garden depends, in turn, on the quality of its engagement with the auction system.

SPLITTING

Despite the vagaries of weather, season, and provenance, companies demand a consistent taste in the tea blends they distribute. To produce consistent blends, buyers must find teas with certain qualities. The seemingly abstract numbers in the auction catalog present buyers trained to read them with the ability to tell the stories of particular teas, to link the differential regime of taste with the abstract regime of price.

Monojit, one of the clerks in the J. Thomas tasting room, used to work for a buying firm. He explained to me that unlike the J. Thomas brokers, buyers have the "stressful obligation" to find teas that the companies who contract them want. These companies can be quite particular, Monojit said. If they say they want a certain tea from a particular plantation, even one that is not considered a quality garden, their agents have to find it anyway. If they want a malty, tannic tea at the start of the first flush, when teas tend to be lighter and more floral, buyers must try to oblige. For these reasons, tasters at buying firms taste much more slowly than the brokers do. They revisit each tea sample several times to make sure that it has the right flavor, color, and appearance. They taste the teas with and without milk.

When buyers taste, they consider their own impressions, the broker-determined valuation price, and each lot's potential to blend with other teas. Much of the black tea that global firms sell is blended from several lots, from multiple regions. To produce consistent flavors, buyers must deploy a complex metrology. They use their memories, palates, and personal relationships to filter catalog numbers representing age, mass, color, place of origin, season of harvest, and grade, making calculated purchases that yield the tastes that their employers desire. They render these composite sensations into their own valuation price—the maximum price they (or their clients) are willing to pay. They must do this in competition with buyers who are also thinking about future blends for their own companies or employers. The skill of buying at auction, then, is the skill of tracing the paths taken by individual lots of tea and deciding when and where to intervene in those paths: when to make a bid, when to hold back, and when to negotiate. This game of singularization and standardization reaches its climax on the auction floor.

Mr. Chetal is the head auctioneer for J. Thomas's orthodox tea catalog. One morning early in the 2009 season, his sales—usually brisk and tightly controlled—had been rather languid. Then, in a scene that was repeated dozens of times during my fieldwork at Nilhat House, a certain lot on a certain page elicited a new dramatic scene.

As soon as Mr. Chetal intoned the lot number, Kaka, one of the major buyers at the auction, could not contain himself. He wanted this lot. "On, on, on!," he screamed in staccato response to other bidders' offers. In the language of the auction, "on" indicates a bid at the price of the previous lot. Kaka was poised with his buttocks just barely touching the top of his auditorium chair, so as not to break Mr. Chetal's strict rule against standing while bidding. To make himself taller, he was throwing his hand toward the stage as he screamed, trying his best to keep contact with the seat.

When the next lot came up, another buyer jumped in almost as quickly as Kaka had. "Drop!," he yelled, indicating a bid of 5 rupees less than Kaka's buying price for the previous lot.

"Ons" and "drops" are common at the orthodox tea auction because lot-by-lot prices tend to fluctuate less here than in the Darjeeling auction, where garden-to-garden and flush-to-flush variability requires more specific bids. (The price fluctuations are even smaller in the CTC and CTC dust auctions that are held simultaneously in the larger auction room on the other side of the atrium.) When especially desirable lots of orthodox tea appear, the whole crowd seems to rock, pencils pointed toward the front of the room, shouts propelling them forward.

On the next lot, a buyer got a little overexcited: "Drop-Drop-Drop-Drop-Drop-Drop!!!," he fired off in rapid succession. The other buyers turned around to look at him and snickered. He was oblivious. As soon as Mr. Chetal announced the next lot, he cried "On-On-On-On-On-On-On-On," asking to buy this lot for the same price he had paid for the previous one.

"No, sir, this is a better tea, *sir*," Mr. Chetal corrected him, with a smirk.

The buyers took this as license to begin making fun of the overzealous bidder. For the next several lots, other buyers mimicked him, calling out their "Ons" and "Drops" many more times than was necessary. Mr. Chetal quickly put a stop to this, staring silently at the gallery from the podium.[31]

J. Thomas's orthodox catalog on this day was fairly thick, so Mr. Chetal's disciplinary gaze was important to maintaining the overall chronicity of the event. Too much comedic license could quickly threaten the completion of the catalog. Nevertheless, just as they did every day at about 10:30 a.m., two white-coated staff members brought Mr. Chetal his morning tea in a disposable plastic cup and melamine saucer, with two Bisk Farm biscuits. Almost in unison, Mr. Chetal and the two other brokers at the front of the room began bobbing their Jay India tea bags up and down in the milk-filled plastic cups. This metronomic motion, keeping time with the pace of the catalog, was echoed out on the auction floor. The Hindustan Unilever buyers did not take the standard Nilhat House tea service. They brought their own tea bags. Today they had a new box of Brooke Bond Taj Mahal, still wrapped in cellophane, and they insisted that the staff bring them fresh cups of hot milk and water. As the tea service proceeded, a few buyers in the back of the room passed around a mobile phone with a joke on it, laughing to each other. Mr. Chetal was forced to bang his gavel to get their attention.

Mr. Chetal reads the room carefully, even when everyone is behaving well. In all the catalogs they publish, brokers try to group lots from particular plantations together. Groups of quality gardens appear together, as do groups of cheaper teas. This, they say, promotes engagement among buyers who they know are interested in particular kinds of tea.

As the tea service wound to a close and the white-coated waiters exited the room, the orthodox bidding escalated again. At the crying of one lot, Mihir Exports called out to the current high bidder, Som Industries, who had been consistently outbidding Mihir Exports on several lots of lower-grade Assam tea.

"It's a special request, leave this one aside," Mihir Exports pleaded. He needed it. Som Industries did not comply.

A few lots later, Mihir Exports finally won the bidding against Som Industries. At this, Mihir Exports turned to Som Industries and placed his palms together at chest level, sending a sarcastic *namaskar* across the room. Som Industries responded by rolling up his catalog and waving it dismissively back at him.

The interactions between Mihir Exports and Som Industries were intentional, and to some degree, they were what Mr. Chetal and the other brokers at J. Thomas hoped for. But the auction was run in such a way that competitive bidding need not result in disappointment for one side.

On the next lot, there was more competition, and Tata ended up being the highest bidder.

"Tata can I have it? Can I have it, Tata? *Taaataaa*?" Blue Tea, a more moderately sized buyer, held up his hand. With his outstretched fingers, Blue Tea made a motion as if he was trying to pull the lots for which Tata was the high bidder toward him.

After a second or two of silence, the Tata buyer asked, "How much?"

"Half," the Blue Tea buyer replied. The Tata buyer nodded his head in agreement. With that, the lot had been "split." Mr. Chetal moved on to the next lot.

Because buyers need to buy teas with particular tastes and aesthetic qualities, lots are often split between two or three buyers. A split is initiated when a buyer calls out to the current high bidder during the auctioning of that lot. While bidding and engagement with auctioneers like Mr. Chetal happen exclusively in English, buyers interested in splitting will sometimes yell across the hall in Hindi or Bengali.

Splitting is always an agreement rather than a foregone conclusion. A current high bidder can stonewall a buyer who asks to split. He does not have to give him anything, but that may mean that the other buyer may try to outbid him. In some cases, a current high bidder might even transfer an entire lot to another buyer, but a split is usually a division of a lot's packages. The number of packages is noted in the auction catalog, but there is no standard way of breaking up a lot. Depending on the plantation, the packages might not even be of the same weight. The number and type of packages, determined at the point of production, thus helps determine how lots can be split. Lot splitting ensures that buyers get at least some of the taste and qualities that they want.

Volume is high in the Nilhat House auctions. In a single week, some of the larger buyers may purchase as many as 3,500 to 4,000 packets of tea. These packets are usually spread across several warehouse facilities. Early on in my fieldwork, I was sitting in the office of the director of the CTTA while he was patiently explaining to me how the auction worked. One of the first things that I noticed while observing the auction were the dialogues around lot splitting. I asked him about this. Trying to understand the logistical challenge of getting the packets from split lots to the right buyer, I was reminded of sitting on an airplane and watching the ground staff move bags on, off, and on to other locations. Some bags went to baggage claim, others to connecting flights. Then there were the oversized items, the dogs, the mail, and so on. My (mostly older, mostly male) interlocutors often tried to explain how the tea industry worked through elaborate, sometimes bizarre metaphors and comparisons. So I offered up my airline luggage analogy to the CTTA director. He laughed.

> It's far more complicated than that. Bags are discrete units. The baggage handlers don't need to pull something out of one bag and send it somewhere else. They don't have to pull out a toothbrush from this bag coming from Delhi and send it with this bag going to Bangalore—a bag that you already stuffed in a pair of socks and something else from two other bags heading in other directions. The lots need to be segregated, and that takes time.

In the end, he explained, each buyer (or more likely, someone from their company) gets the tea they bought in the split by going to the warehouse where it is located and picking it up. This could mean going to any one of seven warehouses in the city. Buyers might leave the tea at the warehouse for weeks or longer. Storage in a CTTA-approved warehouse costs 90 paisa (Rs. 0.9) per packet per week. When I spoke with the director in April 2009 he told me that people were only then starting to pick up tea they bought or split in fall winter 2008 in order to blend it with teas they acquired more recently.

Back at J. Thomas's orthodox auction, Mr. Chetal was working his way toward the end of the day's catalog, and the splitting continued.

At one point, a buyer from Cosmos called out to the current high bidder, Parvati Imports. "Milega! Milega!," he cried. (This is a form of the Hindi verb *milana,* which translates as "to mix," "to conjoin," or "to get.") "Give me ten, please," Cosmos said, raising his hand in a beckoning "come here" motion. "Ten to me." Parvati kept his eyes forward and did not engage him. "Milega!," Cosmos implored. Parvati continued to ignore his calls and took the whole lot.

"Thank you, Parvati," Cosmos called out dismissively after the lot was finished.

On the next lot, Parvati was again the highest bidder, and again Cosmos wanted part of the lot. Again Cosmos called out for a split. This time he actually got a response. "I cannot divide this, I need the full lot," Parvati said, coldly.

"Please?," Cosmos whined. No response. Gavel.

On the next lot, the current high bidder, Tripathi, agreed to split with another buyer. "Tripathi! Three ways!," Cosmos called out to him, but Tripathi, like Parvati, did not engage the request. Cosmos hemmed and hawed, visibly annoyed.

Mr. Chetal banged the gavel to try to settle him down. "I know that you are a very large buyer, Cosmos, but you are not the only bidder."

Cosmos mumbled something about needing the tea to produce a particular kind of tea bag. He needed this tea, but he could not bid any higher than the current bid. Or, perhaps, he did not want to get stuck with the whole lot.

Splitting can be quite political. Buyers I interviewed tended to agree that you did not want to split with your competitors. By "competitors," they meant buyers who were working within the same kinds of markets. For example, buyers who were both working with companies that made larger-leaf tea bags sold in Germany and other European markets might be competitors, as would the several buyers buying for cheap domestic packet teas sold in West Bengal.

Splitting is like a sports match, spread over a day or even weeks, months, or, perhaps, entire careers. It is a socioeconomic interaction akin to the Bengali (masculine) intellectual tradition of *adda,* a spirited debate, full of vociferous disagreement, whose end is not enduring animosity but collegial understanding. This kind of grappling reaffirms rather than undermines the integrity of the larger system of which it is a part. Buyers I observed trading insults and barbs during the course of a splitting negotiation frequently returned together to the auction room after taking a cigarette break, both with fresh pastries from one of the vendors outside.

LIQUID STORIES

One morning in September 2009, an all-woman Spanish film crew was in the small auction room videoing the proceedings. One of the taller, younger, and more dapper buyers was charged with walking around with them and answering their questions. The auction continued without much attention to the filming. Visits from local and international media are a fairly regular occurrence. Like the J. Thomas boardroom upstairs, the auction is a stop for many wide-angle documentary views of the tea industry. There are numerous YouTube videos not only of Kolkata's outcry auction but also of those of other centers across the world. Mr. Chetal even once played himself, the expert tea taster, on an episode of the reality show *The Amazing Race,* sponsored by Snapple (though on the show he traded in his belt and tie for a crisp white kurta).[32]

The performative nature of the auction clearly makes it attractive to observers. One reason is its combination of novelty and familiarity. Whereas the origin, flavor, texture, and aroma of the teas listed in the auction catalogs vary, the process by which all tea is sold, from cheap CTC to pricey full-leaf Darjeeling, is highly ritualized. And what is ritual if not a storied, collective performance designed for quality control? Stories and rituals distill the radical particularity of social life into order, making things and concepts commensurable and comparable, allowing people to make intelligible normative judgments. As Bestor notes, while "the outcome of a given auction may seem mechanically calculable . . . the participants can make such calculations only after the market's underlying codes of competition, fair play, exchange, and transaction have been created or routinized."[33] Evidence of such coded behavior appears in the ways that brokers and buyers work together.

Numbers are central in the language of every auction, but while traders who buy and sell wheat, pork bellies, or even coffee futures can easily keep numbers and things separate, at Nilhat House numbers can never be insulated from the embodied experience of the tea they represent. The numbers in tea catalogs are both material and ideological inscriptions: other brokers can see them and think, through their own histories of physical contact with tea, about what they signify. The tea auction catalog is thus not only a site of time-honored ritual; it is also a site of experimentation in which a doubling of abstraction and differentiation, opacity and transparency, becomes apparent.[34]

A market, however, needs more than numbers. A market is also brought into being by experts (e.g., brokers) through their experimental use of the communicative instruments that record and measure it (e.g., auction catalogs).[35] Catalogs structure and script auctions, making economic exchanges legible and archivable, but the form of the catalog is itself structured by the unspoken, tacit rules of etiquette that govern relationships among traders.[36] While it may be surprising and even disturbing that the communicative practice that governed trade at Nilhat House during my fieldwork seems so similar to (and indeed reverential toward) its colonial antecedents, the deep connection to the past makes sense if we see market behavior as governed through a communicative infrastructure. Nilhat House, after all, is part of a tea production system that relies on a colonially derived plantation complex, where fixed capital includes century-old coal-fired machinery, laborers' villages, and dirt roads. The auctions make direct and indirect references to these other, more material forms. Adherence to communicative norms not only affirms the material quality of tea lots; it also affirms the broader quality of the market. Such norms work to fix colonial institutions to each other and to the material and sensory qualities of mass-market black tea itself.

With the complexity of a water, transportation, or electrical grid, the numbers in the auction catalog crisscross one another.[37] The auction catalog is a script that guides buyers from the start of the day's sales to its end, but the numbers it contains also lead buyers through other scales of time and space— to the warehouses spread across the city, to plantation fields and factories, to tasting rooms, and even to the contents of the bags of tea that bounce up and down in their cups with the rhythm of the gavel. As systems for maintaining the literal and figurative liquidity of both tea and ideas about quality, communicative infrastructures have many entrances and exits.

This returns us to the boardroom and the miniature museum on the second floor of Nilhat House. What looks like a spatial anachronism is a sedimented and embedded and yet thoroughly contemporary form of relating. Fixed capital is not just machinery, then. It is a force that binds together notions of gender and identity. Fixed capital requires constant care and maintenance. The quality of markets is discernible in the quality of the communicative norms that govern them. These norms are not modular platforms. They are integrated with the divisions and systems of care that structure plantations.

THREE

The Problem with Blending

AFTER TEA IS BOUGHT AT AUCTION, it is sold again to companies that may be based close to or far away from the auction house. Most tea is eventually packaged in blends. The rise of blended tea was a direct result of the growth of European empire. Before British colonial tea manufacture began, the bulk of tea on the market came from China. Consumers bought tea from their local grocers, often bringing their own receptacles in which to carry it home. "A housewife herself," wrote Gervas Huxley, chief publicity officer of the Empire Marketing Board in London in the mid-1930s, "sometimes blended the teas she bought and might have by her some fine Flowery Pekoe or choice Gunpowder to add to her Bohea or Souchong for special occasions."[1] This tradition of home blending subsided after the introduction of Indian tea to the British market in 1836. By the mid-nineteenth century, retailers were blending China and Indian teas before they sold them.

By the turn of the twentieth century, tea grown in British colonies—particularly India—had overtaken the market. In 1867, British consumers purchased 104,500,000 pounds of China tea and 6,250,000 pounds of Indian tea. By 1907, British consumers purchased 9,750,000 pounds of China tea and 162,500,000 pounds of Indian tea.[2] Even amid what might have appeared like a successful market takeover, tea planters in India and consumers in Britain worried openly about how well the quality of Indian tea measured up to that of Chinese tea and tea from other competing regions. Just as Indian tea was surpassing Chinese tea in terms of market share, it began to face stiff competition from tea grown in the Dutch-controlled islands of what is now Indonesia. In response, the ITA launched a public campaign to promote the consumption and trademarking of "Empire Tea." The campaign included pamphlets and news reports that told consumers that Empire Tea was a commodity whose mass production and consumption were not only crucial to the British economy but also central to the economic well-being of the colonies.[3]

What blended, packaged tea offered was consistency—regularity of flavor and texture. But the fact that tea over the course of the nineteenth and early twentieth century increasingly came to consumers in the form of blends raised questions about consistency in a different sense—that of physical makeup. At the same time that the ITA was actively promoting Empire Tea, Britain witnessed a flurry of scientific studies and negative advertising about the health effects and material constituency of tea blends. Medical journals linked the increased consumption of malty, astringent teas being sourced from British colonies to a population-wide rise in indigestion and constipation. These digestive woes were linked in turn to the environmental conditions of colonial industrial production. For marketers and medical professionals, the culprit in this wave of indigestion was tannin, a little-understood chemical compound that was thought to give tea its characteristic bitterness and color. Debates about what tannins were and what effects they might have on human health played out in the pages of medical and trade journals from the 1890s to the 1930s. Medical writing from the period cites the British Pharmacopeia, which placed tea tannins in the category of *acidum tannicum*, a classification tea tannins shared with tannic acid used in leather tanning. Fears grew that tea tannins did to intestinal tracts what tannic acid did to the hides of animals. (Black tea did, after all, seem to have an ability to "tan" the table cloths and teeth of those who consumed it.) In response, the ITA and allied producer organizations summoned experts from the burgeoning science of industrial chemistry. Investigations into tea's chemistry worked to manage the interface between metropolitan consumers, colonial landscapes, and the colonial subjects who plucked, processed, and packaged tea. The goal of these investigations was to render plantation production palatable, normal, and safe.

The rise of tea packeting and blending helped usher in an entirely new orientation to quality within the industry. The history I recount in this chapter shows how quality was produced both ideationally, through a dialectical relationship between consumer desires and marketing discourses, and materially, through a dialectical relationship between the physical methods of bringing tea to market and the physical experience of digesting it.[4]

It was just as blends began to dominate the market that notions of quality began to go beyond the palate and deeper into the digestive tract. During this same period, a vision of the biophysical body as a kind of "human motor," and of food and drink as a set of lubricating, energetic, or corrosive inputs to that motor, took hold in Europe and the United States.[5] Medical experts, food producers, and consumers began to consider how, through the intake of food, the body was materially entangled both with the urbanizing landscapes in which it lived and with the increasingly extensive and increasingly transnational systems of agrarian provision that sustained those urban landscapes.[6] This new consumer consciousness gave rise to a new governmental regime of food safety, which tracked consumable goods and their microbial, nutritive, and chemical contents from farm to table.[7] Early food safety sought to maintain the moral and material "purity" of bodies and products, a goal that had particular salience in the age of Euro-American empire.[8] The drinking of tea was not just an encounter between human bodies, nonhuman plants, and the chemicals that constituted them. Contact with tea, whether in the cloistered laboratories of chemists or in the drawing rooms of consumers, also entailed contact between white metropolitan bodies and the bodies of racially marked field laborers.[9]

Teas grown under colonial plantation conditions raised new scientific questions. Their successful integration into the market through blending was not just a matter of ideological or aesthetic work, the work of marketing and messaging. It was also ontological work, the work of establishing what could (and could not) be known and said about the world. The story I tell in this chapter is one of how discussions of quality shifted, in the words of the Empire Tea Board, "from being concerned with tea *qua* tea ... into a rivalry ... between different kinds of teas. Into the discussion both the chemist and the doctor were drawn. Argument centered in particular on the pharmacology of tea—and its chemical composition."[10] What counts as quality tea today is both a product of colonial difference making and a product of scientific and discursive efforts to make colonial differences disappear.[11] As the uncertainty about tannins played out, tea was rematerialized not as a singular, unified product but as an active assemblage of chemical agents.[12] The process of scientifically determining the harms or benefits of blended black tea was freighted with the baggage of the colonial racial order that brought it into being.[13]

BLENDING OUT DIFFERENCE

The idea of tea blending arose from the experience that a beverage more pleasing, more satisfying, and less costly could be produced from a variety of teas scientifically mixed than could be obtained for any one tea used by itself.

THE ART OF TEA BLENDING, 1893

Tea production in British colonial India began in the 1830s. Initially, Indian tea planters adopted a model of production they observed (or, more likely, heard about) while trading opium, silver, textiles, and tea through the East India Company hub of Canton. In this model, small farmers grew green leaf and brought it to a centralized location for processing and packaging. British planters quickly set out to shift to an industrial economy of scale, carving out plantations first in Assam and later across the Himalayas, the Northeast, and South India.[14] Soon after, planters switched from hand processing tea to the use of faster, more efficient coal-fired machines, located in factories on plantations.[15] The colonial penchant for agricultural "improvement," however, did not stop at the gates of the plantation.[16] Railways and warehouses moved crates of processed tea to brokerage houses in port cities. Botanical gardens and agricultural experimental stations tested the viability of crops in newly annexed regions while also working toward the improvement of the crop itself.[17]

As an 1893 instructional text, *The Art of Tea Blending,* explained:

The cultivation of tea is in India much more a matter of science than it is in the Celestial Empire. The Chinese, from time immemorial, have grown their teas on every little available space—sometimes on hillsides, sometimes on patches of land comparatively barren. They have used little or no manure; in fact, the son has followed in his father's steps without attempting to excel. On the contrary, *the growth of the tea industry in India has been fostered by many experiments*—experiments as to the climate most suitable to tea growing, as to the soil most congenial to it, and the manure by which it is most nourished; experiments as to the best methods of manufacture, and also experiments to ascertain the best kind of plant to cultivate. All these problems have been solved to a certain extent, but there is no doubt much progress will still be made.[18]

Previous histories of tea have noted that much of the colonial British tea industry's capital during the nineteenth and early twentieth century was devoted to convincing consumers that tea from India and Ceylon were possessed of tastes and aromas that were not only just as pleasing as those of Chinese teas but also (due to the introduction of mechanization and standardization) safer and purer.[19] What I want to emphasize here is how British colonial tea planters explicitly invoked an ethic of experimentation in their efforts to tout the superior quality of their product.

Colonial science gave birth not only to the vertically integrated plantation system but also to a rigid system of ethnic hierarchy. The ranks of field and factory labor in British plantations were dominated by racially marked and marginalized groups, such as Nepalis in Darjeeling, Adivasis in Assam, and Tamils in colonial Ceylon. Management was, unsurprisingly, white and European. The result of these transformations was not just a new system of industrial and racial inequality, or a dramatic spike in tea supplies in the West, but an entirely new kind of taste. Colonial plantation production methods and the cultivation of the indigenous Assam variety of tea (*Camellia sinensis* var. *assamica*) yielded a malty, dark, "black" tea whose flavor was immediately distinguishable from the light, floral taste associated with "green" China teas. In the face of this variety there emerged an entirely new way of preparing tea for consumption: blending.

The 1894 guidebook *Tea and Tea Blending* explains:

> [Indian tea's] great strength was a valuable quality which would not allow them to be ignored; while on the other hand, their harshness made them unacceptable to the public by themselves; hence they were mixed with China tea, at first in small proportions, but, as the production increased, and improved cultivation and manufacture removed many of the objectionable qualities possessed by some of their earlier imports, the proportion of Indian tea used became larger and larger. . . . As tea-blending became more and more general, the producers, especially in India, gradually ceased to aim at turning out teas which should possess a combination of qualities rendering them suitable for drinking by themselves, and became specialists aiming to secure for their teas some one striking and distinctive quality; thus one strove to produce tea which should draw liquor of very dark colour; another, to secure a delicately fine aroma and flavor, a third, to secure intense pungency, and so on.[20]

Blending was thus an extension of the experimental work that began on plantations. Blending was about managing—or perhaps more accurately, masking—ecological difference across European colonial occupations and making that difference palatable.

For example, the guidebook highlights that knowledge about the water in the region in which blended tea would be steeped was essential. Hard water "fails to draw out the characteristics of fine teas." For hard water, more "strong, rough kinds" of tea had to be included in a blend. In soft water, by contrast, "all that is in the tea comes out, and the strong, rough kinds, suitable for hard water, taste coarse and rank, and the fine flavoury kinds are more suitable."[21] Plantation owners started planning the manufacture of teas knowing full well that they would be blended and drunk in combination rather than alone. Indeed, with the exception of some Darjeeling teas, from high-altitude plantations that could viably grow the Chinese jaat (variety) of tea (*Camellia sinensis*), most tea grown in colonial India and Ceylon was blended either with Chinese teas or with other South or Southeast Asian teas before it was steeped and served.

Getting a blend to taste right remained difficult. As *The Art of Tea Blending* explains, "No two parcels of tea are exactly alike, and although teas may be chosen of about the same quality, chosen from those grown in the same districts, and blended in exactly the same proportions as the mixture they are designed to succeed, the difference may still be so great as to cause dissatisfaction."[22] To meet this challenge, a commercial tea packeting industry arose. The English businessman John Horniman started blending teas on the Isle of Wight as early as 1826. His packets were so popular that his operations quickly expanded and moved to London.[23] By the 1880s, Horniman's, as well as Lipton, Brooke Bond, and other brands still recognizable today, had proliferated on the market.

Something changed as the practice of blending migrated out of homes, first to the backrooms of grocery stores and later to the packeting facilities of industrial enterprises. As Gervas Huxley wrote, "Both grocer and customer may no longer have any idea of the special characteristics which distinguish the teas of Assam, Darjeeling, Travancore, and Ceylon. Almost forgotten is the housewife who selected her tea as she would her meat or vegetables, and brought small quantities of the various growths to blend them herself at home."[24] But although the commercialization of blending may have relieved people of the need to understand the geographic diversity of the empire, it did nothing to assuage their anxiety about the empire's human diversity—anxiety rooted in racism and xenophobia.

Huxley explains that the tea packet served "to protect the consumer against fraud.... Cunning Chinese merchants, to enlarge their profits, formed the practice of coloring their teas with artificial powders of Prussian blue, green-grey and red, in order to disguise the common brown flavorless leaves, which were thus rendered, in appearance, equal to the best tea and sold at a much higher price."[25] While tea's value throughout the 1700s and early 1800s came largely from its association with the exotic and mysterious world of "the East," and China in particular, by the early twentieth century, fascination had given way to fear.

The industrial plantation complex that grew up in British colonies yielded unfamiliar, tannic, malty flavors, even as racially charged suspicions about unscrupulous traders adulterating teas made the once more prized flavor of China tea suspect. As the historian Erika Rappaport explains, promoters of Indian tea argued that the use of machinery on plantations, while it might have yielded different tastes, actually prevented contact between Nepali, Adivasi, or Tamil workers' hands and feet and the processed tea that would be drunk by white British consumers.[26]

By shifting the emphasis from tea's diverse origins to its consistent taste, blending temporarily resolved these racial anxieties. The blended tea packet became wholly British. Blending was explicitly about making the abstract notion of quality—a combination of fair price, consistent taste, and safety—commensurable with an increasingly complex, racially and ethnically diverse, and geographically variable supply chain. This message was not subtle. A Horniman's advertisement from a turn-of-the-century London newspaper warned consumers:

> DON'T TAKE UNNECESSARY RISK.—When buying tea, always ask for HORNIMAN'S. You cannot be too careful in the selection of food and drink. The predominant feature of the present time appears to be cheapness. The so-called "Cheapness" is in reality "Dearness," because a cheap price is paid for an inferior article. "Real Cheapness" is purchasing a good article at a fair price.[27]

OF BLENDS AND POISONS

Though racially charged claims that tea grown on industrial plantations was purer and safer than tea from China must have aided the steady growth of empire-grown tea's market share, consumers could not help but notice that the black tea blends that had become so popular by the end of the nineteenth century left notable stains on teacups, teeth, and tablecloths. As blended tea grew in popularity, so too did claims that tea tannins had a permanent effect not just on porcelain, but on human digestive tracts. According to many industry insiders, consumers were to blame for what seemed like a growth in indigestion because they oversteeped and overbrewed their tea. As *Tea and Tea Blending* explains:

> After they [blends] leave your hands, you, to a great extent, have no control over their fate, and the result of all of your skill may after all be well-nigh spoilt by careless or improper brewing; therefore, it is well to print clearly on every tea wrapper brief hints as to how tea ought to be made, in which the following points should be insisted. . . . Use water the minute it boils, not

before, and don't boil it again. Tea should not stand under a cosy indefinitely. It is a great and far too common mistake in brewing tea to allow it to stand too long—the first five minutes bring out the quality, the next five minutes add to the body, and after that the longer it stands the worse it gets.[28]

Tea tannins became the focus not only of friendly advice to consumers but also of a series of comparative laboratory experiments, carried out by doctors and industry scientists over roughly forty years from the late 1800s through the late 1930s. In these experiments, the sensations of consumption, from taste buds to intestinal tracts, were linked (negatively this time) to the industrial landscapes of production.

An 1893 report, "*The Lancet* Analytical Commission on Tannin and Theine in China and Indian Teas," began by enumerating the various caffeinated substances popularly consumed at the time: coffee, tea, mate, guarana, and kola nut. The report noted that

> tea is practically the only member of the foregoing group of plants in which [tannin] occurs in any important quantity. The proportion of tannin in tea appears to depend on climate and upon the nature of the soil upon which it grows. Thus the Indian teas commonly contain the largest proportion of tannin, the Ceylon teas an intermediate amount and the teas of China the smallest quantity.[29]

According to the authors, the tannin in tea was a "marked poison," "known to produce well-marked gastric and nervous disturbances."[30] They explained that tannins were a "kindly provision of nature intended to warn the drinker when the tea is too strong and when it contains more theine [caffeine] than is good for him."[31]

By the time of the 1893 *Lancet* study, theine had been widely discussed in the scientific literature. Seventeenth- and eighteenth-century writing on tea and health focused on its stimulant effects: its ability to "cheer but not inebriate."[32] The novelty of the *Lancet* study rested in its attention to brewed tea rather than dry leaf, which had been the object of analysis in the earlier theine experiments. The researchers compared one sample of brewed Indian tea with three brewed China teas, and "a breakfast-cup was taken as the standard measure of the water employed and a teaspoonful the standard weight of tea."[33] Samples were steeped in just-boiling water for five and fifteen minutes, after which they were examined for the presence of tannin, theine, and "total extracted matter." The price per pound for each tea was also indicated, with the Indian tea being the cheapest by almost a shilling.[34]

The results of the experiment showed that after five minutes, the Indian tea yielded slightly more tannin than the China teas. After fifteen minutes, the tannin levels increased marginally in the China samples but rose considerably in the Indian sample. The theine levels, after five or fifteen minutes, stayed almost the same. What was surprising to the scientists was that when the experiment was repeated with distilled water, the tannin levels across all four samples went up—doubling across the three China samples and increasing two-and-a-half-fold in the Indian sample. Theine increased minimally across the samples. The scientists concluded that the fifteen-minute steep "practically represents the total amount of tannin and theine." As the *Lancet* scientists wrote, "Tannin, of course, imparts astringency to tea," but Indian teas are "undesirably rich in tannin."[35] Their recommendation: "Tea should never be allowed to stand longer than fifteen minutes at the most and probably half this time is sufficient to dissolve nearly the whole of the theine, whilst less than one half of the total tannin will be taken up."[36] Ordinary tap water, they added, could deter tannin release. If that water was hard, it would prevent full tannin take-up, while soft water dissolved tannin more readily.

The report did little to quell debate about the digestive impact of tea tannins. As the pages of subsequent scientific papers show, this debate was not only about the taste or toxicity of finished products (though cases of "tannin poisoning" were reported in the *Lancet* and other venues) but also about the means of their production.[37] As a 1908 *Lancet* article explained:

> A controversy which has long been settled in the minds of scientific men has been revived by trade partisans. The persons, on the one hand, whose business it is to sell China tea affirm that Indian tea was long ago tabooed by medical men because unless it is prepared for use under very careful directions it contains an excessive amount of astringent substances known to chemists under the generic name of tannin. On the other hand, the parties interested in the sale of Indian and Ceylon teas declare that China tea is objectionable because the leaf is prepared under unwholesome conditions, that it sustains in fact contamination owing to its manipulation by hand, whereas Indian and Ceylon teas are immaculate in this respect because nothing is concerned in their manufacture and production for the market but machinery. To this view many tea connoisseurs reply that the aesthetic qualities of the tea leaf are injured considerably by the mechanical means adopted.[38]

While the authors doubted that the hand-finishing of tea common in Chinese production could cause it to be adulterated with harmful bacteria, they were quick to declare it "idle and impossible" for advocates of Indian tea to deny that their favored product contained more tannin. Scientifically, the authors declared, China teas were "more suited to the requirements of persons with delicate digestive apparatus."[39]

In response to these claims, a reader by the name of H. W. G. MacLeod, introducing himself as the holder of a medical degree from Edinburgh, a member of the Royal College of Physicians, and a doctor of public health, penned a letter to the editor of the *Lancet*. MacLeod wrote, in defense of Indian teas, "It is known that much of the China tea exported is artificially coloured, or 'faced.'" Facing, according to MacLeod, was "a filthy process . . . carried on by the Chinese." In facing, "dyes were smeared on the perspiring back of an 'assistant,' and the dried leaves were rubbed over him to give them the necessary colour. No doubt, as you remark in your article, all germs are destroyed by boiling; yet the idea of imbibing the secretions from the skin of an unhygienic Chinaman is repulsive enough to put one off drinking 'green' tea."[40] MacLeod went on to claim that tannin content also had to do with the age and size of tea leaves. He suggested that the smaller leaves of the highest grades of tea (Orange Pekoe, for example) were richer in tannin. These leaves, collected from "the tops of tea bushes," were more desirable, compared to the Souchong or Congou grades, which were made from larger leaves collected from lower parts of the bush.[41] The association of Indian tea with excessive tannin, then, might actually have something to do with the qualities of the leaves available to British consumers and scientists. "The *best* China tea," MacLeod hypothesized, would also be "collected from the top of the branch." Presumably, this tea, too, was high in tannin. MacLeod proposed that this finer tea was "never exported, but is preserved for the Emperor and highest officials. The adulterated [and less tannic] article is sent abroad!"[42]

While the Sale of Food and Drugs Act of 1875 ensured the inspection of imported tea and other food products, MacLeod's letter highlights how the imperial project that put British Indian tea in competition with Chinese tea continued to provoke racial anxieties that food safety regulations could not fully quell. Images of dyed teas and unhygienic producers persisted in the popular imaginary.[43] At issue in the debate over tannins, then, was the impact of an encounter between white metropolitan bodies and the racialized and potentially polluting bodies of Asian field and factory laborers—an encounter mediated by tea itself.

By the 1920s, the amount of tea produced in India and Ceylon was stagnating, while imports of cheap (if, according to most experts, inferior) tea grown in the Dutch East Indies were booming.[44] Blenders began "breaking down" India and Ceylon teas with teas from Java and Sumatra in order to keep the prices of their packet teas as low as possible.[45] Alarmed at this trend, British planters' groups operating across the empire warned that Dutch tea's "encroachment" would "harm the goodwill of Indian and Ceylon teas in that consumers attribute the poor quality of the tea which they purchase to Indian and Ceylon teas which they suppose it to be and not to the presence of a filler of an inferior quality."[46] The problem for planters in India and Ceylon was that Dutch tea was never sold as such; it had no real value on its own, apart from its "qualities as a filler" in blends.[47] While wholesale prevention of the importation of Dutch tea into the United Kingdom was impracticable, British producers in India took active measures to discourage its uptake in blends. To do this, producer organizations applied for protections under the Merchandise Mark Act (MMA) of 1926. According to the MMA, the government could require certain products to carry "marks," or labels, indicating locations of origin. The ITA, along with allied planter organizations from South India and Ceylon, petitioned to have all teas sold in the United Kingdom marked as "Empire," "Foreign," or "Empire and Foreign."[48] These categories of origin would be "printed in a conspicuous manner" on packages of tea (including blends), "so that the place of origin may be clearly shown to the consumer."[49] If given the choice, producer organizations argued, consumers would choose the empire-grown product.[50]

In late 1928, British imperial tea planters made their case before the UK Board of Trade. Their application was opposed by the Tea Buyers' Association and British tea interests in Java and Sumatra.[51] It was also opposed by the Joint Parliamentary Committee of the Cooperative Congress, which claimed to represent the "experience and interests" of "growers, blenders, and packers of tea." At the time, the cooperative movement had over 5.5 million members, from retail to production. As plantation owners, members of the English and Scottish Joint Co-operative Wholesale Society (part of the Joint Parliamentary Committee) grew tea on thousands of acres of tea plantations in India and Ceylon. The society was, at the time, the largest single distributor of tea in the United Kingdom, supplying about one-sixth of the total consumption. Of this consumption, 90 percent was blended packet tea.[52]

Though much of the five-day hearing dealt with the question of whether consumers would actively select tea based on its place of origin, the documents and transcripts from the hearing outline a parallel conversation about what can best be described as the ontological status of blended tea.[53] Both sides agreed that the taste of tea—even tea from a single plantation—varied throughout the season and over the course of the year on account of soil, climate conditions, methods of cultivation, plucking, and other factors. "'Quality,'" as the applicants for the marking order wrote, "is elusive. It varies from time to time throughout the year but there would in fact be no difficulty on the part of blenders in establishing a standard quality from empire-grown tea."[54] Seasonal variation could be overcome only by blending.

But was blended tea materially, chemically *distinct* from its constituent parts? Empire Tea advocates and manufacturers applying for a marking order had an answer to this question. As they stated in their written notes in preparation for the 1928 hearing:

> It is admitted that tea blending is the work of a specialist but to say that the blending of tea in this country is "the product of a complicated and difficult process of manufacture" is not admitted, for the simple reason that the tea does not change its form. The blending is just mixing, nothing more, having regard to the appearance of the tea and to the liquor product of the mixed tea. There is no process of manufacture whatsoever of raw materials into another form for us so far as the blender is concerned; he handles and mixes the tea but he does not manufacture anything.[55]

In addition to making an economic case for the marking order, then, the applicants had to establish that the tea that drinkers purchased was the same tea that was packaged, shipped, tasted, and auctioned. If tea was unchanged by the process of blending, then it was traceable and therefore could be labeled.[56] Put in terms of contemporary sociological theory about the logic of markets, the question at hand was how tea was to be "qualified" before it came to market.[57]

Tea blenders themselves were, perhaps not surprisingly, the most vociferous of the opponents in the case. They marshaled evidence to show that blending *was* transformative—that the tea sold in packets was something distinct. The tea buyers' "Statement of Opposition" made this case in a way that mixed economic argumentation about maximizing value from raw material with scientific argumentation about chemical constituency.

The extraordinary art of the tea blender will be the more appreciated when it is considered that he has always to keep in view not only the dry leaf which he handles but the liquor product of such leaf when the tea is brewed by the ordinary public. The result is that the blended tea sold in this country is the product of a complicated and difficult process of manufacture and the chemical constituents of blended tea will differ in varying degree from the several raw teas of which the blend may be composed. Not only is blending essential from the consumer's standpoint, but it is also vital to the producer as unless the coarse and fine crops are suitably blended, it would not be possible profitably to utilise the entire product. It is on the art of tea blending that the prosperity of the English tea trade is wholly and entirely dependent. In addition to nature and quality the tea blender has constantly to have before him the question of price, and he has above all things to secure that the public shall receive at a standard price a standard quality of tea. It is by the successful achievement of this object (by the blender's skill) that the great fame and reputation of English tea has been built up.[58]

The tea that consumers purchased was, according to the blenders, thus a fully transformed product: "The blended teas are goods which since importation have undergone treatment of process which has resulted in so substantial a change in them that *their identity is wholly destroyed,* and their chemical constituents when brewed in the blend are proportionately varied."[59] Blenders positioned themselves not just as intermediaries, but as essential producers of quality, in terms of taste and price. Through their own careful study of flavor profiles, the market, and brewing techniques, they subjected their blends to repeated "trials" designed to ensure its reliability.[60]

What made English tea English and what made Scottish tea Scottish was not the fact that it was produced on plantations owned by English or Scottish firms but that it was materially altered by blenders to match both the desires of consuming publics and the ecological contexts of consumption. Blending manuals suggested that a knowledge of water's material makeup had to precede an appreciation of local taste preferences. It was due to the consideration of both the mineral contents of local water (hard water with high quantities of "lime and other minerals in solution" versus soft water with fewer of these) and local gustatory trends, for example, that Irish consumers encountered a higher percentage of Indian tea in their blends, while "the greater portions of the English people like in every blend at least half China tea."[61] For blenders, quality came from the ability to effect a simultaneous transformation of economic value and material makeup.

The blenders had good reason to make this assertion. Their claims were rooted in the debate from decades earlier about the health effects of tannins.

Back in 1911, the ITA had enthusiastically endorsed another *Lancet* study, "The Chemistry, Physiology, and Aesthetics of a Cup of Tea." This study claimed that what expert tasters defined as "good tea"—whether it originated in China or India or Ceylon—was possessed of a balance between those two all-important chemicals, caffeine and tannin. The authors explained that "good tea"

> is good because the caffeine and tannin occur together as a definite neutral compound, practically neither caffeine nor tannin being present in the free state. On the other hand, the cheaper commoner classes of tea, according to the experts' category, did not in the experiments we record show evidence of the equilibrium being preserved between the two substances, one or the other being in excess. In the common tea it seems probable that the bitterness of the free caffeine is evident to the taster's palate, or the astringency of the free tannin, as the case may be. The good tea is classed as such because there is a balance of these two constituents. . . . It would therefore appear that when the taster decides upon the quality of a sample (apart altogether from its flavour) he is guided largely by the fact that in a good tea the caffeine and tannin are present in properties which mutually extinguish the bad qualities of each other, and these bad qualities refer not only to taste but to physiological effect.[62]

At the time, the ITA and other producers of Indian tea actively used the *Lancet*'s findings to promote sales, but seventeen years later at the Board of Trade hearing, those same findings were mobilized by opponents of the Empire Tea movement to label blended tea based on its origins.

On December 11, 1928, the second day of the hearing, the board heard evidence from a Mr. John Parry, an analytical chemist with forty years' experience specializing in food and a fellow of both the Institute of Chemistry and the Chemical Society. A lawyer for the Tea Buyers' Association, one of the groups opposing the petition for a marking order, asked Mr. Parry whether there was "any method of detecting the presence of a particular tea of a particular country in a blended tea."[63] Mr. Parry testified that he knew of no such method. The lawyer then asked, "Do the tea blenders and tea tasters know what they are doing chemically when they select a given blended tea?"[64] Parry explained that while blenders might not know what was going on at a chemical level, "their rule of thumb methods get them there pretty well as if they did. Their object is to get an infusion of tea in which the caffeine and tannin are properly balanced and which are the proper balances of straight teas. . . . [A]lthough the tea taster and expert is not much concerned with the percentage of caffeine or tannin . . . he probably does better than if you consulted an analyst to decide on the blending."[65] The lawyer next asked Mr. Parry whether he believed that it would be possible to use chemistry to separate the constituents of a blended tea after they had been mixed. Mr. Parry guessed that "in a blend of China tea with other tea it is just possible for someone to sit over it with a lens and pick it out leaf by leaf with a pair of tweezers" but that otherwise, de-blending a packet of tea would be impossible. Moreover, he testified, the "ratio of the principal chemical constituents" in the blend becomes permanent the moment tea is infused in hot water.[66] Parry then echoed the findings of the 1911 *Lancet* study, telling the court that "a badly blended tea might result in a certain amount of tannate of caffeine with an excess of tannic acid or caffeine."[67] Parry's testimony used a combination of chemical and aesthetic judgment to validate the blenders' claims that their work produced a substantive transformation of "straight tea"—a transformation that was as important to tea's taste as it was to its safety for the consumer.

TANNIC GEOGRAPHIES

After the five-day hearing, the Board of Trade denied the tea planters' organizations' application for a merchandise marking order. The decision was made on the grounds that since almost all tea was blended, such an order would "hamper the blenders in supplying the needs of the public, and would probably raise the price of tea to the consumer."[68] The board agreed with the applicants, however, that British consumers were both aware of the existence of empire-grown goods (including tea) and potentially willing to purchase them over so-called foreign ones. In 1931, an Imperial Economic Committee (IEC) report reviewed the 1928 marking order case and reasserted the need for some kind of effort to promote the consumption of empire-grown tea. In the context of the Great Depression, the IEC's call was one of many efforts to bolster "home" industries.[69] The ITA circulated a leaflet to its members and members of the applicant organizations in Ceylon and South India. It urged the recipients to contact their Members of Parliament, and it encouraged planters themselves (and those around them) to contribute in everyday activities as well: *"Active help can thus be given if you will ask for Empire Tea, recommend your friends to purchase Empire Tea and, if possible, insist on obtaining such teas."*[70]

Even amid the depression, China remained a concern for Indian tea producers. Despite racist derision of Chinese tea as produced in an "unscientific" manner and of Chinese merchants as prone to secretly adulterate teas on the market, a sense lingered that Chinese manufacture possessed innate superiority over British colonial manufacture.[71] On November 17, 1931, Sir Charles McLeod, chairman of both the Imperial Tea Committee and the National Bank of India, gave a speech at the Royal Empire Society in London titled "A Plea for Empire Tea." As Sir Charles explained, the dominance of branded, packaged teas on the market took advantage of "ignorance in the public mind in regard to the origin of the tea drunk here and of the contents of the blends which are placed on the market." His argument was, like much discourse about tea consumption, pointedly gendered:

> It is a common experience ... to be asked in hotels and tea-shops whether you will take "Indian" or "China." If you demand the Indian product, you might get a blend of Indian, Ceylon, and Java tea; if your preferences go for the China article, Heaven knows what you will be served. There is an amusing story of the two ladies who, going into a tea-shop, ordered "One pot of Indian tea and one of China, please." The waitress, in her turn, called down to the kitchen: "Two teas—one weak!" And it may well be imagined that the lady concerned, like all other people in similar circumstances, was satisfied that the weak beverage supplied to her was made from genuine China leaf.[72]

Later in his speech, Sir Charles described how an "enthusiastic lady who was anxious to respond to the appeals now being made by some of the most eminent personages in this land, recently wrote and asked where she could [obtain] good Empire China tea."

A copy of the letter to which Sir Charles referred, written to the Indian Tea Association by a Mrs. Henry Bayly, is housed in the British Library along with a copy of Sir Charles's speech. Mrs. Bayly was one of many middle-class consumers targeted in the ITA's campaign to promote Empire Tea. She wrote:

> Gentlemen,
>   Having received your circular ... [I am writing to inquire] whether I can get China tea which is grown within the Empire? I live in a small flat and do not like weak tea myself, but I have it for my friends who prefer China tea, [but] I cannot buy it in large quantities. [I have gone to the Army Navy store looking] for China Tea grown "within the Empire," [and they said] they could provide it, but were curious to know where it could be got. If I could let them know, they would be very grateful.[73]

For Mrs. Bayly and interwar consumers like her, "China" was less a place than it was a flavor profile. As Sir Charles explained in his speech, Mrs. Bayly was trying to do a patriotic duty: purchase this flavor from the empire and for the empire.

Though Sir Charles did not mention it in his speech, the response to Mrs. Bayly's inquiry from the secretary of the Indian Tea Association is instructive.

> Dear Madam,
> I have your letter of the 20th . . . but beg to advise you that China Tea is not grown within the Empire and that the article you require (namely Empire Grown China Tea) cannot be obtained.
> Might I suggest that you use Darjeeling Tea which is famous for its characteristic flavour.[74]

What the secretary did not make explicit to Mrs. Bayly was that Darjeeling's reputation for quality and delicacy came in large part from the fact that it was made up exclusively of leaves from the Chinese jaat of tea, *Camellia sinensis*. Other teas grown in India often comprised in large part leaves from the Assam jaat, *Camellia sinensis* var. *assamica,* a variety that, among other things, was thought to contain higher levels of tannin.

After more than three decades of scientific reports and analyses of the safety of empire-grown *assamica* teas, tannins continued to be viewed as health threats. By the onset of the Great Depression, notable brands such as Typhoo and Brooke Bond were marketing "digestive" teas that they claimed were free from harmful tannins. In 1931, G. H. Harden, a principal in the company that marketed the most famous of these, Doctor's China Tea, published the *Treatise from a Medical Point of View on Various Facts Relating to Tea*. Harden clarified in the introduction to the *Treatise* that although he was not himself a doctor, "in setting out to write the present treatise, I have been actuated very largely by two separate considerations. . . . My primary object has been to draw attention to the extraordinary extent to which indigestion due to tea-drinking has increased in this country within the past fifty years, and to put forward what I believe to be the cause of this increase and the methods by which it may most effectively be counteracted."[75] Harden traced this mass indigestion to what he called "a 'speeding up' process" that had taken hold in Europe and America during the previous century. "For this pace to be maintained with comfort," he wrote,

> some sort of stimulant was increasingly necessary. Alcohol, except in most moderate quantities, had already been discouraged by all the leading dieticians of the day; and tea—previously restricted to China tea, and therefore, rightly regarded as non-harmful—was welcomed everywhere as the only suitable substitute. Unaware of the lurking danger, the consuming public felt that here, at last, was exactly the beverage that it required.[76]

During this speeding-up process, "as China tea 'went out,' so indigestion and nervous affections 'came in.'" The difference lay in the tannins. "As is well known," Harden wrote,

> tannic acid forms with the . . . contents in the stomach . . . a leathery insoluble compound upon which the digestive ferments cannot easily act, and hence excessive tea-drinking becomes a primary cause of indigestion. The human system is capable, under favorable circumstances, of coping with a small amount of tannic acid without ill effects; but the cumulative effect of habitually exceeding this "small amount," to say nothing of the inveterate habit of large doses, is little less than disastrous.[77]

Because of its effects on the "muscular coating of the intestines," tannic acid "arrests their normal gradual movements and so induces constipation." According to Harden, tannic acid's "astringent effect" also caused gastritis, various ulcers, dyspepsia, and even stomach cancer.[78]

China tea, Harden argued, was free from these risks because of the way it was produced. As he explained:

> The conservative habits of the Chinese have prevented them from adopting modern methods of extensive cultivation, and their tea is almost entirely grown by the small farmer who has no difficulty in carrying out the necessary manuring from the ordinary farmyard sources, in the natural if primitive way. He also clings to the old-fashioned method of making his tea by hand, the ineradicable Chinese conservatism resenting any changes. In many cases only a very small area—perhaps the corner of his farm—is planted with tea. . . . Large plantations of a thousand acres or more, such as are common elsewhere, are practically unknown in China, as are also even the most rudimentary forms of tea-making machinery. It is no doubt partly due to these old-fashioned methods of cultivation and manufacture, as well as to the differences in the soil and in the nature of the plant itself, that China teas should vary so greatly from those produced in any country. . . . Although I realise that my view may be disputed, I do not think that the use of modern machinery has improved the quality of tea in general. I believe, on the contrary, that it may actually be detrimental, and it is significant that in other directions our diet has certainly lost in quality through the introduction of mechanical methods, however much may have been gained in quantity and economy.[79]

Harden's *Treatise* harkened back to the "digestive geography" of tea and tannins that had consumed *Lancet* authors and caused consternation to Empire Tea promoters at the turn of the century.[80] In most respects, his claims were both hyperbolic and anachronistic. At the hearings at the Board of Trade and in numerous scientific studies over the preceding decade, the concern that tea tannins caused the kinds of digestive problems he described had been largely placated.

What Harden presented was a more redemptive (if also differently racialized and essentialized) view of tea production in China. His message was that heavy industry and the drive for efficiency—both in the factories of England and Scotland and in the plantations of India and Ceylon—wreaked havoc in the digestive tract. Later in the *Treatise,* Harden lamented that producers of Devonshire and Cornish butter had abandoned hand methods for machinery, which in turn "banished the delicious flavor." He suggested that the "food value" of common products may have been reduced as well. Beer made by hand with "pure" ingredients "was certainly more wholesome than now." Bread made with natural yeasts obtained from the village inn following beer brewing and baked in a wood-fired oven also "had little enough in common with the modern machine-made loaf." But "it is at any rate some satisfaction to know that we can still obtain unspoilt China tea which has been grown, made and packaged by methods traditionally dating back more than two thousand years before the Christian era. I hope the evil day will never arrive on which the Chinese make use of modern tea machinery."[81] For Harden, the problem was not just the machinery used to process tea. The industrial organization of factories in England also played a role in the indigestion epidemic. Harden tells the story of "a young girl suffering from chronic ulceration of the stomach." The London factory in which she worked had a custom whereby "each girl [would] bring a teaspoon full of tea wrapped in a piece of paper. These papers were emptied in the morning into a gallon pot, which was then filled with boiling water. During the day the pot was constantly refilled as the contents were exhausted, and each girl in the factory consumed at least six cups of this astringent concoction during working hours."[82] The longer tea steeped, the more astringent (or "tannic") it got, and the greater the chance for ulcers.

Advertisements for Doctor's China Tea appeared in medical journals and popular media outlets. These were accompanied by testimonials from "medical men," including doctors who themselves suffered from indigestion before making the switch to this "tannin-free" brand.[83] In one of these vivid testimonials, a woman who was a devotee of Doctor's China Tea describes being on holiday and being given another tea, whereupon she immediately started vomiting.[84] In its own way, the Doctor's China Tea company even joined in the push to promote Empire Tea. The small print on a half-page advertisement that ran in UK newspapers read:

More than 2,000 medical men recommend The Doctor's China Tea to nervous, dyspeptic patients—and use it themselves. The Doctor's China Tea is prescribed universally as a refreshing and health giving beverage in cases where ordinary tea is forbidden. It is the *only* tea that thousands of our people can use, because it cannot cause indigestion. And remember, China sends us her . . . tea to pay for the goods she buys from us and which otherwise *she could not purchase.*[85]

In large letters framing this testimonial, the ad read, "For its Health and for its Wealth the Empire *must* have China tea."[86] Harden's *Treatise* might seem like a typical, if extreme, example of aggressive direct marketing, but the ITA and other proponents of Empire Tea saw Doctor's China Tea and similar products as a serious threat. They considered "tannin-free" marketing pitches harmful "propaganda," even if in all likelihood these products probably contained at least some Empire Tea, given both its market saturation and the nature of blending at the time.[87]

The ITA's response to these health-oriented, antitannin marketing pitches consumed much of its work over the course of the 1930s. In a campaign that was part scientific, part legal, and part commercial, the ITA set out to push back against the direct causal connection that Harden made between tea drinking and the "epidemic" of indigestion. The ITA did not dispute that such an epidemic existed, but it maintained that claims of such a connection, as a letter sent to Harden from the ITA secretary shortly after the publication of the *Treatise* asserted, "[ignore] the vital changes in the whole habits of the people that have occurred in the past half century."[88] More important for the ITA, it was not valid to compare Doctor's China Tea to what Harden calls "strong coarse growths of other countries." The secretary continued:

> The few who may be tempted to drink Doctor's China Tea are among those who probably now enjoy a good Darjeeling or a flavoury Ceylon—teas produced under scientific and cleanly conditions, no dearer, much more palatable and certainly no more harmful (if there is any harm in good tea) than China tea of equal class. To attempt to oust Darjeeling and fine Ceylon by substitution of Chinas is, to say the least, an unpatriotic action, especially when accompanied by misleading and derogatory remarks directed against Empire growths.[89]

The ITA did not limit its opposition to Doctor's China Tea to scolding private correspondence. In fact, it considered taking Harden to court. In October 1931, however, the ITA's lawyers informed the organization that it had little in the way of recourse.[90] On the advice of its lawyers, the ITA set out to produce an alternative, health-oriented pamphlet. For this, ITA officers turned to scientists in the Tocklai Experimental Station in Jorhat, Assam.

Tocklai was the center of the ITA's Scientific Department, which spanned from British universities to offices in London and Calcutta. Experimentation at Tocklai was initially focused on field production: maximizing yields and increasing overall efficiency on plantations.[91] By the turn of the twentieth century, however, tea science was reoriented to maximizing quality. Even before the onset of the Great Depression severely reduced demand, the ITA had resolved to limit total production, seeking to reduce what it termed "coarse" plucking and other plantation practices that might compromise taste and texture.[92] Competitors in Java, Sumatra, and elsewhere referred to this move as an unfair "crop restriction," but the ITA maintained that it was an effort to increase quality.[93] A central task of the new depression-era tea science that held quality as its object of analysis and intervention was to recast tannins as benign flavor-producing substances.

TANNINS, REMATERIALIZED

The objective of the ITA scientists was neither to prove that the coarser, hardier *Camellia sinensis* var. *assamica* tea was somehow innately superior to China tea, nor was it to deny that tannic black teas could leave stains on tablecloths, cups, and saucers. Instead, their aim was to recast tannins as palatable and even valuable constituents of plantation-grown tea. Their audience was not consumers, necessarily, but the "medical men" who were the targets of aggressive marketing by the likes of Doctor's China Tea.

A 1932 handwritten response to Harden's treatise explained, "During the rolling process of black tea manufacture, the oxidized tannin is mixed with the leaf proteins and is largely precipitated. The result is the *removal* of much soluble oxidized tea tannin from the tea leaf."[94] Reminding readers that the tea they were drinking was the product of industrial machine manufacture, however, did not prove to be the most effective way of validating tea's health and safety. Changing course, the ITA enrolled P. H. Carpenter, Tocklai's chief scientific officer, and C. R. Harler, the scientist who would also push for the establishment of a fixed glossary of teawords, to draft a scientific article that would refute the claims in Harden's *Treatise*. Early drafts of Carpenter and Harler's "The Chemistry and Pharmacology of a Cup of Tea" began with a belabored discussion of the technicalities of tea manufacturing, describing the different processes that yielded green and black tea. The substance of the article, however, traced tea tannin in its journey from steeping to mixture with milk to ingestion in the mouth and through the intestines and out of the body. Essentially, Carpenter and Harler were attempting a "digestive geography" that would counter that of antitannin crusaders like Harden.[95]

As Carpenter advised in a January 1932 letter to the assistant secretary of the ITA, "since medical men appear generally to have a misunderstanding of tea," the article should be submitted for publication in the *Lancet*. Carpenter wanted the findings published in the leading medical journal of the day because he and Harler believed they had identified a fundamental chemical difference between "tea tannin" and the tannic acid associated with leatherwork and other dyeing processes.[96] Carpenter emphasized that if it could be published, this finding would be a corrective to the oft-cited 1911 *Lancet* study, which had treated the two substances as a singular compound.[97] Carpenter and Harler were not just defending tannic tea from allegations of toxicity; they were suggesting that tea tannin was itself a chemically distinct entity.

With the ITA's blessing, Carpenter and Harler submitted "The Chemistry and Pharmacology of a Cup of Tea" to the *Lancet* later that year. The article went through multiple rounds of peer review by scientists and industry professionals. Ultimately, however, the *Lancet* rejected the submission. A version of "The Chemistry and Pharmacology of a Cup of Tea" was eventually published in the *Quarterly Journal* of the ITA. Many of the same findings were also published in Harler's 1933 book, *The Culture and Marketing of Tea*.[98] Even though Harler's book proved to be quite popular (three editions—1933, 1956, and 1964—were eventually published), the ITA remained concerned that its message was not yet reaching the right group: "medical men." So-called digestive teas continued to claim a considerable share of the market, and their manufacturers continued to promote these teas as medically preferable to conventional black teas.

In a letter to the secretary of the Indian Tea Cess Committee, the committee in charge of the Empire Tea campaign, the ITA's London secretary, W. H. Pease, complained about this. The major problem from the ITA's perspective was that

> by stating that "DIGESTIVE TEA" is free from excess tannin and consequently does little harm to people who suffer from indigestion and such like troubles, [advertisements] infer that all other tea is harmful. This idea is being

steadily cultivated by the proprietors of Doctor's China Tea, Typhoo Tips and Messrs. Brooke Bond & Co. Ltd. and the impression is, it is believed, steadily gaining ground that ordinary tea is harmful because of its tannin content.[99]

These companies, Pease continued, "do not seem to realise that their propaganda while it may be building up a business for this particular type of tea cannot but do grave harm to their other business in *ordinary* teas and to the Industry in general."[100] Pease's use of "ordinary" is significant here. Antitannin "propaganda" made medical professionals suspicious of the whole process by which the majority of tea on the market was grown. This propaganda drew negative attention to the conditions of plantation production.

Pease suggested that the Drink Empire Tea Campaign should do something to counter such messaging, namely, fund a new scientific investigation into the effects of tea on the human body. Even though the Drink Empire Tea Campaign was ostensibly about marketing to consumers, Pease solicited funding from the Tea Cess Committee in the amount of 500 to 1,000 pounds to pay for such a study.[101] In 1933, the ITA contacted the *Lancet,* asking its editors to help identify scientists who might carry out new research on the effects of tea on human health. The *Lancet* agreed, and it found scientists at the University of Leeds who were willing to participate.[102] The ITA responded with appreciation, but it then insisted that it be able to block the publication of the Leeds study if it did not agree with the findings.[103] The *Lancet* refused, and the study did not move forward.[104]

Though it failed to seize editorial power over the *Lancet*'s studies of tea's pharmacology, in 1936, the ITA did finally succeed in publishing a pamphlet under the auspices of the Empire Tea Bureau. *A New Essay upon Tea: Addressed to the Medical Profession* began with a lengthy dedication to John Coakley Lettsom, "who published the first important Medical treatise in English on tea-drinking, in 1772."[105] It next offered a short history of the tea trade, from the East India Company's exchanges with Chinese merchants to the founding of tea plantations in India and the entrance of Dutch tea into the market and the rise of packet teas.

The core of the *New Essay* was Part II, which outlined tea's "effect on the human frame." The section began by stating that in the recent controversies over the relative merits of Indian, Ceylon, China, and Dutch East Indian tea, and of the relative safety of various blends, "minute and unimportant differences in the composition of teas came to be exaggerated." Aiming to set the record straight "in light of modern knowledge," the *New Essay* zeroed in on "the nature of tea tannin, about which so much misunderstanding seems to exist."[106] "Tea tannin," the essay stated, was primarily a force not in coloration or staining but in flavoring. It conferred "pungency and . . . taste to the tea." While it was true that Indian and Ceylon teas were richer in tannin (as well as caffeine and oils) than China teas, what was of most importance was not tea in isolation but tea in combination, or the blend. Here, the ITA quietly ceded the point made by Mr. Parry during the Board of Trade hearing. "The composition of the infusion," wrote the essay's anonymous authors, "is of much greater practical importance than that of the leaves from which it is made."[107]

Gone were the efforts to distinguish Empire Tea as preferable on its own. Instead, the *New Essay* recounted evidence from clinical studies of the health effects of "the cup of tea, as usually drunk with milk and sugar."[108] These clinical studies were carried out by analytical chemists, and their results had been published and disseminated in trade journals such as the *Spice Mill* and at meetings of the American and British Chemical Societies. While the ITA made use of the results of several studies, the *New Essay* cited no scholarly sources. Indeed, at least one of the scientists whose work was indirectly referenced in the essay, a Dr. Bach, refused to have his name associated with it.[109] Bach's studies found that in human subjects, while a "10-minute infusion" of tea drunk without milk caused "marked discomfort," "the discomfort was less . . . with good quality tea than with poor quality." The addition of milk and sugar to the infusion reduced the reported "discomfort" to zero.[110] Subsequent laboratory studies confirmed that while tea tannin "had a definite effect in reducing peptic digestion," "milk is found to be a completely satisfactory antidote."[111] The *New Essay*'s scientific review ended with the definitive statement that "the cup of tea as normally drunk has no ill effects on the human body."[112]

The conclusion to the *New Essay*'s scientific section listed four important points.

1. Good tea, properly made, is in every way harmless.
2. Poor tea, badly made, may have slightly unpleasant effects.
3. Good India, Ceylon or Java-Sumatra tea produces no other symptoms and signs and no more harmful effects than does good China tea.
4. If milk is added to the cup of tea, even the effects of excessive consumption and bad preparation are counteracted.[113]

The final two paragraphs of the scientific section took up the question of "tanninless" tea. It cited a report reproduced in the *Lancet* by a Mr. H. H. Bagnall, city analyst of Birmingham. Bagnall had analyzed a range of supposedly tannin-free "digestive" teas and found that "the tannin content was the same as the average tannin content of ordinary teas of the same class."[114]

The ITA ultimately rested its case for the health of tea produced in large, industrialized, mechanized plantation environments on notions of the "goodness" or "quality" of the product. Good quality tea—tea that had a refined, aromatic flavor (and was also likely more expensive)—was also healthy tea.[115] "The better the tea, the better for you." So-called common tea could only be saved with a healthy dose of milk.[116]

The ITA considered the *New Essay* a success. In December 1936, the *Lancet* published its response, confirming the assertions in the pamphlet, including the main findings: first, "poor quality" tea caused more digestive distress than "good" tea; and second, tea tannin could even promote digestion in the right circumstances.[117]

A PROGESTIVE SOLUTION

By the end of the 1930s, these discussions of what tea contained, both as a blended beverage and as a chemical amalgam, had transformed the very idea of quality in the market. The experiments that attended the rise of Empire Tea yielded not only new substances (factory-finished black tea and tea tannins) but also new ways of calculating value. Among other things, these experiments provided a medical and scientific rationale for a particular style of consumption. In his classic study of the place of sugar in contemporary Euro-American life, Sidney Mintz outlines the parallels between the making of the industrial British working class and the formation of the British Empire, both as an idea and as a vast commercial infrastructure.[118] Mintz's argument is that taste is as much a matter of political economy as it is regional or group customary practice. Behind the seemingly quintessential British practice of drinking steeped black tea with plenty of sugar and milk lies a violent history of capital accumulation and dispossession. The debates over blending, digestion, and market share I have recounted in this chapter underscore that the establishment of scientific consensus on the chemical outcomes of industrial processes, from field to factory to infused cups, cannot be divorced from that history.

But it is not only forms of consumption that are rooted in a blend of imperial political economy and imperial science. The very terms on which substances are judged and valued are also rooted in those processes.[119] The transformation in the value of tannins is a case in point. Consider "Observations on Tea," a pamphlet written by E. A. Andrews and published by the Empire Tea Bureau in 1939. Andrews writes:

> The best quality teas are made from the youngest portions of the young shoots, the bud and the first open leaf, and it is found that the proportion of both tannin and caffeine is highest in these.... Of recent years the plucking of tea has tended to become finer and finer, and existing conditions of regulation of the crop ... have emphasized this tendency. Present-day Empire teas are therefore produced from the portions of the shoot that contain the highest proportion of tannin present [and] ... give a refreshing and stimulating liquor.[120]

Just a decade after they had lost their bid to establish "Empire Tea" as a trademark and after over half a century of efforts to link tannins to indigestion and ill health, British tea interests had managed not only to equate tannins with quality, but to do so while touting the superiority of plantation production. It was the training of the conscripted or indentured labor force to delicately pluck "two leaves and a bud" that remade plantation tea as "good tea." The image of the brown fingers of Nepali, Adivasi, or Tamil women gently pulling away the tender, green sprigs that now grace the packages of countless tea brands, too, is a product of imperial technoscience.

By the end of the 1930s, the days of "digestive," or tannin-free, teas were numbered. They had been supplanted on the market by a new product: Brooke Bond's Pre-Gestee Tea. Though the blend was ostensibly the same as before, the tannins in this tea were acknowledged as a benefit that helped consumers digest their meals. Grocers found the brand name "Pre-Gestee" overly cumbersome and shortened it to "PG Tea." In keeping with the new science of quality, Brooke Bond added "Tips" to the brand name to indicate a material correlation to good quality.[121] The message was that this brand contained only the "good," tannic, young sprigs of tea. Today, PG Tips remains among the most popular brands of tea in the world, itself a kind of symbol of contemporary British and American consumer culture.

FOUR

The Science of Quality

SEEN FROM THE WINDOW OF A SHARED TAXI rumbling through the mountains of Darjeeling or Assam, the rows and rows of tea bushes on plantations appear homogeneous, orderly, even monotonous. But even though we call them monocultures, these landscapes are far from uniform. I return to the topic of monoculture in the next chapter, but for now, I want to emphasize that even the most uniform-looking tea plantation is a product of a particular form of agricultural scientific experimentation. The purpose of this experimentation is to maximize the quality of each plant. For tea industry scientists, quality means flavor, but it also means viability, or yield. One view of quality holds that a crop with a good flavor might be rare or at least difficult to produce in economies of scale. After all, people will pay more for something that is less abundant. A high-yielding crop, by contrast, may not have a distinctive flavor. Its value comes from the sheer volume of its productivity and its desirability across socioeconomic difference. How, then, has quality come to have these two conflicting connotations?

In 2009, I interviewed an official from the Tea Research Association, the institution tasked with overseeing scientific research on tea in Northeast India. He filtered his explanation of the work of producing quality through the story of plant hybridization. Echoing the view of early British planters, he told me that although many of the tea varieties planted in India today came from China, the nineteenth-century Chinese industry was unscientific and "erratic." The Chinese made no attempt at controlled propagation. Seeds just floated around the fields and "cross-pollinated with each other willy-nilly." Since the Chinese did not cultivate seeds systematically, there was no way, he explained, to know which ones were yielding the most productive tea bushes or the most flavorful ones.

To answer this question, in 1911, the ITA established the Tocklai Experimental Station, base of the tannin experiments discussed in the previous chapter.[1] Today, Tocklai remains in operation under the auspices of the TRA, and its laboratories and experimental plots have introduced hundreds of clonal varieties of tea and distinct seed stocks. Tocklai's network of scientists advise tea plantations across West Bengal and Northeast India about which clones will thrive best, depending on altitude, soil composition, pest insect populations, rainfall, and—crucially—factory finishing method. Tocklai contains not only laboratories and experimental plots but also an entire model tea factory, where the methods of drying, withering, fermenting, rolling, and processing that turn green leaf tea into "made tea" can be replicated, tested, and refined. When TRA advisers affiliated with Tocklai visit plantations, they recommend that clonal teas make up 50 percent of the total tea cultivated. The TRA classifies clones on a scale that delineates between those that have desirable flavors and those that produce high yields. It recommends that plantations select a combination of flavor clones, yield clones, and "standard" clones (clones with qualities somewhere in the middle of the scale).

An official history of Tocklai describes tea research as "the first private-public venture in the subcontinent."[2] Now something of a vogue in international development and public policy, public-private partnerships (PPPs) operate on the premise that the interests of private industry and those of the public good can be reconciled. Frequently, science is seen as the neutral ground on which a settlement between public and private interests should be made.[3] The contemporary TRA is supported in part by the Government of India's Tea Board and in part by voluntary contributions from "members" (private tea companies), but the science of quality straddles much more than the simple divide between public and private. It also bridges the disciplinary domains of biochemistry (focused on flavor, texture, aroma, and appearance) and agricultural engineering (focused on efficiency of production, size of harvest, cost of labor, and market expansion).

Perhaps more significantly, the science of quality developed amid a tension between regimes of colonial and postcolonial governance. This chapter discusses a nearly forty-year set of bureaucratic, economic, and epistemological struggles over the organization and regulation of science in the Indian tea industry.[4] Over the course of this history, debates about whether quality tea was a chemically discrete and isolatable entity crisscrossed with discussions of how (and even whether) the production of tea in more efficient ways might lead to the growth in the quality of life for Indian people, particularly work-ers on tea plantations.[5] As I have been arguing throughout this book, the story of tea is not one of a smooth transition from crop of empire to crop of national development and prosperity.[6] Rather, this story illustrates the entan-glement of empire and development.

The volatile period of the 1930s to the 1960s can be productively read as a series of attempts by British tea industry leaders to keep quality subject to European scientific authority and by Indian government officials to exert sovereignty over the direction of industrial science. The work of the TRA and its predecessors is (and was) done in the service of a plantation system devised by European capital. Scientific knowledge about quality is (and was) assumed to be a product of European reason. By the logic of the TRA official I interviewed, such reason stands in contrast both to the "erratic" practices of Asian "others," such as Chinese farmers, and to the subjective tasting prefer-ences of brokers and blenders, such as those I profiled in chapters 1 and 2. Such dichotomies between science and nonscience, according to Gyan Prakash, "justified colonial dominance, but . . . also conceded that the colo-nial project would never achieve complete success."[7] As the anthropologist and historian of science Francesca Bray has argued, science, technology, and technique were central to both agricultural development and the consolida-tion of state power in imperial China well before Europeans began their incursions into East Asia. Bray defines "science" "as knowledge about natural, material processes expressed in declarative, transmissible form; its representa-tions generally aspire to be authoritative beyond the time and place of their production." She defines "techniques" "as the skilled practices that go into the material production of knowledge as well as the production of artefacts," while "technology" "denotes social-material networks or systems, including sets of techniques and equipment, but also trained personnel, raw materials, ideas and institutions."[8]

Transposing Bray's framework onto the story of Indian tea in the period directly before and after independence, I show how the skilled work of tea brokers and tea plantation laborers became partially grafted onto the labora-tory work of chemists and the designs of industrial engineers. Bray suggests that technologies contribute both to the making of goods and artifacts (tea, for example) and to the establishment of scientific facts about the "nature" of the world. Along the way, technologies of production and experimentation work to sustain (and, I would argue, reformulate) social relations.[9] Tea became a subject of scientific interest precisely at the moment when colonial dominance in India began to erode. The story of the science of quality shows how science plays a role not just in the making of colonial orders, but in their reformulation as national and even global ones. Scientific attention to quality helped to convert tea in India from a sign of colonial extraction and exploitation to a seemingly natural component of national mass consumer culture.[10]

Seen from the vantage point of the tea industry, it is difficult to identify a clean historical break between "colonial" and "postcolonial" science. India's Foreign Exchange Regulation Act, which stipulated that all business profits made in India (including those from tea) must stay in India, did not go into full effect until 1973. This means that British capital remained heavily invested in Indian tea nearly thirty years after independence. But it was not just for financial reasons that tea took a slow, meandering path from crop of empire to crop of national development. Science—particularly chemistry and mechanical engineering—also played a role in shaping that path.

In our 2009 interview, the TRA official drew what I considered at the time to be a curious distinction, between flavor and taste. He told me that each clone produced at Tocklai is tested and rated according to a "flavor index." For raw, green tea, the flavor index comprises six criteria: astringency, briskness, brothyness, color, appearance, and aroma.[11] Over the past eighty years, scientists, first in London and later at Tocklai itself, developed techniques for associating these qualities with what they called the "chemical constituents" of tea. Tocklai scientists can tell you that caffeine confers a bitter taste, while theaflavins and thearubigins make tea astringent. A "sweet" tea tends to have more linalool, while a "floral" tea contains higher levels of phenylacetaldehyde.[12]

While tea can be understood as the sum of some two dozen biochemical compounds, the TRA officer told me that even if the flavor index of two different clones is exactly the same, they will still taste different when brewed. As any J. Thomas tea broker will tell you, taste might be affected by the time of plucking, the coarseness of the leaf, and—most significantly—the factory manufacturing process. Earlier in this book, I described the embodied techniques through which professional brokers arrive at judgments about astringency, briskness, color, appearance, and aroma. Tasters send comments on each tea they taste to plantation managers, and often those comments have to do with plucking or manufacturing techniques. A gap exists, then, between the chemical composition that imparts a flavor index and the aesthetic, sensory, and market logics that refract flavor into taste.

For the ITA, this gap became a point of interest beginning the 1930s, at the onset of the Great Depression. From the 1930s until the end of the 1950s, the ITA funded and promoted a science of quality by constructing a transnational experimental infrastructure that linked its outpost at Tocklai to state-of-the-art facilities in London. This science of quality was forged amid a series of existential crises within the British Empire. Over this period, ITA scientists worked to enact a theory about quality as lodged in biochemistry, but their work was not simply chemical. Scientists were also aiming to affirm organizational theories about the viability of plantation economies. Improving the quality of tea bushes meant improving efficiency and the outputs of human labor, often through mechanization. After independence, the results of the scientific work—in the form of biochemical isolates and manufacturing techniques—themselves became the terrain of a struggle for sovereignty between the ITA and the Government of India. Even as Britain's political dominance over India waned, the British-dominated ITA sought to maintain control of the production of scientific knowledge about quality. The public-private partnership today known as the TRA was forged at the awkward conjuncture of ITA and government efforts to make a place for a colonial crop in a postcolonial context.

CHEMISTRY, TASTE, AND THE OBJECTIFICATION OF QUALITY

By the onset of the Great Depression in 1929, Tocklai was well established as the ITA's principal scientific outpost. During the 1930s, thanks to the rise of blending and packaging, purportedly scientific facts about tea—specifically about its health and safety—were regularly circulated in the market via direct-to-consumer advertising as well as pamphlets and informational material sent to doctors and grocers.[13] As science came to have a larger place in the industry, its focus broadened beyond health and safety to quality. In a 1932 article in the ITA's *Quarterly Journal,* C. R. Harler argued that tannins, far from being harmful to health, were "responsible wholly or in part for such cup qualities as *rawness, briskness, pungency, strength, colour and thickness.*"[14]

But what exactly was briskness, or strength, or pungency? What substances or material processes brought these qualities into being? Harler argued that if chemical compounds could be linked directly to linguistic descriptors, then quality could be maximized. One role for science, then, was to sequester quality from the market: to understand tea's material attributes as knowable, reducible elements that could be adjusted, augmented, reduced, or eliminated prior to sale. This shift in attention to quality occurred during a time when ITA leaders had become worried about an oversupply of tea in the global market. With consumer buying power lowered, tea plantations in India, facilitated by the ITA, agreed to curb production and focus on making *better* tea. These crop restrictions lasted until World War II.[15]

From a scientific perspective, however, the criteria on which quality judgments were being made in the early 1930s seemed irrational. In his article, Harler pointed out what he saw as useless descriptors.

> There are a good number of terms used by individual tasters which convey little or nothing to the average planter. Thus, in one case, a tea infusion was described as tasting like a "bandsman's tunic." Such an expression connotes unpleasantness, and may denote sweatiness, but gives no definite guidance to a planter who wants to trace a shortcoming in his tea to some incorrect factory procedure.[16]

Phrases like "bandsman's tunic," while long on a poetics, were short on material corollaries. Chemistry could more accurately mediate the relationship between materiality, linguistic referents, and quality. As Harler conceded:

> The analyst will never be able to compete with or replace the tea taster, but, in spite of this, a tea analysis, if it distinguished teas according to their quality, would be of great use. By means of such an analysis the changes occurring in the tea leaf during manufacture could be followed, and used as a basis for recommendations regarding factory procedure. A complete analysis would also indicate ultimate differences between teas from various districts, and useful conclusions might be drawn regarding methods in different areas.[17]

The aim of the early science of quality, then, was to improve plantation production in the context of a deliberate reduction in crop yield.

In 1931, the British government's Imperial Economic Committee (IEC) published a pivotal assessment of the industry. The IEC's report suggested that science and production should be seen as two "branches" of the industry that had to work collaboratively. "Adequate organization" was crucial.[18] Following the publication of the report, the ITA appointed a commission of enquiry to identify priorities for scientific tea research.

Initiated in 1935 under the leadership of Frank Engledow, a biologist and professor of agriculture at the University of Cambridge, the Commission of

Enquiry (which came to be known as the Engledow Commission) visited India, as well as Ceylon and Indonesia, to assess the state of tea science.[19] Its charge was to suggest reforms in Tocklai's constitution, governance, and research program.[20] Initially, Engledow, whose previous work had been in the development of high-yielding wheat varieties, raised questions about "the relative amount of research effort which should be devoted to yield of tea in its broadest sense in contrast with quality of tea." His early view was that quality—seen as taste—was a subjective and unscientific concept. As he later wrote, "No more obscure subject for research on crop products could, perhaps, be found."[21] An overemphasis on quality might undermine the potential of scientific techniques and technologies to expand tea consumption within India, which Engledow saw as a vast and largely untapped market.

Around the time of Engledow's visit, the Indian Tea Market Expansion Board was formed to explore the possibility of tapping this market.[22] Up to that time, tea consumption within the subcontinent itself was not particularly common, and tea was certainly not the nearly ubiquitous item of mass consumption it would later become. But ITA officials made clear in internal memoranda and correspondence that they would not entertain an expansion into India if that expansion meant a sacrifice in quality. As ITA officials repeatedly told Engledow, they did not want to build the industry on the back of "cheap tea," even if that tea was high yielding.[23]

As part of its initial survey, the Engledow Commission issued a questionnaire to ITA members.[24] Some respondents noted that they wanted "practical research" on pests, manures, blights, pruning, plucking, and machinery, and others asked for interventions that would allow them to "save labour." Perhaps because of his previous work on the development of more efficient food crop production systems, Engledow argued strongly that conserving soil, attending to the health of bushes, and mitigating disease were imperative, so that when planters did agree to increase output they would be well positioned.[25] Engledow's final report advocated more research into plant breeding and the development of new varieties, or "improved jaats." These varieties would be high yielding, more uniform, and "specially adapted to the various climatic and soil regions of Northeast India."[26] The results of the survey made clear, however, that the "improvement of quality" remained the membership's highest priority.[27]

The ITA London General Committee held a meeting in October 1935 to discuss Engledow's study. Engledow again asked the attendees why it was necessary to bother with quality at all, but he agreed to devise a method for scientifically understanding it.[28] One planter, a Mr. Masefield, suggested that while the problem of quality likely began in the fields, there was no test for quality except for the broker's palate, an instrument whose sensitivity might differ from day to day and from individual to individual. Engledow responded that one of the things that the commission would be looking into specifically was chemical investigations on made tea, of the kind Harler had proposed a few years before. Engledow argued that professional brokers had to be involved in any scientific study of quality.[29] Since brokers' opinions were notoriously varied, Engledow called for the formation of a "panel of valuers" that would taste teas and send its comments back to Tocklai.

For Engledow, quality's enigmatic nature came in part from the fact that it was "largely predetermined" by "any one set of soil, altitude and climatic conditions."[30] "In tea tasting," however, "quality is one of those undefined components, body, aroma, etc., being others, by which the market value of a tea is determined."[31]

> Quality at the present time can only be defined as a conception, more of art than of intellect, of which tea tasters are the repository and by the aid of which teas are valued in commerce. . . . Their judgement is decisively expressed by price and they explain it by reporting on certain components of quality such as pungency, colour of liquor, etc. In reporting on these components they make use of a great number of descriptive words and phrases. The list of components referred to is not necessarily the same in reports by the same taster on different teas or by different tasters on the same tea. Of the relative monetary importance of the individual components of quality nothing is said. . . . The descriptive words and phrases used in connection with the several components of quality exceed seventy in number. Some are synonyms, some are variably used by different tasters and some are, at any rate outside tasting circles, obscure in meaning.[32]

Engledow thought that this mode of valuation created a "dangerous situation."

> The broker's report is passed onto the planter. If the price be unexpectedly low he naturally wishes to find out the particular characteristics in which his tea was faulty. He would then, of course, connect the faults with the circumstances of the leaf or the manufacturing and take immediate steps to improve his quality. But in many such cases the report is obscure and, indeed, virtually meaningless, leaving the planter entirely without guidance. We think it of the greatest importance to the industry that the broker's report should not be limited . . . to a cash valuation. He should give such information as to the

faults and merits of the teas on the market ruling as to guide the planter in his policy. This he cannot do unless he speaks in terms as to which the planter has no doubt.[33]

The Engledow Commission proposed "a new specification of quality," in which the professional taster "becomes a key-member of the scientific staff."[34] As the commission explained:

> It must always be an aim of science to connect cause and effect. Let us take, for illustration, an experiment on the effects of nitrogen, potash, and phosphoric acid on quality. It will be necessary to apply varying doses of these three substances and various combinations, e.g. nitrogen only, nitrogen and potash together, and so on.... The whole elaborate experiment must now be consummated by the tasters' deciding on the quality of tea from every plot. With the present practice the only information in a tasters' report which has for all teas a constant purport is the price. But price does not meet scientific requirements. It is essential to know how each manurial treatment has affected each component of tea quality—briskness, the colour of the liquor, the body. Moreover, this information must be given under the same headings and in the same form for all teas from all experiments.... Two teas from an experiment may be worth the same price one being outstanding in one characteristic and one in another. Price would thus not help in connecting individual causes with individual effects in the way which has been explained to be necessary.[35]

Engledow envisioned two ways to solve this cause-and-effect problem. The first was "fundamental" research.

> Quality, however wide its range and obscure its nature, must depend on properties of certain chemical substances present in tea. These in turn, are derived from certain chemical substances in the green leaf as a result of chemical and physical changes during manufacture. If these substances could be identified and if their effects on the palate could be fully worked out, it would be possible to make exact scientific definitions of all grades and aspects of quality.... If exact physical and chemical tests of quality can be devised they will be of great value in research and so lead to increased control over manufacture.[36]

The commission suggested undertaking "investigations with the object of discovering the chemical substances in the leaf, the chemical and physical changes they undergo during ... manufacture and the ways in which these substances and changes influence the market value and the components of quality of tea."[37] It further recommended that tea chemistry experiments should be conducted not at Tocklai but in London[38] This preference for locating work in London would have important political consequences after Indian independence.

Engledow's second recommendation was the rollout of a "uniform and analytical system for specification of quality" that went beyond price.[39] For this, Tocklai would play a role. Its botanists would create new "experimental teas," which they would send to London, where they would be evaluated by a panel of professional brokers based on a limited number of quality characteristics (Engledow's report suggested no more than six and noted that if "appearance" was to be one of them it would need "careful specification"). The Engledow Commission suggested that the panel should evaluate each of these characteristics on a numerical scale, say, 1 to 10, using a sample from a control plot as a standard and comparing all other teas to this standard as "equal to, better than, or worse than the control."[40]

The ITA's London Advisory Commission (a body primarily composed of tea company executives who advised on scientific matters) met in 1938 to discuss how to enact the model suggested by the Engledow Commission.[41] It appointed Dr. A. E. Bradfield to lead what it dubbed "investigations into the chemistry of made tea."[42] Bradfield was hired on a five-year contract, funded jointly by planters' associations in Ceylon, the Netherlands, South India, and the ITA.[43] Although the tea corporation J. Lyons and Company provided laboratory space in its London headquarters, from 1939 to 1943, Bradfield worked without much attention from the industry.[44] In 1943, Bradfield, with Lyons's chief chemist, Leslie Lampitt, finally released a report that was circulated to the funders.[45]

In the report, Bradfield and Lampitt argued that the discussion of tea chemistry—and of quality generally—was still overly consumed with the idea of tannin. It was generally assumed, they explained, "that the strength and body of a tea infusion is dependent on the amount of 'tannin', and several methods have been devised for estimating the 'tannin.'" But after Bradfield's own investigation into the chemical constituents of tea, he concluded that quality could not "be related to the amount of tannin, or to any other *single* parameter."[46]

The report describes an experiment in which Bradfield took five teas from different regions of the British Empire—each thought by brokers to be of better or worse quality. Tea A was an "ordinary Sylhet tea"; Tea B, "a very good Upper Assam tea, showing good tip"; and Tea C, a "high grown Ceylon tea." Tea D was a Dooars tea, and Tea E was a Nyasaland tea. All of these teas, irrespective of region, contained both soluble and insoluble polyphenols.

"Why then do these teas differ in quality?," Bradfield asked. Quality of liquor, he explained, depended on the "total relative amounts of the soluble and insoluble polyphenols." His experiment correlated "astringent taste," "thickness," "pungency," "brightness," and "strength" to relative polyphenol content. The two higher-quality teas, A and B, had similar amounts of "insoluble polyphenols, gum and inorganic salts." Tea B had a much higher proportion of soluble polyphenols and caffeine. Bradfield concluded that it was "clear that the strength, pungency, and brightness of the liquor from Tea B arises from the presence of this higher proportion of soluble polyphenols. A fundamental correlation between composition and quality is thus established."[47]

Due to the stresses of World War II and the deterioration of Bradfield's personal health (caused by chemicals used in the laboratory, according to his doctors), the ITA's London experiments provided little more in the way of new outputs between 1943 and 1948. By the end of the 1940s, it was still not "possible to define conclusively the various chemical factors in Tea which contributed to ... flavour quality."[48] But Bradfield and Lampitt had brought Engledow's vision for a science of quality closer to fruition. They integrated professional tasters into experimental algorithms alongside polyphenols and linguistic indexes of quality such as "thickness," "pungency," and "strength."

QUALITY AND POSTWAR PRODUCTION

After the Japanese occupation of Java during World War II, Dutch tea manufacture all but ceased. In response, British-owned plantations in India finally agreed to lift the self-imposed production quotas that had been in place since the 1920s. During the war, the UK Ministry of Food purchased tea in bulk from East African, Indian, and Ceylonese plantations and rationed it to British consumers. Since the ministry was purchasing all tea produced in bulk, the London tea auctions were closed.[49]

The London Tea Auctions Joint Committee, a group representing all parts of the industry, formed in 1947. In that year, its leaders wrote a letter to the Ministry of Food requesting the reopening of the London tea auction. To the committee, reopening the auction was a matter of restoring quality in both the market and tea itself: "Tea is not a necessity of life. It is a beverage which depends for its popularity on quality. For without quality it becomes little more than tainted hot water. No industry which fails to give honest service to its customers can hope to survive. The tea industry most certainly cannot hope to do so unless it provides quality.... [Bulk buying by the Ministry of Food] represents ... a disservice to its customers."[50] The letter suggested that it was brokers' senses of taste, ratified in the auction rather than the laboratory, that ensured quality. Continued closure of the London auction might mean permanent loss of brokers' authority.[51]

The Tea Auctions Joint Committee was equally worried about the possibility that without proactive reinvestment in the London auction, there could be a permanent shift in the global center of the trade from England to India. The Joint Committee was formed, after all, in the year of Indian independence, 1947. What the ITA and others called "postwar planning" comprised a series of moves to manage British tea interests' role in the handover of political sovereignty, with an eye to maintaining British control of the tea industry to the greatest possible extent.[52] The story that transpired in the two decades following independence was not one of decolonization—a steady stripping away of the trappings of empire from tea's mode of production, image, and taste. Rather, and despite the fact that Indian firms did take majority ownership of all tea companies by the 1970s, British-led experimental investigations into tea's quality continued and even expanded during the postindependence years.

These investigations were crucial to the growth of a unique Indian mode of tea consumption on the back of an essentially colonial mode of production.[53] Before the 1960s, most Indians were not avid tea consumers, and the now-stereotypical association of Indian social life with the liberal consumption of milky, sweet, spiced chai did not exist. By the end of the 1960s, however, the industry's landscape had shifted, and a majority of the tea produced in India would soon be consumed within the country.

Before the war, the International Tea Agreements and crop regulation schemes encouraged planters to replant sections of land instead of extending into new areas, in order to limit outputs while keeping plants viable and quality high. As a result of these restrictions, plantations were in a position to increase production when the Indonesian market collapsed. In order to support this increase, however, plantation owners also began providing more facilities to keep laborers in place and to ensure that there was enough food, medicine, and other supplies to keep them working.[54]

The wartime surge in productivity was followed by a generalized crisis in the early 1950s, as Europe's economy struggled to recover. As independence neared, many smaller British plantation owners sold to Indian companies or simply abandoned their land. With the prospect of losing one of its main sources of export revenue, the new Government of India came to see active intervention in the tea sector as a matter of national urgency.[55] If the market continued its downward spiral, thousands of plantation workers would starve. For India's regulators, inspired by a combination of nationalism and a commitment to state-led development, plantations were a site where the violence of postcolonial abandonment was most palpable. Instead of calling for a turn away from the tea plantation economy, however, the government's moves in the early 1950s served to cement and even expand the place of tea and the plantation in the national economy and imaginary.

In 1951, India passed the Plantations Labour Act, which enshrined the wartime provisions for plantation workers' housing, food, healthcare, and education in national law.[56] The Tea Board Act of 1949 replaced the Indian Tea Market Expansion Board, a creature of the European colonial tea associations, with the Central Tea Board. The Central Tea Board began collecting a new export tax, or cess, on all tea grown in the country and to "arrange for research, collection statistics, fixing of grade standards, improving the marketing of tea and bulk buying on behalf of Government."[57] Exports were again curtailed by international trade agreements, and voluntary crop restrictions were reintroduced in 1953 in Northeast India.

The Central Tea Board was subsumed by the Tea Board of India in 1953.[58] The Tea Board of India continued much of the promotional work that the Central Tea Board had done, but it was granted expanded regulatory powers over the industry. Promotional work included the extension of a network of "tea centres" where Indian citizens could taste and learn about tea and the peppering of public spaces with advertising that promoted tea as a Indian, or *swadeshi,* drink.[59] As the Tea Board of India's head of propaganda, J. Mukherjee, noted in the mid-1950s, "Indian tea is now doing a roaring business," but "as long as an Indian tea is an international commodity . . . [w]e must accept the fact that its fortunes must to a large extent vary with the dictates of the overseas market which, in turn, are primarily influenced by the laws of supply and demand and in competition with other producing countries." Unless tea growers were able to "get more and more prospects in our own country interested in tea, we may be forced to accept the inevitable—a stalemate for consumption."[60] As early as 1950, the Central Tea Board called for the provision of additional warehousing facilities for tea in Calcutta and the inclusion of Indians in the ranks of brokerage and tasting firms.[61] It also provided tax relief to plantations that built new worker housing. As

Mukherjee wrote, "Our internal expansion can be commensurate with our ever increasing population. It is primarily a question of encouraging future generations to accept a higher standard of living."[62] The state, in other words, would use tea production as a vehicle for improvements in quality of life—both for rural plantation laborers and for urban consumers.

Government regulators saw scientific research as essential to this national effort. By 1956, the Tea Board of India reported that while 62 percent of Indian land under tea was still managed by British "sterling companies," a growing number of tea plantations were owned in part or in full by Indian "rupee companies" or by individual Indian citizens.[63] Many of these new owners, convinced that the Indian tea industry was poised to make a comeback after the crisis of the early postwar years, had overpaid for marginal land. These new Indian tea growers were saddled with old and nonproductive tea bushes and decaying factory machinery. An Assam government study lamented that "little attention" was paid by these new owners "towards improving the quality of tea."[64] This lack of attention to quality was not entirely surprising, since "the number of Indian nationals recruited to the Industry's cadre of officers is painfully low."[65] These new owners, like nearly all Indians before independence, had been excluded from scientific training in tea management and agronomy. As a result, prices were low, and owners were financially unable to provide workers with the welfare provisions now guaranteed to them by law.

Instead of focusing tea science on chemistry, Indian government regulators recommended that scientific work be reoriented to land management, machine engineering, and plant breeding. As the Central Tea Board's Ad Hoc Committee on Tea wrote in 1950, "Clonal material, derived by vegetative propagation on selected bushes, is available, capable of giving crops of 20 [maunds] or more per acre," as opposed to the 16 maunds a planter might have hoped to get before. Such clonal material, the committee wrote, was "equal in quality to the product of the best commercial seed available from professional seed growers. Genetical work shows promise of producing even better yields and greatly improved quality."[66]

But the infrastructure of tea science remained almost entirely in the control of a private, British-dominated organization of tea growers, the ITA. Even though the Tea Act of 1953 had granted India's government a great deal of regulatory power over private tea companies, the Indian state's approach to the ITA was diplomatic. "It is a legitimate function of private industry," the Tea Board of India's 1956 Plantations Inquiry Commission wrote, "to organise the scientific research necessary for its own progress. . . . To duplicate the work that is already being done would be a waste of money and effort."[67] Still, it was clear that the work that had been done at laboratories in Tocklai and in London up to that time was carried out primarily for the benefit of the ITA's British member companies, not the Indian economy. Since Indians were rarely recruited into the ranks of management, the extractive and exclusive nature of tea science was all the more apparent. The Tea Board wanted not only to train Indians to manage tea plantations but also "to review the field of research and advisory work already covered, and to supplement and expand it to the extent necessary so that *all sections of the industry* . . . get the benefit of scientific information."[68] Scientific knowledge needed to be made public if tea growing was to be an engine for driving the country toward a higher standard of living. The science of quality would only be of benefit to India if the meaning of quality could be expanded beyond biochemistry to include viability, productivity, and yield. An increase of these, as much as isolation of the chemical roots of flavor, appearance, and texture, would lead to better quality of life for tea consumers and plantation workers alike.

A RETURN TO CHEMISTRY

Between 1953 and 1954, the ITA sponsored a second commission of scientific inquiry, again headed by Engledow. The second Engledow Commission Report offers a revealing glimpse into how British capital understood postindependence conditions.

> There is a wholly new labor situation; bulk buying induced changes in plucking; on some estates the weather and other operations have been considerably modified. . . . Of all the factors influencing quality of teas from Northeast India at the present time fineness of plucking is most surrounded by factual uncertainty. Conditions between 1939 and the return of the free market altered greatly the old range of customary standards of fineness. The extent to which there has been an attempt to return to pre-1939 standards and what degree of success has attended the attempt, are unknown. Fineness of plucking is connected with yield which can be influenced by manuring and other controllable circumstances: but it has also acquired significance in relation to labor and labor costs.[69]

From the perspective of Engledow and the other scientific advisers to the ITA, the wartime push to increase yields had led to deterioration in quality at several levels. Land was being pushed beyond its carrying capacity. Plucking was "coarse" (meaning that long sections of the bush were plucked, not just the "fine" tips containing two leaves and a bud), even as Indian plantation labor law was driving the costs of compensating field laborers ever higher.

The second Engledow Commission agreed with Indian government regulators that if the postindependence trends continued, domestic demand for tea in India was likely to increase, but as the commission's report said, "certain consumer markets . . . will go for cheapness of product, always provided a certain minimum standard of quality is maintained, but in the main consuming countries, quality will be rewarded by premium on price."[70] While the Indian regulators were pushing to increase domestic markets, the second Engledow Commission held that continued orientation to the needs of the European marketplace remained the way forward—at least for the British firms represented in the ITA.

The second Engledow Commission also noted that planters were still unsatisfied with the "excessive number and the obscurity of terms used by tasters and brokers."

> Planters' criticisms to us on this score . . . are fewer and milder than those of predecessors received on the subject. But, once more, this misleading nature of the cash valuation (influenced by short-term market fluctuations) is insisted on and "standardized" terms, i.e. having a reasonably constant meaning, are asked for. Some planters evidently expect tasters not only to name specific defects but to identify the causes. To do that will . . . become generally practicable in measure as understanding and control of manufacture are advanced by research.[71]

"It is therefore important," the commission concluded, echoing the recommendation of Engledow's 1936 commission, "that in our research special attention should continue to be given to quality."[72]

In 1951, the ITA's London Advisory Committee appointed E. A. H. Roberts as the research manager for a revival of its chemistry experiments. As in the period before the war, these experiments would be principally carried out in London, but this time, rather than use the laboratories of J. Lyons and Company, the ITA set up its own facility, at Butler's Wharf.[73] Butler's Wharf was the largest tea warehouse in the world. Within the wharf, customs and excise duties were not applicable, either for the tea that would be tested or for the imported ethanol that was essential to experimental procedures.[74] Effectively, this made Butler's Wharf not only a proto–free trade zone but also an extension of the already blurry border between the ITA and the states (India and the United Kingdom) within which it operated. During the course of discussions about the appraisal value of the property at Butler's Wharf, in 1959, the ITA London issued a circular outlining the reasons the space should not be considered a laboratory but an extension of the industry. The space "should be accepted as an industrial hereditament as Dr. Roberts work is not research for research's sake." Instead, "the results of [this research] will be applied to actual manufacturing processes. Although the laboratory is some thousands of miles away from factories[,] . . . [it] is essential as Dr. Roberts must have tea as it is sold for consumption and have available all the scientific advice which can only be attained in London."[75]

Roberts would receive samples of tea from Dr. Wood, the senior biochemist at Tocklai. Butler's Wharf and Tocklai operated as part of a single (British) operation. Following the model of Bradfield's prewar experiments, Roberts and Wood integrated professional brokers into their experimental design, convening panels of tasters both in London and in the growing brokerage sector of Calcutta.

Research on the chemistry of quality advanced more under Roberts and Wood than at any previous time. Their experiments were becoming increasingly precise. While Bradfield had succeeded in breaking down the broad category "tannin" into the narrower bifurcation between soluble and insoluble polyphenols, Roberts was the first chemist to isolate a single polyphenol, theogallin, and to prove that it was a "desirable constituent of tea."[76] In one experiment, a small amount of crude theogallin was added to a sample of tea liquor, and a panel of tasters observed a noticeable improvement in liquor quality, even if they also detected a "foreign flavor" due to the "trace solvent remaining in the crude theogallin."[77]

Roberts's isolation of theogallin had important ramifications for the study of tea quality. The next step would be to devise a way to detect the presence of theogallin in processed tea. This would necessitate more extensive collaboration with Tocklai.[78] Though tasters and scientists now increasingly used the same terms (e.g., *briskness, strength, color*) in their evaluations, they still differed in their view of how these terms related to quality. As Roberts noted, "quality" in both science and industry alternately denoted individual characteristics and a more holistic relative market value.[79] In general, scientists were more interested in the former, while brokers remained interested in the latter. Repeating what had become a chorus of frustration that began with Harler's writings about tasters two and half decades earlier, Roberts explained in a

1957 lecture in London that "a taster's palate is obviously less reliable than a precise scientific instrument, for the values obtained [by scientific instruments] are not dependent upon fluctuations in the market nor are they complicated by the fact that different tasters may be valuing teas for different markets."[80] With this in mind, Roberts and his colleagues at Tocklai turned their attention to creating a technique for measuring the chemical constituents of flavor at the point of production—the plantation—where they presumed that tea would be more insulated from fluctuations in the market.[81] Their "hope" was that "in due course it will be possible to provide a planter with a simple practical method of testing for the presence or absence of desirable characteristics in the tea that they manufacture. In other words, it is hoped that the planter will be able to have scientific confirmation or modification of the judgments that he now makes day by day on the basis of his own experiences and observation."[82]

By the mid-1950s, the Butler's Wharf and Tocklai laboratories were able to isolate and measure not only theogallin but also two other polyphenols, theaflavins and thearubigins. They hypothesized that the quanta of these substances could be measured with a simple test, to be used in combination with tasting, such that "where a garden wishes to rectify faults in manufacture, following an adverse [taster's] report . . . the tasting may well be followed by chemical analysis. The two methods of assessing a tea, taste and analysis, are therefore complementary to each other."[83] Roberts and Wood's ultimate goal was to make it possible to predict the eventual polyphenol content of manufactured tea from examination of unprocessed green leaf.[84] If, as many planters feared, quality was deteriorating over time, such a test could prove this in quantitatively measurable terms without the input of subjective (and excessively market-sensitive) brokers.

By the mid-1950s, Tocklai was developing its own experimental tea varieties and testing them with a panel of tasters in Calcutta. Tocklai developed these varieties with an eye to achieving what Wood and Roberts considered an optimal balance of theaflavins and thearubigins. But just how these samples should be evaluated was unclear.[85] "It is questionable," scientists wrote in 1952, "whether brokers' opinions on new or unconventional types of tea can, by themselves, be relied upon to give a complete picture of the acceptability of such teas." A broker, after all, had to think about how blenders and dealers would value the tea, so until blenders "have had an opportunity of examining a particular type of tea a Broker is in no position to say what their opinions will be."[86] Tocklai scientists were "perplexed" by the fact that certain tasters put more or less weight on the various characteristics of tea, "according to how it affects their market."[87] To account for this, Tocklai hired its own in-house tasters, who made regular visits to Calcutta to meet with brokers in major firms, including Carritt Moran, J. Thomas, and A. W. Figgis. The principal taster, a Mr. Trinick, was encouraged to study "the universal fundamentals of taste and flavour" from a "rational" scientific perspective as well.[88] Trinick, and later an assistant taster, Ranjit Chowdhury, would remain part of the experimental team into the 1960s.[89]

Tocklai clones were released to around 177 plantations in West Bengal and Northeast India between 1949 and 1954.[90] Scientists then sought to measure the performance of these clones in evaluations by both Tocklai's in-house tasters and tasters working for brokerage firms. In a 1957 test of a new "continuous rolling" machine, "[one] sample, in spite of its high theaflavin and thearubigin values, was marked down in price on account of its appearance and limited demand." Another sample "received an enhanced valuation, presumably on account of the good show of golden 'tip.'" For the panel of commercial tasters, appearance mattered in an overall evaluation of quality, especially when different grades were tested simultaneously. "If, however, each grade of tea is taken separately, the sample with the better [laboratory] determined quality is found to have the higher valuation." The ITA scientists used this finding to conclude that "the chemical valuation ... of these teas gave a truer indication of their intrinsic qualities, i.e. of their value to the consumers, than the tasters' valuation."[91]

These attempts to prove empirically the capacity of chemistry to verify quality, however, never fully succeeded in unseating the authority of the tasters, whose opinions held sway in commercial brokerage houses. The ITA needed more resources and more money, but its membership was continuing to dwindle as British plantation companies sold their interests and left India. Many of the rupee companies joining the tea business did not pay to become ITA members. Instead, they looked to the Tea Board of India for support. Reluctantly, the ITA concluded that if research on the chemistry of quality was to advance, then it, too, would need the help of the Tea Board.

SCIENTIFIC SOVEREIGNTY AND INDIAN TEA

Tocklai's position as a de facto field station for the London laboratory at Butler's Wharf had long been a source of disquiet for the Indian government.

As early as 1954, officials in the Central Tea Board had noted that while the biochemical department at Tocklai had conducted extensive work on quality and chemistry, it had done little to foster dialogue and collaboration with chemists based in India.[92] In 1958, the ITA dispatched Engledow to meet with the Tea Board's chairman, Mr. Chatterji. The Tea Board's chief concern, Chatterji told Engledow, was the fate of "common tea," which was being grown in marginal regions such as the Dooars and Cachar, on smaller plantations increasingly owned and operated by rupee companies. Chatterji himself had visited these regions, and he queried Engledow about what might be keeping them from making a profit. As the Indian government had noted years earlier, even if the quality of field plucking could be improved, the quality of output on such plantations would still be constrained by ecology and seasonality. They admitted that "there is apparently little that can be done to produce liquor quality in a non-quality growing district." Chatterji wondered if planters might be planting the wrong varieties or if their machinery was outdated. Since even these marginal plantations had once been profitable, Chatterji wanted to see "real and fundamental" research done on these questions.[93] Essentially, Chatterji was soliciting Engledow's assistance as a development consultant. Engledow, who still represented the ITA, was able to use the prospect of sharing British agronomical expertise with Indian counterparts to the British association's advantage. By the end of the 1950s, thanks in part to Engledow's intercession, the Government of India was providing supplemental funding for the work of Roberts and Wood. Even if Engledow had intimated to the Tea Board that the ITA might provide technical assistance, the ITA London Committee assured its membership in 1959 that "every endeavour would be made to guard against interference by Government or the Tea Board in the affairs of Tocklai."[94]

Roberts and Wood's discoveries about the role of polyphenols in conferring color and flavor in manufactured tea proved highly influential, just not in the sector of the industry to which they had intended to contribute. Throughout the late 1950s and early 1960s, Roberts was repeatedly approached by representatives of major tea corporations, including Lipton, Nestlé, and Finlays. While the ITA's stated aim for its scientific efforts since the 1930s had been the maintenance and improvement of quality in what came to be known as "orthodox tea," these corporations were all pursuing the development of water-soluble instant teas. The corporations had become interested in using lessons from Roberts's biochemical work to produce a portable, easy-to-make, economical product that could be sold in markets where hot tea was less desired. In particular, they had their eye on the American market, where iced tea had long been popular. They sought to develop a soluble, tealike product—something akin to instant coffee crystals—that Americans could make simply by adding water. When instant tea makers spoke of quality, it seemed, they were speaking Roberts's language. They were talking about the quantum of desirable characteristics—a color, a bitter or floral flavor—that could be reduced to a set of discrete chemical components, synthesized, and standardized.

Roberts's superiors at the ITA were just as ambivalent about the idea of sharing his knowledge—the ITA's *proprietary* knowledge—with the developers of these new products as they were about sharing it with the Government of India. As one ITA official noted when Roberts asked if he might be allowed to consult with instant tea makers, "If we could be assured that instant tea would *increase* the consumption of pucca [orthodox] tea, it might be to our advantage to let Roberts cooperate."[95] Even though there seemed to be a direct chemical connection between the science that went into improving "pucca tea" and the science that permitted the stable production of instant tea, many within the association doubted that there would ever be a *market* connection between instant tea and "pucca tea." As Roberts wrote in an internal report on Nestea, "Nestea ... does show certain differences from the normal product of commerce, and these differences would be expected to detract from quality, although many consumers not blessed with a palate would probably find that this would not prove any great deterrent to its consumption."[96]

Instant tea was also problematic for the Government of India, albeit for slightly different reasons. In 1959, the Tea Board set a new production target for the industry: 900 million pounds by the end of 1966. This target was included in India's third Five Year Plan for development. The plan was focused on the expansion of agricultural production through scientific methods, mostly by the use of fertilizers and mechanization. While the plan is most commonly associated with the production of food crops, particularly wheat, the legal restructuring of regulation during the 1950s put tea production under its remit as well. In setting these targets, the Tea Board was interested both in meeting export demand and in growing the domestic tea sector. Instant tea was not a part of this plan. Indian producers—even producers of "common teas"—were entirely excluded from the instant tea market. To produce instant teas, companies were purchasing the majority of their tea from East Africa.

The interest of instant tea makers in Roberts's expertise, then, underscored a fracture in the postwar, postindependence tea trade. British firms maintained majority interests in African and Indian tea, but they were competing with one another for market share. The governments of former colonies found themselves competing as well. Even if the ITA did lend Roberts's expertise to the perfection of instant tea, doing so might, as one ITA official wrote, give the Government of India an "excuse for declining to sanction the remittance required to pay Roberts' salary and other expenses."[97] The ITA had managed to make the case that Roberts's work would have positive applications for India's economy, but why should money made on Indian soil support research that would enrich European companies? While the ITA continued to request (and receive) supplementary funding from the Indian government for its research activities, the Indian Exchange Control authorities continued to press the ITA to make the case for why Roberts's scientific work still had to be based in London. These authorities came to see the ITA's insistence on keeping cutting-edge chemistry in London as a backhanded means of extracting value from one of the independent country's most important agricultural resources. The ITA's internal correspondence confirms that the Indian authorities were correct. The minutes of a 1961 ITA London committee noted, "All we see on the ground at Tocklai and a lot we do not see comprises an asset of the greatest value.... If we calmly accept a subvention and proceed harmoniously in tandem with the government of India we shall have lost the opportunity of saving this great asset."[98]

For the ITA, maintaining the technoscientific apartheid that had long kept chemical knowledge about quality in the hands of British plantation owners remained a priority, but the steady exodus of British planters, especially smaller operators, made that apartheid harder to sustain. In 1962, the Tea Board of India and the ITA came to an agreement on the formation of the Tea Research Association, a multisited research institution for Northeast India whose headquarters would be at Tocklai. The government would provide part of the TRA's funding, with the remainder supplied by subscriptions from member plantations, both sterling companies and rupee companies. Though the laboratory at Butler's Wharf was shut down soon after the formation of the TRA, it would take another fifteen years and continued threats by the Indian government to withhold funding before the main center of laboratory research on tea was transferred from the United Kingdom to India.

Chemistry was not the only branch of tea science to which the Indian government wanted more access. The ITA had also spent much of the 1950s pursuing methods for improving tea processing machinery. An engineering department was formed at Tocklai under the directorship of D. W. Tull in 1949.[99] Tull and his team were charged with finding ways to make factory processing faster and cheaper. The rationale for the addition of engineering to botany, entomology, biochemistry, and the other branches of Tocklai was rooted in postwar economics. The chairman of the ITA Development Committee charged with overseeing the engineering department wrote in 1951 that the "whole economic background of industries" had changed. Standards of living—and the cost of maintaining those standards—had risen across India.[100] When the industry "began to move back to more normal conditions after the war," planters found that the cost of manufacturing was draining profits.[101] Mechanized plucking, rolling, sorting, and firing could cut the number of Indian workers ITA-affiliated plantations had to employ. But by the 1950s, most processes in tea making that could be done by machine were already being done by machine. The task, as the 1954 Engledow Commission put it, was to improve existing machinery.[102]

Though the dream of a mechanical plucker that would replace fieldworkers loomed large for years, perennial crops like tea were much more difficult to harvest mechanically than annual crops like wheat. The Tocklai engineering department thus focused its research on factory machinery, introducing new dryers, rollers, and withering technologies, all with the aim of ramping up production. Until the establishment of the TRA in 1962, all of these innovations were, like the chemical knowledge produced by Roberts and Wood, the sole property of the ITA. Tocklai sold licenses for improved machinery to plantations, but revenues from these licenses were not sufficient to keep the ITA's scientific operation running.

Innovations in processing technology were also central to the effort of India's government tea regulators to promote domestic consumption. To supply domestic demand, they needed to find an economical way to process tea grown on marginal land, where the production of high-quality orthodox tea was difficult and where most rupee companies were operating. Initially, the Tea Board's domestic marketing efforts had entailed distributing "liquid tea" in households, villages, and shops across the country. The Tea Board inherited this direct marketing strategy from the Indian Tea Market Expansion Board, which had adapted it from the "Empire Tea" marketing campaigns of the 1930s.[103] A direct-to-consumer approach proved ineffective in expanding the Indian market, since it required that the people targeted already think of themselves as tea consumers. It might have worked on Indians who were already regular tea drinkers, but for many, tea was a foreign and perhaps even dangerous concoction.[104] These *potential* consumers, the Tea Board reasoned, needed to be educated not just about tea's flavor, but about its mode of preparation. As J. Mukherjee, the Tea Board's head of propaganda, wrote in 1955, "The real factors that will stand immediately in the way of a wider acceptance of tea will be (a) its quality and (b) its price."[105] In its later educational campaigns, the Tea Board raised public awareness about the importance of buying tea from "genuine stockists." The Tea Board created tea centers, which Mukherjee likened to "tea ashrams," where curious consumers could learn about the "standard preparation of tea" and "what a cup of good tea should be like."[106]

But as Philip Lutgendorf explains in his work on the history of Indian chai, many Indian consumers, particularly the less affluent, were not impressed with the British "standard preparation," which entailed gently steeping cylindrical twists of orthodox tea leaves in hot (but not boiling) water. Without teapots at their disposal, many poorer Indians preferred to crush orthodox leaves into a powder and boil them, not steep them, in a combination of water, sugar, milk, and spices. For this kind of preparation, "low grade" tea was not only acceptable, it was preferable.[107]

While Mukherjee and the Tea Board worked with limited success to promote "proper" tea preparation, Indian engineers and entrepreneurs were quietly reviving what many British tea planters had long considered a failed technology. The growth in Indian consumption of chai in the 1950s and 1960s was facilitated in large part by the reengineering of cut-tear-curl, or CTC, machinery. As its name indicates, CTC processing yields a tea that is already crushed and rolled into a tiny, dustlike consistency. CTC tea could be rendered into a dark malty drink that took well to the addition of fatty milks, ample sugar, and pungent spices.

Until the 1950s, however, the CTC machine was regarded within the industry as a cautionary tale about excessive ambition. It was invented in 1930 by a Scottish engineer, Sir William McKercher, superintendent at Amgoorie Tea Estate in lower Assam. As an unpublished history of the CTC machine written by the Amgoorie planter F. G. Johnson explains, the plantation had a quality problem: "Amgoorie teas produced up till then had been wishy-washy liquors," with an undesirable gray color and little distinguishable flavor. McKercher hypothesized that if the "'bloom' on the leaf [could be] retained instead of being lost during the dry cutting of leaf," then a better liquor could be obtained.[108] McKercher designed a machine that would cut, tear, and curl the leaves, producing a stronger, maltier, more flavorful cup.

Though McKercher's machine was cumbersome and prone to breaking (people who were present when it was first brought to life recall holding their ears to block the sound of roaring metal and ducking to avoid projectile screws), Amgoorie put it to use during the 1931 growing season and saw its sale prices go up. As Johnson explained in his recollection, "Those from upper Assam look down their noses at our tea areas, factory leaf houses, etc. And rightly so, as everything left a great deal to be desired, and they marveled at how we could possibly retrieve such results!"[109] The CTC machine seemed capable of giving new value to marginal tea. In the early 1930s, there was a short-term craze among planters for McKercher's machine, but its tendency to break down caused nearly every plantation that bought one to abandon it within a year or two.

The engineering department at Tocklai was well aware of the story of the quick rise and fall of the CTC machine, and much of its work was dedicated to finding ways to achieve what Tocklai's director, Mr. H. Ferguson, called "the continuous factory."[110] According to Lutgendorf, however, it was actually Indian engineers from the Small Tools Manufacturing Company in Calcutta who first patented a modified version of McKercher's design that overcame the flaws that led to its failure in the 1930s.[111]

It was tasting and chemical work at Tocklai that helped turn CTC from a rogue experiment into an official category of judgment and valuation. Tocklai began sending experimental samples of tea processed by the CTC method to tasters in London and Calcutta. These tasters soon developed a set of criteria for valuing CTC to go along with those for valuing orthodox teas.

CTC provided a mechanical fix for the postcolonial tea industry, even as it further entrenched the plantation itself into the economic fabric of India. The rise of CTC paralleled the birth of the TRA, a merger of the ITA's private, export-driven, proprietary model of science with the Indian Tea Board's nationalistic, yield-driven, publicly oriented model. One result of this set of meandering, often incidental arrangements between postimperial trade protectionism and state-led agricultural developmentalism, then, was a new, hybrid means of producing quality. A divide in the market between orthodox and CTC teas remains to this day. As a result, two kinds of quality—quality as flavor and distinction and quality as efficiency in production and growth in standards of living—are able to coexist. A tension between these two kinds of quality lies at the heart of contemporary, postcolonial tea production in India.

Over the course of the latter part of the twentieth century, CTC steadily overtook the domestic Indian sales market and overall production. CTC accounted for 90 percent of output by 1999.[112] Yet CTC tea is not simply the massive, undifferentiated "bottom end" of a global market. Despite CTC's quantitative dominance, much of Indian tea's image is still suffused with a colonial nostalgia that sanitizes plantation production as an idyllic and "natural" state of affairs. Even if some orthodox tea plantations—all of them now owned and operated by Indian companies—have managed to keep this nostalgia alive in tea shops and stores in the Global North, the realities of life on plantations tells quite a different story.[113] As I show in the next chapter, even producers, sellers, and buyers of "cheap tea" are consumed with the question of quality. Indeed, it is in the ostensibly marginal plantations, factories, and auctions of the CTC market that the uneasy settlement between quality as taste and quality as standard of living is most visible, and most problematic.

FIVE

The Quality of Cheap Tea

THE NIRAJ TEA COMPANY IS LOCATED DOWN a dirt road in a remote industrial corridor outside Siliguri. The company's factory is surrounded by cement walls, painted in different shades of blue. Niraj blends and packages CTC for the domestic Indian market. The company sources thousands of different invoices of tea. In the factory, workers run these teas through a machine that first uses large magnets to remove nails and shards of metal lurking inside the packages. The tea then enters a chamber in which it is shaken to remove strips of plastic or paper. Now free from extraneous material, the tea is sent by conveyor belt to the floor above for "packeting" (figure 9). Niraj Tea is a relatively modest operation, but it produces a number of different CTC blends, with different brand labels, and markets them at several price points across West Bengal and North India, from 4-gram, Rs. 1 sachets to 5-kilogram (about 11 lbs.) loose-leaf tubs.

CTC tea like this, produced for the domestic market, is cheap. Really cheap. Strings of those little perforated Rs. 1 sachets hang alongside colorful strands of single-use dishwashing soap and paan in tiny storefronts in villages and towns across India. The plastic, machinery, electricity, and factory labor that go into making these sachets arguably cost more than the actual tea leaves encased inside.

Niraj Tea mostly buys teas from the Dooars, the narrow strip of land that hugs the India-Bhutan border, to the north of Siliguri. The Dooars links India's Northeast with the rest of the country. The British annexed the land that now comprises the Dooars from the Kingdom of Bhutan in 1865, and almost immediately, they established tea plantations there. Today, the Dooars is blanketed in plantations. While other major tea-producing regions in India, such as Assam and Kerala, produce a combination of orthodox and

FIGURE 9. One-rupee packets of tea. Photo by author.

CTC teas, in the Dooars, production is devoted almost exclusively to CTC. The state of West Bengal produces 300 million kilograms of tea per year. Of this 300 million, 9 million is orthodox tea from Darjeeling, and the rest is CTC produced in the Dooars and the small Terai region just to the west of Siliguri.

When people refer to tea as India's national beverage, they are referring to kernels of CTC, boiled with milk and sugar to make one of many variations on chai.[1] This beverage takes many forms and punctuates everyday life across an economically and socially diverse subcontinent. It is consumed in homes and at roadside stalls. It is carried out to fields in reused bottles and drunk out of porcelain cups in urban offices. In India, tea (usually CTC) is a staple, along with rice, daal, oil, or salt.

The Niraj Tea factory manager, Mr. Sarkar, explained to me that even though the company's blends of tea are cheap, a lot of work goes into making them taste and feel a certain way. "Every packet is produced for a certain quality," he said. "And the taste is also different. We have to taste. It is all about taste." Tea aimed at middle-class urban markets has to be blended differently than tea aimed at the rural poor.

Continuing from the previous chapter's discussion of the postcolonial technoscientific fix for the plantation that led to the rise of CTC in India's domestic market, this chapter is about how ideas of quality, even at the bottom end of the market for Indian tea, have long worked to reinforce, and even hold together, the plantation system. But the place of quality in cheap tea production has changed in the context of market liberalization. Since the early 2000s, quality has become a conceptual cornerstone in an industrial reform effort aimed at changing field-based tea production and even eliminating the plantation system.

These agrarian reforms are summarized in a corporate-driven platform launched in 2013. Under the name "Tea 2030," Tata Global Beverages (maker of Tetley, Good Earth, and Tata Tea) and Unilever (maker of Lipton, PG Tips, and Brooke Bond) have united with companies like Yorkshire, Finlays, and Twinings, as well as nongovernmental organizations (NGOs) such as Rainforest Alliance and Fair Trade International. The objective of this global corporate-philanthropic partnership, which spans beyond India, is to alter the way tea is valued and produced. By systematically addressing a long list of what the Initiative terms "challenges"—from climate change to women's empowerment—Tea 2030 aims to turn tea from a problematic colonial legacy into a vehicle for development.

A 2014 Tea 2030 report states:

> [There is a] real opportunity for tea to become a "hero" crop. A hero crop delivers more than just a commodity. It also delivers major benefits to the millions of people involved in the sector, the planet, and the wider economy. Central to this transition would be a move away from a long, linear supply chain, to a value network that takes into account everyone involved in the tea sector and . . . works together to create a more sustainable industry.[2]

To break the "chain" holding tea supply captive, Tea 2030 proposes recalibrating two numbers. The first is the price of tea, formulated by brokers not only in India but also in Sri Lanka and East Africa. Removing the control these brokers have over the formulation of prices is a key element of reform. I discuss this aspect of industrial reform in the next chapter. The second number—the one that provides the context for this chapter—is labor costs, which refers to the compensation tea plantation laborers receive. This compensation includes both monetary wages and nonmonetary in -kind payments such as housing and food rations. While Tea 2030 promotional materials note that workers' wages are relatively low, they also claim that labor constitutes the bulk of production costs (70 percent according to the estimates of Forum for the Future, the NGO in charge of the rollout of Tea 2030). In Tea 2030's narrative, this rate is unsustainably high. Devising "new remuneration models" is a goal of Tea 2030 reform.[3] Tea 2030's premise is that the process of brokerage keeps tea prices too low, while the plantation model, with permanent laborers working under arrangements that net them fixed daily wages and in-kind benefits, keeps labor costs too high.

The resonances with the history I recounted in the previous chapter are worth noting here. The concerns of Tea 2030 reformers with price and labor costs are eerily similar to those expressed by the ITA in the postwar years, when quality was seen as deteriorating and when new labor standards were driving many British planters out of India altogether. And like the Tea Board of the 1950s and 1960s, today's Tea Board supports Tea 2030's idea of turning tea into a vehicle for national development. Whereas modern laboratory science and mechanical engineering were seen in the mid-twentieth century as the best experimental tools for achieving these aims, the early twenty-first-century reforms have focused more on experiments in agricultural policy.

For Tea 2030, the answer to the problems that beset the industry lies not necessarily in the abolishing of plantations, but in the extension of the tea monoculture *beyond* plantations, through the promotion of small-grower tea farms. The Tea Board has framed the push for small-grower tea farming in regions including the Dooars as a form of sustainable development. By endorsing the hypothesis that nonplantation agricultural systems can and should produce tea, the Tea Board sees itself as inviting an unorganized, unprotected agrarian sector into the stability of a market for tea.

Elizabeth Povinelli argues that contemporary politics are hamstrung by the assumption that there should be programmatic alternatives—a "what then?" to a "not this."[4] Small growers have become the "what then" to the "not this" of the Indian tea plantation. But the insistence among self-styled corporate and state reformers on a "what then" for the Dooars and for the plantation system has only strengthened the hold the tea monoculture has on the region's landscape and lives. This agrarian conversion has arguably not brought significant development gains for farmers. More important for my argument here, the promotion of smallholder tea production has not ushered in an end to the plantation system. The extension of a tea monoculture to smallholder farms in the Dooars, born out of a concern about the quality of the market, has generated new questions about quality in the two senses I discussed in the previous chapter: the quality of things produced for the market and the quality of life for the people who produce and consume those things.

MAKING MONOCULTURE IN THE DOOARS

Intentionally cultivating plants is a means of making place and a reason to stay there. Plants conscript humans into relationships. Monoculture is what happens when "plants" become "plant." Think of the singularized nouns *soy, cotton,* and *rubber* that are used in commodities markets and in everyday speech. These refer to generic objects, but they also, if indirectly, refer to homogeneous landscapes and industries.

To understand how monoculture is changing in the twenty-first century through the advent of phenomena like smallholder tea cultivation, it is necessary to go back: to see how the plantation, as a form of human-plant intimacy, was put into motion and how it has managed to persist. In the mid-nineteenth century, Indian-grown tea joined other colonial plantation crops like sugar, coffee, and tobacco in an arsenal of what Mintz once called "proletarian hunger-killers": the cheap energy that fueled the early carbon-based economy of British and American mills.[5] The extension of plantations hinged on massive agrarian transformations. Before they could build tea factories, for example, European planters had to plant tea in a way that ensured a steady supply of raw material; they had to make a monoculture.

Champions of imperial expansion hailed monoculture as a triumph of science and technology over "wild" landscapes and people. Key to the success of monoculture was the vertical integration of the entire production process. Tea fields, factories for processing freshly picked leaves, and—importantly— housing and basic social services for the hundreds of laborers needed to staff an individual tea plantation were part of this vertical integration. This model of production was heralded by European tea planters as the sociotechnical apex of a colonial vision of efficiency.

For these European planters, as I noted already in previous chapters, the plantation stood in stark contrast to the mode of tea production that prevailed in China. The Chinese mode of production was distinguished by small production plots where farmers grew green leaf on land that was held collectively or privately owned and brought it to a centralized location for processing by hand, not machine. From these processing locations, tea was sold, packaged, and sent to market.[6] While early tea production in India looked similar to production in China, thanks partly to the British conscription of Chinese laborers to work in the tea fields of Assam, by the time Dooars plantations first opened in the mid-1800s, the system had changed. Planters were clearing forest, conscripting laborers from around India, and building on-plantation factories.[7]

Within twenty years of the first tea planting in the Dooars, the vast majority of indigenous Mech and Bodo people living in the region were relegated to a 30.7-square-mile reservation near the town of Jalpaiguri.[8] To build and staff the Dooars plantations, planters conscripted Adivasis, and later Nepalis, from outside the region. European planters deemed these groups more suitable for plantation labor than the indigenous population.

The anonymous author of *Tea Cultivation,* an 1865 instructional manual for would-be tea planters, outlines the steps that need to be taken in order to build a plantation. "Tea will grow better in virgin soil," the author explains. "Village lands have long ago had all of 'the goodness' taken out of them." The author observes that "the germs of all kinds of weeds, deposited by the wind, by birds, and in the cattle manure" sap the "strength or power of sustenance left in" formerly "cultivated" soil. Such soil requires five times as much labor "to keep." "The shade of the forest," on the other hand, "has checked vegetation, the wind has less power to deposit on the surface seeds of wild grasses, and perhaps, more than all, no manure (always so fruitful in the propagation of weeds) has been spread onto the land."[9]

"It is then necessary," the author concludes after weighing the up-front and back-end costs of planting on "village lands" against those of planting in "virgin soil," "to clear forest and jungle land."

"How is this best done?," he asks.

To complete the task of turning forest into monoculture, you must pay close attention to ecology. In eastern Bengal (the Dooars and Assam), as the author of *Tea Cultivation* explains, you must first cut the bamboo, grasses, and small trees, leaving them on the ground to dry for two to three months, rendering them into kindling. Next, bigger trees can be removed by "ringing," or carving a six-inch to two-foot circle of bark around the trunk. Sap circulates under tree bark, like blood under our skin. Ringing halts this process by choking the vascular flow of nutrients to the upper reaches of the tree. Ringing is a slow death.

Anticipating the would-be monoculturalist's concerns about the time and cost of this work, the *Tea Cultivation* manual warns about the dangers of the alternative: unchecked biological diversity. White ants make homes in large trees—even after they have been felled. The author opines, "Were I to commence a garden in Bengal, I would, in spite of the expense, cut down, cut up, and burn the big trees with all the others, and thus, I believe, much decrease the possible chance of damage from these insects." He adds that in the hills, the planter-to-be can save time by cutting these large trees up and "flinging them down" into the ravines.

Once bamboo and grasses have dried up, and trees have died, it is time to burn.

> It is a grand sight to see—the fire leaps along, urged by a strong wind, which is generally waited for, and the quantity of combustible material is so great that the moderate sized trees, which have been felled and which would not burn themselves, are completely consumed. A curious accompaniment to these fires is the sound emitted by the burning bamboos. It resembles incessant discharges of musketry. As I lay in bed one night, in the neighborhood of a blazing jungle, I might easily have fancied myself in action; in fact I did fancy so; for as sleep stole over me, the volley upon volley transported me to scenes far different from the evergreen tea gardens around.[10]

The military overtones—flashbacks, of course, but also flash-forwards to the voracious flames of forests from California to Indonesia—are apt. Creating a monoculture is about eradication (of undesirable flora, fauna, and people), even if eradication is carried in the pursuit of preserving *some* forms of life (i.e., human).

Monocultures are place based and climatically sensitive. The work of making tea plants (*Camellia sinensis* or *Camellia sinensis* var. *assamica*) grow in the Dooars has always been distinct from the work of making them grow in Darjeeling or Assam or Kerala. But, as the author of *Tea Cultivation* explains, tea is less picky than most cash crops: "The tea plant is a very hardy one, and will *grow* in various climates and in almost all soils."[11] Tea's monoculture remains viable in part because of the endurance of the tea plant. It is tenacious, persistent, and forgiving of less-than-ideal placement.

Low-lying, with little shade and nearly no frost or snow, the Dooars offered tea planters a long growing season. This geographical location, however, affected quality. Plantations in nearby Darjeeling produce a delicate, aromatic, floral product prized by connoisseurs, and those in Assam produce sought after "golden tips." (Full leaf second flush Assams can have a golden end—a "tip"—on one end of the twisted leaf.) Dooars plantations are known for nothing in particular—just perfectly adequate mass quantities of black tea, ideal for processing in CTC machines.

In Anna Tsing's influential formulation, monoculture is an emblem of the "ruination" wrought by capitalist excess, a "landscape modification in which only one stand-alone asset matters; everything else becomes weeds or waste."[12] Even if the plant is a hardy one, like tea, getting an "asset" to "stand alone" turns out to require lots of work.[13] The story of tea planting in the Dooars underscores that resources—even monocultured ones—do not "stand alone" as much as they are held in place. They are held in place by the work of tens of thousands of marginalized laborers, as well as systems of valuation and normative assumptions about quality: the way things should taste, look, and feel.

In the Dooars, keeping the Adivasi and Nepali laborers reasonably alive and available to work required an elaborate infrastructure: a company-run system for housing, clothing, feeding, and providing medical care. Planters settled their permanent workforces in "labour lines," simple wooden structures that later grew into villages. Each laborer or family received domestic space as part of their compensation for work in the plantations' fields and factories. Houses were as integral as machinery and fertilizers to the vertically integrated production infrastructure.[14] After independence, the provision of domestic space was codified into plantation labor law. Since the passage of the Plantations Labour Act of 1951, housing has comprised a significant part of workers' compensation, but like factories, domestic structures remain the property of plantation companies.

In the Dooars, as in other Indian plantation districts, these postindependence national plantation labor laws—which are rooted in preindependence, colonial practices of compensation—reinforce the entanglement of plants and people.[15] They have fixed people to the plantation and fixed the plantation as an agricultural mode of production. According to those laws, laborers who pluck tea and process it in factories can be paid in a combination of cash wages and in-kind remuneration. Workers and their families are permitted to live in plantation-owned houses, and they also receive biweekly rations of rice and wheat flour, as well as a monthly ration of tea. Upon retirement, workers are given a gratuity and "provident fund" payments. When not in the fields, workers must maintain houses, roads, and schools—all of the human support structures that, like the tea bushes, they do not own. On the tea plantation, this "socially necessary unpaid work" and waged work are thus collapsed.[16] The laws that codify this blend of in-kind and cash compensation keep people like the Nepalis and Adivasis who staff Dooars plantations marginally alive but firmly in place.

The plantation system was developed and refined to ensure maintenance: to keep the ants, grasses, and trees at bay and to keep houses, food stores, crèches, and infirmaries standing. Depending on the monoculture, maintenance work can include harvesting and replanting (in the case of annual crops like sugar, cotton, and soy), or pruning and watering (in the case of perennials like tea, coffee, or grapevines). Monoculturing is equal parts caring and killing: pesticides and fertilizers, spades and sickles, irrigating water and combustible fuel.

The tea plantation monoculture also endures because it is generative of the material and sensory qualities of tea that blending companies have come to expect (the association of "quality tea" with "quality gardens" and "quality regions" discussed previously). The plantation monoculture is central to how mass-market black tea came to be normalized, standardized, and desired as a thing of quality. Taste is certainly ineffable and unquantifiable, but certain tastes (whether of Indian chai or the British cuppa) have become normalized as social and ethical goods that express a collective identity or sense of togetherness. Senses of how tea should or should not taste are linked to the standardization afforded by the plantation's vertical integration, including its provision of housing and welfare services for workers. A resource's capacity to endure can foster particular sentiments not just toward that resource, but toward its potential to provide a suitable living for those who produce it.

Tsing positions her work on the abandoned timber monocultures of the Pacific Northwest of the United States at the end times of extractive relations, brought on by the exhaustion of the landscape. The monocultures oriented to the production of mass-market cheap black tea highlight a different temporality. Povinelli notes that the term "exhaustion" has an "implied antonym," "endurance."[17] We cannot understand how monoculture fosters ecological, bodily, and market exhaustion without also considering monoculture's equally remarkable capacity for endurance and coherence. Monoculture persists through tensions between endurance and exhaustion, intimacy and alienation, fixity and liquidity. "Internal to the concept of endurance," Povinelli writes, "is the problem of substance: its strength, hardiness, callousness; its continuity through space; its ability to suffer and yet persist."[18]

Those sensations of calm and reliability that come with a "nice cuppa" hinge on the maintenance—the fixing—of monoculture and the social and ecological relationships that are part of it. The maintenance of monoculture extends far beyond the fields. When we consider that tea does not so much stand alone as it is held in place, we can ask what institutions, practices of valuation, forms of labor, tastes, flavors, ideas of quality, and expectations do that holding.

THE PROBLEM WITH ABANDONMENT

In the view of Tea 2030 reformers, the price of tea, the cost of labor, and even tea itself are all held captive by a "linear supply chain," of which plantations constitute the anchor. Once liberated from this chain, tea might have the power to liberate people. Tea 2030 proposes that breaking the plantation's hold on the industry can be a transformative development intervention, improving the quality of the tea market, of the lives of tea laborers, and of tea itself.[19]

Since the early 2010s, the Indian and international media have reported on what appears to be a mounting epidemic of starvation and malnutrition on tea plantations in the Dooars.[20] Health problems like malaria, diabetes, and tuberculosis have long plagued plantations in India, but this coverage highlighted something else: arresting visuals of emaciated bodies lying on the dirt floors of the small one- or two-room huts that house workers and their extended families; ribs, eyes, and stomachs bulging; tuberculosis treatment sporadic, diabetes unmanaged, and otherwise unremarkable intestinal infections unmedicated. The plantations on which the workers in these stories live have closed. No work means no pay, and workers quickly run through their meager savings. Workers have to choose between food and medicine.

These stories describe the human costs of the abandonment of plantations by capital. They rarely, however, point singular fingers of blame. In much of this public discourse, state- and national-level bureaucrats and politicians, plantation owners, labor unions, and even workers themselves are all implicated in the crisis. This wave of abandonment is linked directly and indirectly to the push to promote smallholder tea production.

When I started working in the Dooars in late 2015, it appeared that the news stories were correct. A mass abandonment of tea plantations was under way. Over the previous two decades, dozens of tea plantations had closed. In 2014, sixteen plantations owned by just one company, Duncans Industries Limited, which was among the first to establish plantations in the region beginning in the 1870s, halted production. Companies like Duncans now claim that operating plantations has become too expensive. As in the years after the production boom of World War II, bushes are old, overworked. The Nepali and Adivasi laborers who pluck leaves from those bushes are also aging. In line with the claims in the Tea 2030 campaign about spiraling labor costs, companies say that they can no longer afford to maintain either plants or laboring populations.

Importantly, however, most of these Dooars plantations have not been *fully* abandoned. As the stories about starvation and sickness attest, many workers remain on the plantations. These workers have not simply resigned themselves to a life of deprivation and decay. Rather, as I found, many remain hopeful that companies like Duncans will reopen the plantations on which they—and often generations of family members before them—have spent their entire lives.

They do this with good reason. Legally speaking, many "closed" Dooars plantations have not been totally shut down. They are instead held in suspended animation. Under Indian law, tea plantation companies can pause production with the objective of getting their finances in order. In both governmental and informal discourse, such plantations are not considered "closed" but "sick." The sickness of plantations, as media accounts show, manifests itself in the sick and malnourished bodies of workers.[21]

A sick plantation is subtly marked. The gate to the factory is closed and locked. Walking past that gate, you are not met with the usual scents of burning coal and freshly fired tea. Instead, the air is quiet and still. Beyond the factory, the fields are verdant. Tea bushes span toward the horizon. People walk the paths that connect the fields with the factory and the villages of workers. Their head baskets are not filled with tea leaves as they would be on a healthy garden but instead with laundry just washed in the river or grasses to feed livestock or to make brooms to sell in town. Children play cricket in the paths between the houses. This might be the scene on an open plantation on a Sunday, the off-day for plantation workers, but on a sick plantation, this is every day. The sick plantation is occupied, but it is not worked.

I began studying plantation closures in the Dooars thinking that I might find evidence of what Tsing has called "feral biologies": new ecological relationships and alternative economies that tend to emerge in "capitalist ruins."[22] But abandonment is rarely a clean break; rather, it is a politically fraught and indeterminate process.[23] Nowhere is this more evident than in the Dooars.

Tsing describes how the makers of monoculture "dream" of alienation, which is "the ability to stand alone, as if the entanglements of living did not matter."[24] It is this dream of alienation that makes the plantation system tend toward sickness. Tsing explains, "When its singular asset can no longer be produced, a place can be abandoned. The timber has been cut; the oil runs out; the plantation soil no longer supports crops. The search for assets resumes elsewhere. Thus, simplification for alienation produces ruins, spaces of abandonment for asset production. Global landscapes today are strewn with this kind of ruin."[25] In Tsing's account, the abandonment of monoculture appears almost inevitable. Eventually, pesticides stop working, carbon goes from the ground to the atmosphere, and weeds and waste take over. Some scholars have asked if the current geological epoch should be called not the Anthropocene but the Plantationocene.[26] Monoculture is an overworked nature. To put it simply, plants, people, soil, and atmospheres in the world's monocultures all seem exhausted.

The sick plantation is a category somewhere between the "cheap nature" of a functioning monoculture and the feral state of an abandoned one.[27] A sick plantation is overworked, exhausted. It needs rest. Sickness is also normalizing. In late capitalism, as David Harvey has argued, sickness has come to be defined as the "inability to go to work."[28] Here, that which is unable to work is a more than human assemblage of hardware, plants, people, and capital. What is sick can be healed, even if it eventually falls sick again. Cycles of plantation sickness and recovery are becoming something of a norm in the Indian tea industry, especially in those areas oriented to the production of CTC tea.

Povinelli's "problem of substance" is again relevant here. We could consider the plantations—particularly closed plantations—as kinds of "capitalist ruins": blasted landscapes unable to provide abundant sources of wealth for capital. But the workers remain, highlighting how plantations—even sick ones—remain spaces of home and belonging. As I explained above, extracting capital and making home in monocultures are intertwined processes. The monoculture is durable in both a material and an affective sense, and the recent epidemic of starvation highlights how difficult abandonment can be.

SICKNESS, EXHAUSTION, AND ENDURANCE

In January 2016, I was at Stellabarrie, a Dooars plantation whose owners had shut down operations the previous September. Citing a lack of profitability, management stopped paying wages and benefits to workers. I visited one Sunday. Getting to the plantation involved crossing a dry riverbed, which was filled with picnicking families from the nearby city of Siliguri. That Sunday at Stellabarrie, members of a Siliguri-based bankers' union were handing out food aid, in the form of 6-kilogram portions of rice, to the workers who remained on the plantation without pay.

The food distribution took place at the plantation factory. Like most factories, it was surrounded by barbed wire and only accessible via a large gate. The workers were lined up single file outside of the gate with empty shopping bags, waiting to hand in little square pink paper chits that would allow them to get their scoops of rice. The workers filed in, ten at a time, collected their rice, and exited the gate. A woman at a table inside the gate signed each worker's chit to prevent them from coming back again to collect more rice.

Outside the factory at Stellabarrie where the workers received their rice rations, a doctor had come for the day, examining workers and distributing medicines. The ad hoc diagnoses included tuberculosis, low-grade fever, and cough. NSAIDs were given out for generalized pain and swelling. Most of the women were anemic. With some stinging irony, they were told to eat more vegetables, and when they could, a little meat.

Stellabarrie had opened and closed several times over the previous few years, and workers to whom I spoke while waiting in line for medicine or food were hopeful that it would reopen by spring. This hope was rooted in both past experience (the plantation did tend to reopen) and a quirk of Indian plantation law. The land under tea plantations in the Dooars is technically owned by the state of West Bengal and leased out to individual companies. When a tea plantation stops operations, its owners have a fixed amount of time to reopen or risk losing their leasehold. If an owner loses a lease, the fixed capital atop the land (the factory, the bushes, the infrastructure) can be sold to a new buyer, but the land stays with the state, and the new buyer must operate a plantation with it.[29]

To avoid a forced sale, owners can declare their plantations sick. Sick status, in this respect, is akin to bankruptcy. The state refrains from repossessing the leasehold, and the original owner has the opportunity to refinance and reopen. Plantations like Stellabarrie, which were chronically open and shut, were sick in this sense. Throughout the rash of closures in the Dooars over the past few years, owners frequently reported to journalists and government officials that they fully intended to resume production. Plantation owners and managers maintained that the closures were only temporary. State and national politicians and bureaucrats as well as local political leaders all looked the other way.

The idea that tea plantations can become sick (and potentially recover) is a powerful one not only for Dooars plantation owners seeking insulation from state sanction but also for workers. The food aid from the bankers was one of many relief actions that took place in the Dooars that winter. The response to stories of starvation from the state of West Bengal and the Indian central government had been lethargic or uncoordinated or both, in part because of the legal structures that legitimized declarations of plantation sickness. Relief thus came from Christian churches (many Adivasis in the Dooars have converted in the past twenty years), local NGOs, and other volunteer groups. The distribution of food and medicine at Stellabarrie had the choreography of a humanitarian intervention, but the mood among the workers was one of cautious optimism. Food relief was just that: temporary relief. A treatment of symptoms alone.

When I asked plantation owners and managers why sickness was so common, they told me a story of ecological and economic exhaustion. The bushes were old and overworked, the machinery was out of date and in need of repair, and the cost of supporting the full-time workforce was too great. The decision by management at Stellabarrie and other Dooars plantations to stop providing wages and benefits when they did (in September) made sense in the context of the ecology and market for tea. By September, as the monsoon reaches its climax, tea bushes still yield leaves, but the value of this autumn flush is much less than the first flush and second flush harvests that take place between March and June.

Stellabarrie's *garden bau,* a leader among the workforce and a liaison between labor and management, insisted that Stellabarrie *could* operate year-round like any other "healthy" plantation, but its owners had neglected to invest in or repair the bushes. On healthy plantations, the winter dormant season, between November and February, is a time when workers prune the tea bushes so that fresh young sprigs will grow when the weather turns warm again. Bushes that had grown old and unproductive were not being replaced with younger, healthier clones, as advisers from the Tea Research Association recommended. The Tea Board of India had actually initiated a scheme to finance replantation on plantations in the Dooars, but Stellabarrie could not take advantage of it because management had missed too many wage and pension payments during its sick periods.

As the garden bau explained, Stellabarrie's management stopped payment at a crucial time not only in the ecological calendar but also in the social calendar. On healthy plantations, management is obligated under plantation labor law to pay each worker a cash bonus in October, to mark the Hindu festival season. The October bonus is vitally important for social reproduction on plantations. October is a time for visiting family, for decorating and cleaning houses, for discussing marriage prospects, and, of course, for eating and drinking. On healthy plantations, reinvestment in tea bushes coincides temporally with reinvestment in household, kin, and social relations.[30] This meant that the September closure at Stellabarrie was particularly painful. At Stellabarrie, workers had already started making arrangements for the festivals, which left them with no cash savings by the time management had stopped paying wages.

The workers in the food line told me that 6 kilograms of rice were minimal, but still, they took it. "We are old and we can't do anything else," one woman explained. "What can I do? I sit in the house and wait." While older women "waited" on the plantation, others looked for wage work near the plantation.

"Most of the people are in the river," said the garden bau's wife, who was collecting chits at the gate. The rivers were wider and flatter here in the Dooars than in the steeper Darjeeling hills. In the dry winter season, riverbeds become spaces of labor and recreation. Picnickers like those I had seen on my way to Stellabarrie could get to them with ease. So, too, could construction trucks, looking to harvest the stones left in the bed. Able-bodied tea workers—mostly women—could walk to the river and break rocks, working them into neat square piles, ready for shoveling into the beds of the trucks. Rock breaking is not easy, but for many in the Dooars, it is preferable to migrating to Delhi, Kerala, or Bangalore in search of wage work. In the big cities, there were little more than domestic service jobs available to Nepalis and Adivasis. In addition, off of the plantations, few people spoke Nepali or Sadri.

There were thus good reasons for workers on sick plantations to remain in place, waiting. These reasons included the geographic isolation of the Dooars, linguistic and ethnic discrimination, the need to care for aging relatives, and the fact that workers' houses were attached to the plantations. That seasonal sense of hope was also important. The first flush of March was coming after all. Immobility is built into the monoculture and inflected by a peculiar kind of intimacy: intergenerational care in a house owned by one's employer and connections to place mediated by the seasonality of ritual, rainfall, and temperature.

In monocultures, this immobility and intimacy creates dangers not only for labor but also for capital. The longer Stellabarrie stayed "sick," the less likely it would be that its owner would find a new buyer. In order to take over the lease, any new owner would need to pay back wages and pension contributions, starting from the date of closure. According to the terms of the lease from the state of West Bengal, the new owner would also have to agree to keep Stellabarrie running as a plantation. To rip up tea bushes and not replant them with more tea would be a violation of the lease agreement.

The lease requirement to keep plantations running *as plantations* exhausts the bushes and the soil, but the promise that a winter's rest will lead to recovery, both of the plants and of the people who care for them, allows the monoculture to endure. On healthy gardens, workers are compensated for aiding in this recovery, but on sick plantations like Stellabarrie, they were not. Insofar as they are connected to the stoppages in wages and benefits, starvation and illness among workers on sick plantations are symptoms of an overworked monoculture. The food aid workers at Stellabarrie, the doctors, and even many women's willingness to break rocks were all attempts to *revive* the monoculture, not change it.

BOUGHT LEAF AND THE QUESTION OF QUALITY

"Dooars tea is not known for its taste," a Siliguri-based journalist told me with the authoritative air of an industry insider. "It is not known for quality." Contrasting plantations in the Dooars to the ones located in the hills of Darjeeling and Assam, he added, "Nobody knows the plantation names." He paused to qualify this. "You *may* know them if they are associated with a happening or a family member."

The journalist had been a reporter in the Dooars for over a decade, and recently he had been writing for a national newspaper on plantation closures. He concurred with other observers that starvation deaths were common on sick plantations but also that "savvy, intelligent people" were moving to Siliguri, to New Delhi, or to Bangalore. Those workers who stayed, waiting, were putting their faith in a plantation system whose time had passed. The journalist insisted that this time, the sickness was terminal. The wave of the future for the Dooars and for Indian tea, he assured me, was smallholder tea production.

While big plantation companies struggling to make payroll lobbied for the rewriting of leases or plantation labor laws, small farmers (the other "savvy" group in the region, according to the journalist), whose land had long been dedicated to rice, pineapple, or other food crops, were planting new tea bushes. They could sell the leaves they picked, first flush through autumn flush, to a new kind of processing factory: the bought-leaf tea factory, or BLF.

Small growers of tea in India, in and of themselves, are not a new phenomenon. In the years following independence in 1947, some plantations closed, and others divested from marginal lands they controlled. People living on these plantations, now finding themselves out of work, could sell green leaf by the kilogram to managers on the adjacent estates. Until the introduction of BLFs, plantations were the only sites where tea could be processed in India. Once bought by a plantation, small-grower tea was mixed with the daily harvest of that plantation for withering.[31] Plantations can still buy small-grower tea in this manner. BLFs are different because they are not attached to plantations. BLF owners purchase unprocessed green leaf directly from growers and process it in their factories before sending it to auction or selling it directly to blenders like Niraj Tea.

"The quality is really good," the journalist insisted. After all, the small growers who sold to BLFs were working with vibrant, young bushes. By the time of our conversation in 2015, the number of BLFs and smallholder operations in the Dooars was exploding. In 1998, West Bengal contained 22 BLFs, producing 7.43 million kilograms of tea per year. By 2006, there were 85, producing 59 million kilograms per year.[32] Today, the number of BLFs in the Dooars is well over one hundred, and production continues to rise. Small growers are now "the growth-drivers of the tea industry in India."[33] Together, the journalist said, small growers and BLFs "are running like a plantation."

There is, however, one big difference. BLFs and small tea growers are not governed by the same labor laws that govern plantations. Small growers sell green leaves on a per-unit basis. The owners of BLFs are not required to provide pensions, benefits, schooling, or housing to their employees. Because of green leaf tea's perishability—its biophysical inability to endure once plucked from the bush—small growers must sell quickly.[34] Small growers can neither leave leaf on the bush for an indeterminate amount of time nor pluck it and hold on to it, waiting to sell until prices reach an optimal level. Once plucked from the bush, tea starts naturally withering. The withering process must be controlled in a factory, and factory machinery depends on a consistent throughput of fresh green leaf.

Journalists and some industry insiders I met in the Dooars and Siliguri frequently suggested that the rise of a network of entrepreneurial smallholders and BLFs presented a hopeful alternative to the vertically integrated plantation system. In fact, it was initially difficult for me to identify a critique of the smallholder-BLF model from within the CTC tea industry in the Dooars. When I did, it came from an unlikely source: the owner of a BLF whom I met at the Siliguri tea auction. When I asked him about the state of play, he admitted, "We need to cut down on production and increase quality." He pointed at the day's auction catalog: "Look. The price is only Rs. 125 a kilogram. You can't pay your workers with that. There needs to be higher price realization. . . . Only when the price of tea moves up [will] we start to see fewer closures and crisis in the industry." The problem, as the BLF owner saw it, was overproduction.

In the Dooars, the dedication of more and more land to the production of tea led both to what he called "stressed" plantations and to the emergence of a class of inexperienced, overzealous, even desperate small farmers. These farmers were at the mercy of both the BLFs and a plant whose perishability made speculation on price difficult if not impossible. As a vision of agrarian reform, the smallholder-BLF model ignored the fact that those who worked most closely with living tea bushes—the farmers—bore a disproportionate burden of economic and ecological risk. Indeed, the disaggregation of factory-based finishing and field-based plucking meant that green leaf's perishable nature worked against farmers and in favor of BLF owners. The purpose of the conversion to the smallholder-BLF model, of course, was not just to promote a better quality of life for small farmers in this impoverished region; it was also to improve the quality of the market—to make it easier to produce cheap tea.

The packaging manager at Phukan told me that in order to make a consistent—and appropriately cheap—product, he bought tea processed at both BLFs and plantations. Blending companies like Niraj Tea buy from the regional auction center in Siliguri, operated by the Siliguri Tea Auction Committee (STAC). STAC opened in 1967 to accommodate increases in production due to the yield-oriented intensification of plantation agriculture in West Bengal and Assam. Over the course of the 1960s, the Tea Board succeeded first in boosting total production (geared largely to domestic demand for CTC) and second in mandating that plantations sell a minimum percentage of their tea at auctions in India. Throughout the 1960s, India-based brokerage firms like J. Thomas and Contemporary Tea Brokers grew as the center of the tea trade moved from London to Calcutta. They opened satellite offices in Siliguri, as well as the other regional auction centers in Guwahati, Assam, and multiple sites in South India. At STAC, the auction and the tasting process are largely the same as those at Nilhat House, but STAC brokers only deal in CTC and CTC dust categories. The Siliguri buyers are described by their colleagues in Kolkata as being rowdy, boisterous, and generally a bit uncouth. Some attribute this to the unplanned development of the border town of Siliguri after independence, or the fact that they deal exclusively in cheap tea, which engenders a certain kind of downhome affect and disposition. There is, in other words, a hierarchy in the tea auction world. Regional auction centers like Siliguri are used as a training ground for junior brokers who will end up at Nilhat House after working there for several years.

In winter 2016, I moved between the closed plantations in the Dooars and STAC. The Siliguri headquarters of Contemporary Tea Brokers is located in an office suite on an upper floor of STAC. I was present for the first sales of the year in 2016. Sales are numbered 1 through 52, corresponding to the weeks of the year. I wanted to know more about how brokers here, who only deal with CTC, tasted and valued cheap tea.

Mr. Bose showed me Contemporary's tasting room. His junior colleague was already there, tasting the selection of lots that had been spread out for Sale 2, which would happen the next week. Sale 1 was already going on downstairs. Just as at J. Thomas, teas were lined up on long, narrow tables, but since these teas were all CTCs, each cup contained some variation of a milky brown hue.

Mr. Bose explained that CTC tasting, like all tasting, was about comparison. "We compare this week's teas with what sold last week. . . . We are looking at the corresponding grade of that same garden. This is how we do the valuation. If these are of inferior quality this week, we drop the price. If it is slightly better," he motioned with his hand upward. "And if it is the same more or less we keep the price as is."

He walked down the line and grabbed a cup of milky tea. "See the liquor? Come here and look. This is a very brown tea. This is a secondary grade. OK? You will find that it is very brown compared to this." He picked up another one to show me in comparison. "But the liquor of this," he elevated the second tea is his hand, "is slightly better."

"Why is the liquor better? Is it the color?," I asked.

He nodded his head in agreement. "This one is what we call *a little pink*." In case I didn't follow, he qualified this description, adding, "This is not a good thing."

"And you can only see pinkness when the milk is there?," I asked.

He nodded. "See again, you can see the difference between this and this." He picked up the upturned lids covered in steeped CTC leaves.

"This one is darker and really discrete," I commented, noticing that there was definition between individual kernels (figure 10).

"But this is discounted," he explained of these darker and more differentiated leaves. "This one," he elevated the lighter-colored, slightly disintegrated tea leaves in his other hand, "is better."

"Why?," I asked.

"This is called *dull*," he said in reference to the first tea. "And anything like this [the second tea] or better, we call it *bright*."

He went down the line and picked up another tea. "This is a dull tea. All of these [he waves his hand down the line] are of poor quality." In CTC, the individual kernels of tea should break down a little during the brewing process. If the kernels were still distinct, this would mean that the brew would not be as pungent as desired and that the color would not be attractive for most blenders. Teas that break down "brew better."

We moved farther down the table. "These are large," he said pointing to the steeped leaves of another cup. "These are BOP grade. Then this is secondary BOP. Then BOPSM, slightly smaller than that (the "secondary BOP"). Then the BP. BOPSM is somewhere between BOP and BP. Largest grade, second largest grade, third largest grade," he said, pointing to each of the three. "And lastly the orange fannings, which are the smallest. OK? And then

FIGURE 10. Comparing BLF- and plantation-produced teas. The one on the left is produced on a plantation. The other is from a BLF. Photo by author.

there are corresponding grades here: OF, OF1. Now we go on to the next garden. BOP. BOPSM. BP. And it continues like that. Sequentially, as it is in the catalog. Lot 199, 200, and so on."

"This is a good tea," he said, picking up a cup from near the beginning of the line and bringing it back to where we were standing. "You see? This is a bright cup."

Then he picked up another. "This is somewhat pink." Referring to the bright cup, he told me, "This is one of the good teas going on for this season. And selling at very good prices, almost 190." "And this," he held up the pinker cup, "is selling at 130 or 140. Either way, 50, 60 rupees difference."

"And this difference is mostly due to the liquoring color?," I asked.

He nodded. "This tea," bringing my attention to yet another cup, "is poor quality." "Between these two," he pointed back to the good, "bright" tea, "there is almost 100 rupees difference. It's because *this* [referring to the steeped leaves] is *black*."

"What makes it black? Is it because it is fired too high?," I asked, remembering the lessons I had learned at the orthodox tea tasting with J. Thomas at Nilhat House.

"No. No. It is a compilation of things, right from green leaf quality onwards. The green leaf, the manufacturing style. But it all starts with the quality of green leaf. The plucked leaf."

"Is it too old or something?," I wondered aloud.

"Yes. They pluck it late. Too late. And the leaf becomes large. There is too much stem, mother leaf, whatever. Then they have to process it, and the processing is not good because the raw material is not good. So the final product won't be good." "But this," he explained holding up our good tea for reference, "is from a well-plucked garden." "And this," holding up the tea he described as black, "is what we call a bought leaf factory."

He picked up another lid filled with steeped tea. "It is small, no?," I ask.

"This is an orange fannings," he explained. "They are always quite small." "But look at this," pointing to this tea's liquor, "this is an indicator that it is a poor tea. It may not reflect so much on this [referring back to the brewed leaf], but this is still better. But the main difference is between this and that [the way the liquor looks]. This is 100 rupees' difference."

"Because of that color?," I asked.

"Yes." Then he went on to explain why some people would want the larger BOP over the smaller orange fannings. BP, which was slightly larger, was the most popular grade. This size tended to blend and brew better than others. All plantations and BLFs were focusing on producing as much of this grade as possible. "But even then," Mr. Bose reminded me, "it's all about comparison. You have to put this with this. See?" He highlighted the color difference between two BP grades. "You see this one? The color is faded. Then see the difference between this, this, and this. Three different cups." At this point, Mr. Bose was clearly quizzing me to see if I was retaining his lesson.

"That's faded. That's good. And that's pink," I answered. "But why is it faded?"

"It is about the manufacturing in some bought leaf factory," Mr. Bose explained.

THE ORIGINS OF CHEAP QUALITY

Both Mr. Bose and the Niraj Tea packaging manager insisted that the best quality tea came from plantations. This was because plantation tea was, in general, sourced from a historically consistent monoculture. The same leaves, harvested from the same places, tended to have a similar taste. The quality of

BLF-produced CTC was inferior because it contained tea from several places. In addition, BLF tea had sat—sometimes for days—between plucking and processing, often in heavy, tightly packed plastic sacks, as opposed to being laid out flat over wire mesh in a factory withering trough. Often, it was clear that BLF tea had been "coarsely" plucked. The challenge for Niraj Tea was to keep tea cheap and consistent in a market for CTC that was now more differentiated than ever. For buyers and blenders in Siliguri, the question of a tea's quality—its taste and texture—still depended on what happened back in the field.

Again, to my surprise, it was the owners of BLFs who seemed the most reflexive about this fact. As one BLF owner told me, "The problem with the BLFs is that they are buying tea of all different qualities and trying to make tea out of that. The quality is all uneven, and people are plucking this much leaf." He pointed to his elbow, indicating a long sprig that would have contained many leaves. His explanation echoed the criticism of the industry made by the Engledow Commission and the Central Tea Board of India in the early 1950s. During the spike in production during World War II, the "fineness" of plucking had also deteriorated. Experienced tea planters know that the length of plucked sprigs of tea should correspond roughly to the length of a fingertip, not an arm. This ensured that only the most tender leaves would be put into processing. "Years ago, during the Britishers' time," the BLF owner continued, perhaps unaware that the problems he was describing were not entirely new, "they used to only pluck two leaves and a bud, and the quality was very good."

A buyer sitting next to us at the STAC auction added, "In some of the places that the BLFs are sourcing from, they are plucking twelve months of the year. There is no rest. There is not proper pruning." Buyers and blenders now had to sort through improperly picked leaves, rotten leaves, and—most problematic of all—leaves so saturated with pesticides that both flavor and safety were compromised. In remarkably short order, the small-grower monocultures around the Dooars were becoming dangerously overworked.

What even the most ardent proponents of "freeing" the tea market from the colonial yoke of the plantation system were coming to realize was that people's intimate relationships to the monoculture mattered to the quality of tea, even cheap tea. It was anxiety over the taste of cheap tea—rather than in the slow-building humanitarian crisis on sick plantations—that sparked the concern of industry leaders. Tea's perenniality, its perishability, and its tendency to reflect in flavor the characteristics of its cultivation could not be ignored, even here at the very bottom of the global market. The subtext of these critiques of taste was that smallholders needed to start behaving more like tea plantation workers. They needed to find a way to maintain, care for, and work with the monoculture. Mutual relations of care between people and plants would yield better sale prices and more long-term connections to BLFs. Only then would the smallholder-BLF nexus aid in the growth and prosperity of the cheap tea market.

Whereas the incentive for such care on plantations came from a paternalistic system of cash and in-kind benefits that was underwritten by a broader system of ethnic and gender discrimination, the incentive for care on smallholder plots was purely economic. As one BLF owner lamented, "Everyone is running for the money. It is about quantity, not quality." Even among those who appeared at first glance to be the greatest beneficiaries of a free market turn in the tea industry, the BLF owners and the blenders and sellers of cheap CTC packets, there emerged a nostalgia for the plantation past. What looked like a solution to "imperial ruination" had, in many ways, accelerated it, insofar as empire's botanical avatar, the tea monoculture, was now more abundant than ever.[35]

The expansion of BLF production is literally changing the taste and qualities of tea. It is also creating a glut in production, which has both exacerbated plantation sickness and kept CTC tea cheap. Despite reformers' desire to recalibrate the relationship between labor costs and the price of tea—to reduce labor costs and raise prices—the average price of tea produced in West Bengal and sold at auction remains stagnant. Much of this can be attributed to the 100-rupee-per-kilogram differences that Mr. Bose identified between plantation teas and BLF teas. One hundred rupees is significant at STAC, where nearly all teas sell for less than 200 rupees per kilogram. Low prices justify not raising wages in step with inflation. The expansion of BLFs, then, has succeeded in dropping labor costs not just in the smallholder farms from which they source but also in the adjacent plantations. The recent reform efforts have changed the nature of labor in the Indian tea industry in an even more general sense. The rise of smallholder tea production is changing the definition of a tea *laborer,* from waged worker to entrepreneurial farmer. Unprocessed green leaf—vulnerable and perishable—is an inherently risky thing. Green leaf tea can provide high yields, but it can also wither and take farmers' livelihoods with it.

From one perspective, the rise of the BLF-smallholder complex signals an abandonment of (or an alternative to) the archaic plantation estates, with their paternalistic and ethnically divisive system of managing labor. It signals a "freeing" of labor and production. From another perspective, the rise of the BLF-smallholder complex signals a different kind of abandonment. When smallholders rip up food crops to plant tea, we see an abandonment of crop diversity, a doubling down on monoculture, and a recapitulation of the violent process of land takeover that occurred in the colonial period. Corporate and governmental faith in tea as a vehicle for development, seasonally and into the future, moves the monoculture forward in time. On plantations, aging workers wait in line for rations of rice, while small farmers transition to the production of a crop that they cannot eat.

But people in Siliguri and the Dooars talked about another sense of abandonment, too. According to some activists and even many longtime tea planters, sellers, and brokers I interviewed, chronic plantation sickness was a sign that tea production in general should be abandoned. In late 2015, I spoke to a Nepali labor activist who was the child of tea plantation workers in the Dooars. Like others familiar with working conditions in the tea fields, he was cynical about the fact that it was only amid the recent spate of "sickness" that national newspapers had bothered to report about starvation, lack of medicine, and other forms of exhaustion. To him, these were not new phenomena. The region and its plantations had been "sick" for some time, even if plantation owners had not publicly declared them so. The starvation, the chronic illness, and the slow loss of profits signaled to him that everyone should just walk away and try something new. Sick bodies and sick landscapes need to be sacrificed, not saved.

As Povinelli argues, contemporary critique and politics are hamstrung by the assumption that calls for abandonment—for example, statements like that of the activist—must always be paired with normative, programmatic alternatives. The defiant statement, "Not this," she argues, must presumably followed by the positive, hopeful question, "What then?" Refusal must be paired with the search for alternatives.

Povinelli suggests, however, that those who refuse to formulate such alternatives are not failing to act politically; they "are acting positively in a social world" in which such an alternative does not readily follow from a critique or identification of a problem.[36] The problem for such actors remains the object of analysis. The activist and others like him instead were saying "Not this" to a colonially entrenched system that generated cheap tea at the expense of soil, water, and marginalized people. The point was to continue to say "Not this." But perhaps this is an expression of exhaustion itself—a form of resistance to the existence and extension of monoculture in the Dooars.

The insistence by industry reformers like the proponents of Tea 2030, the Tea Board of India, and liberal-minded journalists on a "what then" for the Dooars has only strengthened the hold the monoculture has on the region's landscape and lives. Yet in the context of the slow-mounting crisis brought on by plantation closures, most industry insiders continued to criticize the BLFs not because they perpetuated malnutrition and deprivation but because they threatened quality. This privileging of quality takes for granted the existence (and persistence) of tea. It ignores the "problem of substance." After all, thanks to decades of colonial and postcolonial investments in clonal varieties, soil science, and new machine manufacturing techniques, quality can (theoretically) be improved. A focus on the quality of tea thus engenders, paradoxically, both a belief that the BLF system can ultimately succeed and a nostalgia for the way the plantation system used to work. Quality and sickness conceptually and materially come together in the market for cheap tea. Technical know-how can heal the sick (plantations as well as people) and raise quality (in terms of taste and life). Enough know-how might allow for tea to become a "hero crop," eliding the possibility—raised by more radical activists in the Dooars—that tea itself is the real problem. An aspiration to quality (of tea, of life) keeps the monoculture together, and a resolve that improvement is always possible allows the plantation to hang on for another day, another year.

SIX

The Quality of Markets

SURROUNDED BY SPRAWLING GARDENS AND STATUES of horse-mounted British dignitaries, Kolkata's Victoria Memorial is perhaps the most iconic relic of colonial power in a city filled with them. Today, in what once was the center of the Raj, the Kolkata police arrange diesel-stained metal road barricades that create a buffer between the capaciousness of Victoria Memorial's grounds and the congestion of Kolkata's streets—from the honking of motorbikes and ambassador taxis to the smells of horse-drawn silver phaetons and fresh *puchka* (figure 11). Each of these barricades is adorned with hand-painted advertisements. These advertisements, for everything from snacks to steel, are usually unmemorable, but while I was doing fieldwork in Kolkata, one stood out. The lettering read "teauction.com," and it was embossed with a little teapot.

Teauction.com named an attempt to change the way Indian tea was traded. Since the early 2000s, reform efforts have blamed the tea industry's woes not only on the archaic plantation system but also on corruption and collusion in auctioning and brokerage. In 2002, the Tea Board of India supported the launch of teauction.com, a private online trading platform, in the hope that digital trading might replace outcry auctions. Though it is a government institution, the Tea Board supported teauction.com and other similar privately run experiments because its leaders believed that with the implementation of digital technologies, trade would become more transparent and lagging prices would surge. Once established, moreover, a digital auction would open the trade to more participants. It would also open it to new kinds of investment. Tea Board officials I interviewed claimed that if the digital transition were successful, the trade would soon revolve around the buying and selling of futures contracts, not individual lots of tea. But first,

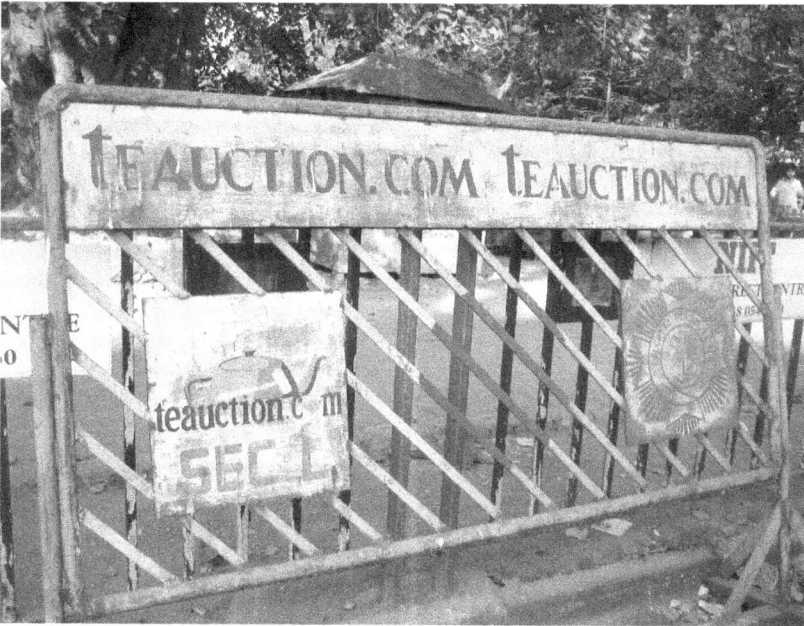

FIGURE 11. Road barricade outside of Victoria Memorial, December 2008. Photo by author.

the power and authority of tea brokers needed to be supplanted by "modern" technology.[1]

So far in this book, I have discussed how expert tea tasters and their apprentices work to cultivate an embodied ability to detect quality, how scientists and blenders struggled to identify the molecular and botanical fundamentals of quality, and how agronomists and proponents of smallholder production attempted to improve the quality of agrarian life in the tea sector through new models of landholding and factory processing. In this final chapter, I examine experimental work on markets themselves. For economic experts and state reformers, electronic auctioning and internet trading promised to improve the quality of the tea market. This experiment in quality might seem to be ushering in a rupture of the colonial system, at least as compared to those experiments discussed in previous chapters. But like that of the plantation, the entrenchment of the auction—and its associated embodied knowledge—is difficult to undo.

Economists have long written about quality as a problem in markets. Classic papers have explored, for example, how the quality of goods on the market can deteriorate when there is an imbalance of information between sellers and buyers, and how to apply "hedonic" value models to ascertain the extent to which expert and nonexpert perceptions of the qualities of fine wines affect sales.[2] More recently, however, some economic experts—including consultants working in the Indian tea industry—have become concerned not only with quality *in* markets, but with the quality *of* markets. In the latter sense, "quality" tends to be defined as a combination of a transparency in trading and a perceived fairness in pricing.[3]

While the concept of market quality may be a relatively new one in economics, at least in formal terms, attempts to improve economies in the developing and postcolonial world through the application of economic theories of efficiency and fairness are well known.[4] Corruption is often a keyword in these interventions, particularly in India. As Mazzarella notes, digital technologies in India have been touted as vehicles for stemming corruption and promoting transparency. Digitization seems to have the power to bring hidden social relationships into the light and to render different forms of relating commensurable, but technological fixes often produce their own kinds of opacities.[5] At an extreme, digitization threatens to supplant social relations with technology.

Ideas about the "impartiality" and "rationality" of digital systems reveal how visions of India's economic future depend on the elimination of cloistered expertise and its replacement by distributed, democratic knowledge. In South Asia, the concepts of transparency and opacity have long been threaded into discussions of democracy and corruption.[6] Calls for transparency in capitalist markets often emerge when publics or regulators begin to feel that something hidden or secret—particularly a secret form of knowledge—lies behind the accumulation of wealth. The harboring of certain kinds of hidden knowledge, or secrets of the trade, is often associated with a bygone, proto-capitalist era of guild-based production.[7] Whether in anxieties over counterfeit goods masquerading as the real thing or suspicions of insider trading on stock markets, secret knowledge appears to fundamentally threaten the quality of markets.[8] Of course, some kinds of secrets emerge not prior to the elaboration of capitalist markets but within them. The global approval of patents for medicines or the genetic codes of proprietary seeds, for example, is seen by some as conducive to overall market quality. A certain amount of protection for knowledge can incentivize innovation and increase productivity. But the consequences of such secrecy, for small farmers indebted to seed retailers or for patients paying astronomical costs for patented drugs, has been devastating.[9]

The practices of brokers were more akin to secrets of this latter type. After all, the communicative infrastructure that was now under attack by digital reformers emerged *within* the colonial system of capital accumulation. At one time—in the living memory of many of the brokers with whom I worked—their esoteric style was seen as an asset to the industry. That style, complete with its complex web of terms and numerical signifiers, was developed to solve a problem created by colonial tea production itself. After all, plantation-based production introduced malty, tannic black tea to the market, and it revolutionized the practice of blending. Without knowledgeable brokers, turning singular, unique lots of tea into standardized blends would be impossible.

Many attempts at the improvement of market quality are self-consciously "experimental."[10] What Callon and Muniesa call market "tests" "are organized to clarify the functioning of the market" (i.e., to observe it) "and act on its organization" (i.e., to change it).[11] Economic experiments are not always successful, of course. The photo of the faded teauction.com advertisement on the Kolkata police barricade sits amid a slew of unfulfilled pronouncements from the Indian and international press about the imminent revolution that technology would bring to the market for the world's most popular beverage. Teauction.com was a notable failure, but state- and industry-led efforts to digitize tea auctions persisted throughout the 2000s and 2010s.

AN AUCTION, A TRADE, OR A MARKET?

At the start of a May 2009 interview—before I even asked my first question—a Tea Board bureaucrat in charge of the rollout of the latest electronic trading platform to be piloted in Kolkata opened up a PowerPoint presentation on her desktop and swiveled her monitor toward me.

"This is a very small presentation," she said.

"Ok . . . ," I ventured, with some trepidation. In my experience, bureaucrats were not known for making "small" presentations.

"Why did we think about going electronic?," she asked rhetorically. "We need to establish a more robust price discovery mechanism, because at present, the price discovery is not actually the *real,* fair price discovery." From a shelf behind her, she pulled a thick spiral-bound consultants' report, commissioned by the Tea Board in 2002 after the failure of teauction.com. "It's all in there. They say the outcry system is completely inefficient—against basic auction principles. The auction needs to be transparent."

Sure enough, the report of the Tea Board's hired consultant, a firm called A. F. Ferguson, had concluded that the outcry system was not actually an auction at all, according to economic principles. The outcry auction's very chronicity—with individual lots coming up one at a time and the labor of auctioneers and buyers choreographed by an auction catalog and its list of valuation prices—allowed traders to buy "with market trends."[12] Buyers not only knew other buyers; during the auction, they knew who the highest bidder was and at what price he (and only on occasion, she) was bidding. For A. F. Ferguson and Tea Board officials, there was no logical explanation for why some lots were aggressively fought over while others needed a broker's coaxing. Buyers and brokers worked in a hidden communicative space that seemed at odds with free trade. A digital, online auction system, reformers claimed, would ensure "natural price discovery."

Economic theory frequently figures the auction as the ideal "spot market." As Bestor explains, spot markets are sites "where cash-and-carry purchases are made of goods available for immediate delivery, where buyer and seller need not know or care about one another, where each transaction is an end in itself, and where the prices at which the market clears—at which supply and demand cancel each other out—constitute irrefutable indicators of market conditions."[13] Many of us probably think of outcry auctioning as a method for selling antique furniture, rare books, or art. These things, at first blush, could not seem more different from warehouses full of mass-market black tea. They are singular items with unique histories. A Sotheby's auctioneer can tell you all about *this* Chippendale sideboard or *that* First Folio of Shakespeare, tracing its provenance across decades or even centuries of ownership. In the outcry auction sales of mass-market black tea, such individualized stories are also important. It is the storied nature of outcry auctioning that distinguishes it from other kinds of commodities trading. Tea's radical particularity and variability are built into the trading process.[14] Even though many of us may think of auctions as exemplars of a competitive and, above all, individualistic capitalist ethic, the competition between brokers at the outcry auctions of Nilhat House is always tempered by a collective desire to find a price for each lot of tea.

Institutions such as India's tea auction are not ideal types. In some ways, they resemble spot markets, but they are also systems of product allocation, in which the things being sold (tea, wheat, fresh fish) will almost certainly fetch different prices on secondary markets.[15] Auction prices, then, are not pure representations of market conditions. According to Jane Guyer, the observation that price is not a "singular amount" but a "composite," or "fiction," resulting from acts of "creation, addition, and subtraction," is now widely accepted by consumers and traders.[16] Prices can keep much "hidden in plain sight."[17] Classically, these hidden terms would include land, labor, capital, and the state—the trappings of the tea production infrastructure I discussed in the previous chapter—but these hidden terms also include a communicative infrastructure through which many auctions operate.[18]

Like those of many experts and regulators seeking to improve market quality, the Tea Board and A. F. Ferguson's worries about inefficiency, fairness, and market principles missed an important aspect of auctions, namely, that, as Christopher Steiner puts it, "rather than reveal market forces and constraints . . . auctions actually *generate* these same forces and constraints within a determining social milieu."[19]

The Indian brokers with whom I worked rarely spoke directly about "the market." They spoke about tea brokerage as "the trade": a social milieu that deserved to be updated, not abolished.[20] As the A. F. Ferguson consultants state in their 2002 report, "Brokers in North India are regarded as 'guaranteed brokers,' (though arguably, this 'guarantee' is by convention rather than as a *legal* guarantee)."[21] The roots of the trade (and of those "guarantees") are, of course, colonial. The habits, terms, and even styles of dress and behavior of tea brokers all maintained, well into the twenty-first century, a distinct British quality. The price of tea emerged from a broader set of colonial practices of enumeration, designed to wrangle what European settlers saw as an unruly India into a translatable and legible form.[22] As Arjun Appadurai suggests, "Numbers became . . . key to a colonial imaginary in which countable abstractions, of people and resources at every imaginable level and for every conceivable purpose, created a sense of a controllable indigenous reality."[23] Tea plantation production provides a ready example of this. Discourses about the sexed and raced bodies of women plantation workers remain woven into discourses about the taste of tea.[24] The cultivated ability of marginalized yet exoticized women laborers to coax flavor from Indian tea sits in direct relationship to the cultivated ability of male elites to properly consume and judge it.

Indian men were not trained as brokers until after independence in 1947. A 1950 report of the Government of India Ministry of Commerce and Industry's Ad Hoc Committee on Tea explained that well-trained tea brokers were "[unlike] middlemen in other branches of trade" because of their "specialized knowledge," including the ability to tell "whether . . . the *particular* type of tea [is] suitable for a particular market."[25] In the handover of the industry from British to Indian control, the Ad Hoc Committee declared it essential to find *Indian* apprentices "with good personality and manners and with a suitable background," whom the four brokerage houses then in operation in Calcutta would train as brokers.[26] Such training, the Ad Hoc Committee emphasized, "cannot be imparted at the Universities and technical institutions."[27]

Even though regulatory power over the auctions now rested with the Government of India, the still British-run brokerage houses initially insisted that if the quantity of tea being auctioned in Calcutta fell below 1949 levels, "the brokers may exercise the option of not confirming" the Indian trainees as "Covenanted Assistants."[28] There was a good deal of dissent over this proviso among the Ad Hoc Committee members (all of them Indian), but the language remained, with the additional guarantee that the government would increase warehouse space and storage capacity to ensure that more tea from Northeast India would be auctioned in Calcutta. While tea auctions had operated in Calcutta since the late 1800s, the Tea Brokers' Association was still based in London at the time of independence. Much as tea science was slowly integrated into—rather than unilaterally taken over by—an independent Indian state through regulatory authority, auctions of Indian tea continued to simultaneously operate in London and in tea growing regions of India until 1998.

Because the transition of the auctions to India took over fifty years to complete, Indian brokers had to master—or, in most cases, have the right kind of cultural capital to already be familiar with—the ins and outs of a communicative infrastructure that was of colonial origins, just as Indian plantation companies had to work within a plantation system that they inherited, willingly or not, from the British imperial project. The process by which Indian brokers did this was not simply one of mimicry but of the maintenance of what Mazzarella calls a "mimetic archive" of tastes and feelings.[29] In what one J. Thomas broker termed "organoleptic valuation," quality prices (the goal of every auction sale) were the products of shared smells, tastes, and memories.[30] Brokers in "the trade" saw themselves as stewards not of a stubborn colonial subjectivity but of a complex web of sensibilities, economic interests, and desires. Each individual tea was like a page from that archive.

Although brokers are often in competition, outcry auctioning requires that they cooperate. They have to work with tea and with one another to see that as many lots as possible find a buyer. Brokers on both sides of each transaction are motivated to see it come to a satisfying end. Brokers collect fees and commissions for completed sales, but there are other reasons that a spirit of gentlemanly collegiality persisted in auction sites like Nilhat House well into the twenty-first century.

Attempting to underscore the importance of organoleptic valuation, the J. Thomas broker told me, "Auctioning may be interesting. In fact, the *form* of the auction *is* interesting. . . . It may be entertaining." Slowing down his speech to ensure that I did not miss his message, he insisted that the behind-the-scenes work of differentiating between individual lots of tea was even more important, "because of tea's var-*ee*-a-bil-i-*tee*." He was referring to several things: the array of chemical constituents that had been identified by chemists at Tocklai and Butler's Wharf; inter- and even intraregional variations in climate, altitude, and soil; and the various grades of orthodox and CTC teas on offer.

This variability leads to volatility, both in price and in taste. Volatility can of course be desirable in finance, but the sheer variety of different styles and grades of tea has long been a source of confusion for would-be speculators. In 1972, the ITA's Tea Futures Market Study Group came to just such a conclusion, insisting that a uniform "Grading Procedure" would have to be applied to all lots of tea if such a market were ever to come to fruition.[31] By 1981, the ITA's annual bulletin indicated that "taking into account the infinite variety and quality of tea being offered for sale[,] . . . there was no prospect of introducing futures trading in tea because the system would lead to huge claims on grounds of quality."[32] It was too much to expect prospective investors to effectively work across the wide array of grades for sale, from Super Fine Tippy Golden Flowery Orange Pekoe to Orange Pekoe to fannings, plus an equally long list of grades for CTC. It was even more onerous to think of investors trying to internalize the lengthy list of descriptive adjectives, from *chesty* to *wiry* to *biscuity,* used in the tasting sessions that traditionally preceded outcry auctions, or trying to understand the numbers in the paper auction catalogs.

In the outcry system, the price of each and every tea had to be discovered individually, even if this meant facilitating parallel exchanges that went beyond the classic image of pure market exchange emblematized in open outcry auctioning. For decades, Kolkata brokerage houses have not just sold tea for plantation companies; they have also helped to finance tea production itself, providing advances on sales. Brokers also arranged the preparation and dispatch of samples of each tea to buyers deemed eligible. Eligibility for samples was based on the frequency with which prospective buyers participated in the auction and the amount they bought. After sale, brokers (especially in Kolkata and Siliguri) routinely extended buyers a generous "prompt period" of thirteen to fifteen days—essentially a gap between sale and final payment. Most important, perhaps, when brokers acted as auctioneers, they could facilitate the practice of lot splitting, whereby two buyers could each agree to take a portion of a single lot. This not only permitted buyers with limited capital to participate but also helped the brokers ensure that they sold as many lots in the catalog as possible.

For brokers devoted to the outcry system, attending to each lot of tea in the catalog individually was essential to getting quality prices. As the director of the Calcutta Tea Traders Association told me:

> The auction is time sensitive, and you need to know the outcome immediately because it will determine how you bid on the next lot. You don't find out the outcome of your railway booking the next day. You want to know if you got that ticket immediately. You need it then, otherwise you would make other plans. What happens if it's not available? Like tea, if you don't get a particular lot, you need to make other plans because you have a set amount of tea you need and often at a certain price, if not an average price.

Outcry price discovery thus depended on a combination of technical expertise and intimate familiarity (the collectively held embodied knowledge of buyers and brokers), as well as the classic economic motivations of supply and demand.

THE DIGITAL "MIND-SET"

Liberal economic orthodoxy, by contrast, presumes that quality prices are a prerequisite to the elaboration of free markets as well as complex financial transactions like futures contracts. Quality prices can only emerge insofar as individuals, not collectives, wield knowledge. Brokers' feelings about the value of tea had to be seen as existing *prior to* rather than *emergent within* the transactions themselves. Central to the Tea Board's reform effort was the basic liberal principle that a quality market is not a place to cultivate and share ideas but a place to act (selfishly) on already formed ideas.[33] For the sake of market quality, it was necessary to reconfigure the communicative infrastructure that governed the tea trade.[34]

The 2002 A. F. Ferguson report commissioned by the Tea Board did note that the "qualitative factors" that went into auction trading could not be ignored. Not everything could be done by computer. Still, the report found fault with nearly every practice of outcry tea auctioning. It singled out the auctions of Kolkata and Siliguri as particularly egregious violators of the auction principles surrounding price discovery. The report stated that the "pressure on all auction room participants to 'complete' the catalog for the day . . . somewhat *dilutes* the quality of the price discovery process."[35] The time-honored practice of lot splitting was even more threatening to market quality, "since it *technically* permits *some* (though not all) buyers to buy their entire requirement of tea without making a single (winning) bid.[36] Even if lot splitting benefited smaller buyers, this problem could be easily solved "*by having 'market oriented' lot sizes*," or, in other words, standardizing the weights and grades on offer.[37] Perhaps more important, the "broker's role as auctioneer and as financier" needed to be "delinked." For the consultants at A. F. Ferguson, the long "prompt periods" given to buyers and the generous advances given to sellers "make[s] the North Indian auction system vulnerable to the potential risk of default."[38]

Even given this harsh criticism, brokers—especially those in Kolkata and Siliguri—managed to resist the calls to turn from outcry auctioning to digital trading. Throughout the early 2000s, they rejected teauction.com and subsequent schemes, and they held fast to their tradition of extending credit to producers and buyers. After all, given that they were "guaranteed" brokers, defaults seemed unlikely.

Then, in 2009, seven years after the publication of the original Ferguson report, Carritt Moran, one of Kolkata's oldest and biggest brokerage houses, folded amid a financial crisis related to unreimbursed advances.[39] In the aftermath of the Carritt Moran default, the remaining brokerage houses were rapidly pushed into the adoption of a "spot payment" or "cash-and-carry" system. A. F. Ferguson consultants were hired to design this system.[40] With its regulatory arm fearful of more defaults, the Tea Board could now revive the experiment in electronic auctioning that had begun with teauction.com.

The Tea Board bureaucrat I interviewed in 2009, on the eve of the rollout of this latest digital auction, explained that while teauction.com had encouraged a voluntary shift to digital trading, it was clear in the wake of its failure that the shift had to be mandatory. The Tea Board's 2005 attempt to mandate electronic auctioning had been undermined by faulty software purchased by the Tea Board from the transnational computer giant IBM.[41] In 2007, the Tea Board contracted the Indian National Stock Exchange

Information Technology (NSE-IT) department to redesign the auction platform. As the bureaucrat explained:

> From our failed attempt, we learned that one should not drive the proposed auction system on an overwhelming desire to get a consensus, because there are so many different stakeholders. We have the producers [plantations]. Then we have the brokers, or the auctioneers. We have the warehouse keepers. We have the buyers. And after buyers, post-auction, we have a system of traders. And different parties have different conflicting interests. The interest of the sellers [plantations] is completely different from the interest of the buyers. So, there will never be a consensus.

She was sure that this attempt at digitization was going to work, even if it had to be unilaterally imposed.

> These buyers ... they can't accept change ... and they are *unscrupulous.* The computerized system will be inherently better because it will be impartial. These buyers all go to lunch with each other and then come back into the auction room. How can that lead to fair prices? They are far too friendly with each other. [The brokers] say that the auction is so personalized; that it is vibrant, exciting. But it needs to be impersonal. The computer is impartial.[42]

Depersonalizing the auction required what the 2002 Ferguson report called "a mind-set change."

In place of a communicative infrastructure that attuned brokers' concerns to the fates of specific, particular lots of tea, the digital auctioning platform would set up a method for attuning them to generic, interchangeable lots of tea. The digital platform was explicitly designed to limit the kinds of information available and the kinds of communicative exchanges that could take place. To do this, the digital platform created preset "price scenarios." Scenarios are, as Melinda Cooper explains with respect to weather risk markets, the elaboration of "multiple future worlds, attendant on alternative actions in the present."[43] Scenarios work experimentally and imaginatively as much as they do technically: they force participants to prepare for events, from crop failures to pandemic emergencies to the prospect of being outbid, that have not yet happened but that potentially could.[44] Instead of linear, one-lot-at-a-time pricing, the digital platform relied on a "parallel incremental" pricing model in which several lots—potentially an entire catalog— would be placed up for sale at once. Each buyer would have to react to a slew of anonymous, generic competitors rather than to particular adversaries. The "mind-set change" effected in price scenarios is temporal. Whereas the outcry auction tuned brokers to a fixed past (comparing each tea in a given sequence to those that had come before, in previous auctions, previous seasons, or previous years), price scenarios tune brokers to an uncertain future.

THE ELECTRONIC EXPERIMENT

The first day of the digital CTC dust auction in May 2009 started like any other. A few minutes before 8:00 in the morning, I walked up to the steel gates of Nilhat House and past dozens of buyers huddled around the dhabas outside the compound, cigarettes in one hand, earthenware teacups in the other. I greeted each of the guards while the brokers and other officials streamed up the marble steps to the auction rooms. But the large CTC auction hall was almost empty, except for two unfamiliar young men standing where the auctioneers should have been. At each empty seat were black laptops. Brokers were milling about outside. Groups of brokers from J. Thomas and other firms had come just to watch.

"What's going on?," I asked a couple of buyers who were standing in the corner and lighting fresh cigarettes, right at 9:00 a.m., when the auction was supposed to start.

"We will go in when we are ready," one responded with a harrumph. "They are trying to replace us with, with—those *things*!," he said, motioning back to the auction room with disgust. The lanky, soft-spoken, and well-respected director of the CTTA had rushed over from his office a few blocks away to usher everyone inside. The brokers tried one last time to convince him that the digital auction was a waste of time. They should just continue with the outcry auction. But the director said that neither he nor they had a choice. This change was sent down from the Tea Board.

The buyers went in but would not sit down. Two young technicians from the NSE-IT department tried to reassure the crowd: "It will work this time.... We have worked out the kinks." With eye rolls and crossed arms, the sea of middle-aged men sat down.

Without prompting, one of the older brokers said, "Years of experience and knowledge, just *tsssss*!" He blew air through his teeth, making a sound like steam hissing from a kettle, and flipped his hand in disgust toward the open computer in front of him. After the technicians went around and ensured that each of the brokers had signed in with his unique password, the auction began, just after 10:00 a.m.

Immediately, thirty-six lots came up at once. Screams and hollers came from the audience.

"What?"

"Why is the whole catalog up?"

"Just take your time and bid," the technicians reassured them.

"I don't know how to bid!"

"It won't take my bid!"

"You have to explain everything!"

"Who's the highest bidder?"

The older buyer I was sitting with was trying to buy tea. He put in a high bid but did not get the lot he wanted. He called the technicians over. "It's not me! It's not me!" He pointed to the screen. "Its New Tea Centre [another buyer]. Where did *my* bid *go?*"

His friend shut the hood of his laptop and pulled out a bag of bhuja, offering him some. Other buyers in front of us were already back at the buyer log-in screen. "It's like bidding in a vacuum. Nobody knows what is going on and that is the way they want it."

One day, during one of the many technological failures that hampered these early experiments, I was talking with two large CTC buyers. One of them said of my research, "All of this must be interesting for your thesis, but it is not so much about tea—it's about *human interactions.*"

The digital auction replaced the linear structure of the auction catalog and the one-lot-at-a-time sequential order with a website that flashed multiple *random* lots at one time, for which buyers had one minute to bid. This led to outrage in the auction hall, but according to Tea Board officials I interviewed, this randomness was instituted to prevent buying "with market trends."

"It has been proven," one Tea Board official told me, drawing vaguely on behavioral economic theory, "that when people don't know what is coming up next, they buy more, and at higher prices." She added:

> We are ensuring the anonymity of the buyer. . . . In fact, we also wanted anonymity of the seller as well, but anonymity of sellers [is] not working out, because teas are in many cases identified by the mark, by the garden name. But, you know, the big gardens, they have a brand name, but the small factories which may also produce good tea because of the brand name, or lack of brand name, they don't get a very good price. So we decided it would be

good to judge a tea only by its *quality,* not by the brand name, but that was resisted. So we said, "Okay, to begin with, let us not have anonymity of seller." But we are insisting on anonymity of the buyer because somebody, just to spite someone, if they see the name of the buyer, just to spite that buyer, they will put a price that is low. These things may happen, so the anonymity of the buyer is extremely important.

This shift in the structure of price discovery was, as A. F. Ferguson made clear, a test, designed to effect a mind-set change. The brokers who were involved in those early electronic auctions were, whether they liked it or not, subjects of a grand experiment in the economics of market quality. In the digital scenario, brokers were being asked to take individual responsibility for their bids and, above all, to keep silent. With no time for open discussion, brokers' knowledge was embodied in a new way.

That new form of embodiment was punctuated by the crunch of bhuja, imitations of tea kettles, and spontaneous outbursts of emotion. Later in the proceedings, a roar of laughter came over part of the room. The high bid for a lot of low-grade CTC was currently at 10,000 rupees per kilogram (about $225 at the time) instead of the 100 rupees at which it was valued. The current high bidder screamed, "I withdraw the bid!! I withdraw the bid!!" This plea, however, could not be answered. The broker up front just shrugged and shared in the chuckle.

On the other side of the room, error messages rolled over buyers' screens, warning that they must only enter bids in increments higher than negative-5.

"Of course, this is what we are doing!," one buyer yelled out, pointing at his screen.

"Just try it again," one of the tech guys said.

"Can *you* do it?," the buyer fired back.

I moved to the back of the room and sat with a broker from Contemporary Tea Brokers. He just looked at me and shook his head. Two buyers in front of us called a tech guy over. "We want to split this lot. How do we do it?"

"Oh, you can't do that like that," he answered.

"But it says 'share quantity.' I want to share." The buyers became angry when the tech guy explained that the computer would decide whom they would split lots with.

As one buyer told me later, "You don't want to split a lot with your competitors. Then you would have the same tea, and you would help him lock it in at a lower price. You only split with your allies, not your competitors."

FIGURE 12. A server crash during the rollout of the e-auction, May 2009. Photo by author.

For buyers, it was the ability to communicate within the space of the auction hall that ensured "transparency." One buyer explained, "[In the outcry system] you know what everyone's bids are, who has the highest, who is in the running for a particular tea and then who got it at what price and everyone is recording it simultaneously on their catalog. The e-auction system is hidden, it's anonymous. You only know the highest bid. The second highest bidder is the only buyer you can split with."

As usual, the staff came around midway through the auctions with tea and biscuits. There were snickers from the buyers about how the refreshments wouldn't fit on their desks, which were now crowded with the computers. Then, one by one, everyone received an error message on their screen saying, "Connection lost." Within a minute, everyone was offline (figures 12 and 13).

"Log back on, log back on," the tech guys told the buyers, until a representative from the Tea Board called to say that "the server crashed in Kullu" and that they would have to do the whole morning's work all over again. The room erupted in yelling and slamming of computers and catalogs. Buyers rushed the brokers' podium and surrounded the tech guys.

FIGURE 13. Laptops stacked up in the back of the auction hall after a failed e-auction, May 2009. Photo by author.

A group of older buyers walked out, passing by the director of the CTTA, who had remained to observe the auction. The buyers joked to the director that they were going out to eat an "e-lunch."

The auction eventually came back online, momentarily. The brokers ran through a few more sets of lots, but soon error messages returned to their laptop screens. An older buyer yelled from the back, "Let's have a moment of silence for the server!" While they waited for the next reboot, some buyers played with their desktop color schemes, but they were quickly reprimanded by a tech guy roving around the room.

"They are trying to fix something that doesn't need fixing!," another buyer yelled out.

While everyone waited, the head of tea buying for one of the large multinationals, which had been diplomatically supportive of the digital auction project, started writing a list of issues to present to the Tea Board. He wanted to know what the contingency plan was "*if* this doesn't work."

One usually quiet buyer from another major corporate player in the Indian market called out to his colleague, "Tell them that they have thought about all of the fine details of plucking but not about what tea is."

What upset the brokers at Nilhat House was that digital trading was a perceived violation of an aesthetic and ethical connection between a style of trading, a style of production, and a style of consumption. Unlike commodities traders in Chicago or London, who have little material connection to the products they buy and sell, tea brokers knew tea—and tea plantations—on intimate terms.[45] The sensory aspects of soils and waters, as well as of aromas and flavors, were as important as the process of calling out lots, splitting lots, and jockeying for particular grades. Brokers felt that tea's idiosyncrasies (the flushes, regions, and grades that caused daily differentiation and took them a career to master) made it a bad fit for a valuation practice based on the spontaneous and individual (rather than collective and recursive) application of embodied knowledge.

The Tea Board and its consultants, on the other hand, felt that the digital price discovery system simply required an attitude adjustment, a change of individual mind-set. In their view, there was no particular reason the auctions even needed to occur in a dedicated auction room. After all, the original model for this particular experiment in digital auctioning was a web-based platform, teauction.com. Whereas outcry auctions draw a small community together within a discrete, shared social and ecological space, generalized price scenarios organize large numbers of people over a vast scale. These people need to share nothing but a desire either to buy or to sell tea. In the course of the experiment, however, brokers and buyers felt not so much a mind-set change as the destruction of the relationship between knowledge, thing, and price. Knowledge about tea was no longer arbitrated *within* the transaction but *outside* it.

Slowly, however, brokers did begin attuning themselves to the digital system. By late August 2009, I noticed that instead of mild protest and tardy attendance, many buyers were positioned behind their computers before the auction started. They would stare at the screen as four lots came up at a time. (Though A. F. Ferguson had recommended that the entire catalog appear at once, the brokers had managed to bargain to have smaller sets appear, in a modified version of the parallel-incremental bidding structure.) Despite the demands by the Tea Board and the NSE-IT tech guys for silence during the auction, you could still hear some buyers mutter "Out" under their breath when lots went unsold. Some rebellious buyers continued to joke about this regulation. One buyer put his finger to his mouth, gratuitously shushing the room. Another buyer yelled out, "No talking in the auction hall!" Others meandered around and visited each other (in these conversations, the linguistic medium was now more likely to be Bengali or Hindi than English), but for the most part, they were participating as the model dictated. Day by day, the chatter diminished.

Silence was essential to a test whose purpose was, to quote Callon and Muniesa once again, to both "clarify the functioning of the market and act on its organization."[46] Through the rule of silence and the attunement to anonymous bids, these early tests of the digital auction sought to coax the rational economic actors that consultants like those from A. F. Ferguson saw as "naturally" latent within the otherwise gregarious, collegial group of buyers and brokers.[47]

THE POLITICS OF MARKET QUALITY

The making of a market—any market—is always a political act. The Tea Board's interest in the tea auction can be explained in part as an effort to preserve it. When the move toward digital trading began in the early 2000s, Indian tea was increasingly being sold outside the auction system. The shift to direct, nonauction trading began in earnest after a 2001 amendment to the Tea Marketing Control Order (TMCO), a national law regulating the industry. On its initial passage in 1984, clause 17 of the TMCO required that the vast majority of tea be sold through one of India's six major auction centers. The 2001 amendment relaxed this requirement, in line with a series of liberal, free-market reforms undertaken in India beginning with the country's economic "opening up" in 1991. While direct trading or private sales initially encompassed mostly specialty, fair trade, or single-origin tea, the auction began to rapidly lose market share after the 2001 liberalization of clause 17.[48]

Auctions remained the trading point for most mass-market tea, but by the time of my fieldwork, nearly half was sold by other means. To keep a regulatory hand in the industry, the Tea Board needed to intervene in the auction: to establish that this "time-tested system" still had "inherent advantages" over private sales, including efficiency, timeliness of payment, regularity of supply, and centrality of organization.[49] The overarching goal of the reforms, then, was to get more tea into auctions. Paradoxically, the Tea Board—a government bureaucracy—used the transparency and free markets promised in the digital auction model to reassert control of the circulation of Indian tea. The reengagement of the Tea Board's regulatory arm in the auctions reflects an important aspect of trade liberalization in India, namely, the tendency of the state to take an active role in the country's move into a global speculative economy.[50]

Buyers, brokers, and sellers alike all told me—with different degrees of sarcasm, support, and criticism—that the e-auction was a step (or a stumble) toward a realization of "Digital India." As the director of the CTTA told me, "IT has unwarranted hegemony in India. If you ask for an ambulance, they won't give it to you, but if you ask for ten computers, they will give you twenty. India will support anything having to do with IT." He continued, "The Tea Board thinks that we are fighting this because we are afraid to lose our jobs. This is not the case." He was insulted that the Tea Board would think of them as so self-serving and narrow-minded. "We are not criminals," he told me, but still the Tea Board continued to "look down on" his members.

The digitization of the tea auction highlighted a clash between not only two technologies but also two kinds of middle-class male subjects. On one side stood brokers, with their esoteric numbered forms, ritualistic language, and gentlemanly habitus that signaled a secret hangover of colonial authority. On the other stood computer-savvy, internet-connected entrepreneurs, who, as wielders of digital information (information that might one day allow them to invest in the future price of an undifferentiated, untasted pile of leaves), harbored a new form of secrecy. One kind of expert seemed to be replacing the other.

Perhaps attuned to this shift in the locus of expertise, just as the digital auction was being revived in 2009, private firms began offering aspiring young brokers a new product: training in tea tasting and valuation. In institutions from the Birla Institute of Management and Futuristic Studies (a subsidiary of the Birla tea company) to Assam Agricultural University, students could purchase lessons in the secrets of tea tasting, preparing to enter a reformed auction system based on standardized scenarios that would welcome a greater number of participants, especially now that those participants were properly imagined less as colleagues than as competitors. It appears, then, that brokers' collectively honed knowledge has been repackaged as a commodity unto itself, yet the repackaging of knowledge as a fungible commodity is rarely so seamless.[51] While neoliberal theorists have drawn on Michael Polanyi's notion of tacit knowledge—knowledge held and passed on without explicit learning—in science to argue that rational economic orders must emerge through spontaneous actions, the Tea Board's move to foment a spontaneous relationship between price and knowledge actually required a great deal of governmental and nongovernmental planning.

The experiment, or "market test," I described above was one part of a plan not only to encourage more participation in the auction but also to shift the trade from a "forward market," in which financiers like J. Thomas gave advances to producers on prospective sales, to a speculative market in futures contracts. As Donald MacKenzie has argued, the futures market is an apt site for seeing how theories about the disentanglement of commodities—a stripping away of the particularities of quality based on production—get put into action.[52] Futures markets rely on a standardized notion of price and of the things (e.g., grain, cotton, or coffee) being priced. This disentangling brings commodities into a rational trading infrastructure. As MacKenzie notes, it is difficult to convince speculators who know nothing about tea (or coffee or grain) to invest, however, unless the auctions that allocate those commodities are already well established as rational cash-and-carry spot markets. The story of Indian tea's resistance to financialization shows how such standardization requires not just a disentangling of commodities at the level of productive infrastructure but also a reworking of the communicative infrastructure of trading itself.

It also bears out Mazzarella's observation that digital technologies in India deployed in the project of stemming corruption and unmasking secrecy often produce their own kinds of opacities.[53] Even though the digital platform would (theoretically) invite more participation by more traders, in the early tests of the platform, it was big buyers like Tata and Hindustan Unilever who dominated. Buyers described the outcry auction, on the other hand, as a space where mom-and-pop tea operations could compete with these corporations. While small buyers were cautious, large corporations continued to buy amid the turmoil. "The e-auction," one large corporate buyer told me, sitting in the foyer outside the CTC hall,

> privileges the big buyers. They have the ability to put a low bid on all of the lots and can see what they get. Small buyers can't do that. They have to bid one lot at a time. They can't get stuck with five extra lots. The big buyers don't even like it, but they have no choice but to participate. They need the tea. The outcry system is far more competitive because more buyers are competing on the lots. With the e-auction this has decreased.

One reason the new digital system favored big buyers like him was that a company could have a primary buyer and four subsidiaries participating in an auction. This allows multiple agents from the larger companies, all acting on behalf of one corporation, to log on together in each auction to buy tea. "But that's not fair. It totally goes against the whole spirit of this," he said, pointing to the auction room.

By the time I returned to Nilhat House in 2016, a Pan-India auction had been launched. Under the Pan-India auction model, buyers were no longer required to limit their bidding to the auction center (e.g., Kolkata, Cochin, or Siliguri) in which they were registered. Once registered with a center, a buyer could bid anywhere. In the previous year, the Tea Board had pushed to amend the TMCO once more, this time to raise the percentage of tea that growers were legally required to sell at auction to 70 percent. Growers resisted, and the number was finally lowered to 50 percent—still higher than it had been after the 2001 liberalization of clause 17. The result of the opening up of buying and the fifty-fifty split between auction sales and direct sales was, for many, a disaster. As Prabhat Bezboruah, chairman of the Tea Board of India, told the trade journal *World Tea News* in 2017, "Because of the freedom they enjoy buyers are gaming the system to drive down prices in auctions. They don't bid for their entire requirement in auctions, and then they buy cheaper directly from the estate at auction benchmark price."[54]

"IT WAS SO MUCH LIKE A MARKET"

In response to these rapid shifts in the landscape of auctioning, brokerage houses have been left in an uncertain position. No longer able to act as financiers due to the cash-and-carry rules and not content to let new schools like the Birla Institute of Management overtake their traditional niche in tasting and valuation, firms like J. Thomas have expanded their consultancy departments. I discussed the consultancy work with Mr. Agarwal one day in summer 2016. We were in his office, yelling over the thumping of his air-conditioner.

Whereas J. Thomas had long marketed the collective expertise of its tasters to tea sellers, its consultancy was aimed at buyers. Mr. Agarwal called this consulting work "organoleptic checking." Buyers would send samples of tea, whether individual lots or blends, and J. Thomas would verify that the markings on the sale sheet matched the tea in the samples. An example of this consulting work was J. Thomas's contract with the Indian army, "a huge market—a market sector unto itself." The army was paying J. Thomas to taste potential "supply blends" in order to help select the CTC blend that would be distributed to every army base. J. Thomas brokers would examine each potential supply blend in an attempt to satisfy the diverse tastes of soldiers from a variety of regional, ethnic, and socioeconomic backgrounds. "It's a hell of a challenge," Mr. Agarwal told me excitedly. "You can't treat one guy or group to his favored tea and not another. It is a heterogeneous market that became a homogeneous market." I asked if this kind of organoleptic checking was something that J. Thomas did for other clients. "Yes, of course," he replied. "We will do anything if they pay us. What we are doing is helping the buyer realize that *value* is important."

The last outcry auction took place on June 14, 2016. I asked Megha, who was the no. 3 broker on stage for the J. Thomas sale that day, about her experience.

"It was heartbreaking," she told me. "You got to know everyone and have this personal relationship. With the e-auction, you don't really know what is happening." A couple of weeks later, while we were sitting in the newly digital Darjeeling auction, Megha said, "It is so quiet. And there are so many fewer people in here. It's bad, isn't it? It used to be so lively, exciting. It's so sad now. It was so much like a market."

Like the efforts to dismantle the plantation I described in the previous chapter, the move to digitize the tea market was essentially an attempt to resolve a contradiction produced by colonial tea production. Both plantations and the outcry auction had once been tools for ensuring market expansion and order, but by the dawn of the twenty-first century, they had become obstacles to just these goals.

The shift to scenario-based price discovery links Indian tea industry reform to broader discussions of the social contexts of technological change in global finance, as well as to other technoscientific changes in the global economy of nature and numbers, from biodefense to epidemiology to climate change models.[55] Putting models into practice through scenarios is a prerequisite to the implementation of new forms of surveillance and control in the future, but it is also central to the elaboration of new kinds of market relationships in the present. Price scenarios work to turn environmental commodities like tea—fickle, particular, and shifting, like pathogens, air, and water—into potential financial instruments.

To conceive of finance as an anthropological object, then, we must think about the physical dismantling of auction houses as much as about the physical opening up of gold mines or hydraulically fractured shale formations. At an even broader level, attention to the technologies of market opening puts the anthropology of finance into dialogue with ethnographic approaches to modernity and infrastructure, which are already rich in attention to how planning accounts for (or ignores) spontaneity and "leakage."[56] Leakages, whether they are what literally flows out of pipe crevices or the outbursts of traders who "don't know what's coming up next," are as common in auctions as in city water systems.

To understand efforts to financialize fields and factories, we must understand how those efforts resonate with similar moves to transform a more hidden communicative infrastructure of price composition in places like the tasting and auction rooms of Nilhat House. Such an analysis enables the anthropology of finance to join studies of environment and development by critically engaging megaprojects that do not take the form of dams, roads, or other modernist structures. Digitization has come along with bold pronouncements about the beginning of the end of the plantation system, with its variable geographies, esoteric factory processing procedures, and archaic labor process. The taste of tea in the broadest sense—its association with refinement but also with enlightened liberal values—is at stake.

The push to expand the digital auction continues, not least because online sales have taken off elsewhere during the past five years. The Tea Board is trying to meld the ethic of speed and seamlessness that marks direct trading with the quality assurance offered by the auction. A growing number of direct traders, who use the internet to cultivate buyers in Europe and America, continue to circumvent the auction, meaning that the high prices Tea Board officials envisioned for the digital auction have not yet materialized. The Tea Board's continued push to get more tea into the auctions is part of a broader attempt to keep tea palatable in India, both politically and socially.

Even though digital auctioning has now fully replaced outcry auctions, brokers and buyers have continued to gather in the auction rooms of sites like Nilhat House and the Siliguri Tea Auction Committee. At STAC in 2016, I asked Mr. Mistri, a buyer whose family firm had been operating in Siliguri since the 1960s, why he still showed up at the auction. Mr. Mistri answered that he was afraid that if brokers and buyers did not show up, the Tea Board would lock STAC up and never let them back in. He made a sign with his hand mimicking a lock and key. As a small buyer, he felt that he had to keep showing up. One reason was practical. Here, there were fewer power cuts and no server problems. In the office, Mr. Mistri would have to make sure that he had backups of power and memory. His was not a big operation.

A more important reason Mr. Mistri kept showing up was that small buyers like him did not have access to preauction tea samples. They needed to be able to speak informally with others, as well as with the brokers. "Here," he explained, "I can see if [the broker] will drop the price a little bit. You can still talk to him. In my office, I can't talk to him and have an idea of what he is thinking in terms of what he needs for a selling price." Even though the digital trading platform only gave him one minute to think about his bid, if he was present at STAC—and if others kept showing up—Mr. Mistri could, in his way, partake in a bit of that collective thinking. Like Megha, he was already nostalgic for the old system. "You saw it, right?," he asked me. "The screaming and shouting. . . . It was so much fun. But I still come, so that I can see people."

Conclusion

THE ENDURANCE OF QUALITY

"NOBODY IS FOCUSING ON QUALITY," the CEO of the online retailer TeaTime told me over a cup of tea in Siliguri. He had agreed to an interview because he wanted to explain his company's take on the state of the trade. He summarized, "In the value chain, everyone takes a margin[,] . . . everyone is an intermediary." An excess of intermediaries, he continued, created an obstacle to "freshness," which, for TeaTime, was at the root of quality. He explained, "For two hundred years, nobody paid any attention to freshness. It takes at least six months for tea to reach consumers. Sometimes, even a year. People are drinking old tea as soon as they get it. This is because everyone is an intermediary. It is not their job to care about the freshness of the tea, or really to care about the consumer's experience." To achieve freshness, TeaTime was introducing innovations in packaging. It sealed every tea it sold in vacuum bags within forty-eight to seventy-two hours of manufacture. It then put these bags in cold storage to prevent damage from what the CEO described—echoing the words of the brokers I had met in the auctions—as tea's "four enemies": moisture, sunlight, oxygen, and heat.

According to the CEO, TeaTime's direct sales approach and packaging technology were intended to yield benefits that would not only be apparent to discerning consumers, but that would also "percolate down" to plantation workers. By buying directly from plantations, TeaTime claimed that it could pay growers 20 percent to 30 percent more than other buyers. When producers are paid more, the CEO went on, "consumers get more value" in the form of "higher quality and fresher tea." Quality of tea and quality of life were connected, on both ends of the value chain.

"TeaTime" is a pseudonym, but the company's approach is representative of a common understanding of quality in the tea market and in many other commodity markets. Specialty tea retailers and enthusiasts increasingly see the improvement in the quality of workers' lives as commensurable with their pursuit of high-quality tea. Over the past decade, I have had many opportunities to talk with those who work in this specialty market. Before these audiences, my stories about plantation sickness, auction reforms, and the entrenched colonial legacies of the plantation are often met with interest, but they are also frequently met with boundary marking. Citing its reputation for poor quality, many specialty buyers in the United States and Europe are quick to tell me that *they* don't buy Dooars tea; they only buy tea of quality. Players in the specialty market have even less sympathy for tea brokers and bureaucrats. Even before the Tea Board of India began pushing for reforms to auctions in the early 2000s, many specialty retailers had already concluded that auctions, whether digital or outcry, were becoming obsolete. They preferred to buy directly from nonauction intermediaries like TeaTime.

Those working on the specialty side of the industry are not unique. Quality can easily seem like the thing that is missing from contemporary capitalist markets. It's hard to find fresh food, just as it's hard to find a mobile phone, or a computer, or an air-conditioner that lasts more than a year or two—even if you can get these things with remarkable speed. Readers of this book are probably all too aware that an emphasis on disposability over durability, on portability over freshness, or on cheapness over dearness *can* have negative implications for the workers who bring commodities into being. To be sure, disposability, portability, and cheapness are qualities unto themselves, but in increasingly fragmented value chains, linking these qualities meaningfully to worker well-being seems harder and harder to do. Proponents of technological innovations like online storefronts and vacuum packaging often see quality as something added, something new that must be brought in from the outside. They portray the pursuit of quality as a way of liberating select consumers, conscientious retailers, and even some laborers from the entrenched systems of provision in which they find themselves. In fact, many of the scientists, bureaucrats, brokers, and planters I encountered in the archives and in my ethnographic work shared the TeaTime CEO's exasperation. They, too, in one way or another, lamented that nobody was focusing on quality.

As I have argued in this book, quality is far from a highbrow concern. Notions of quality are lodged not just in the rarefied, high-end, or "ethical" teas sold for their distinction, but in the words, numbers, laboratory techniques, and labor practices that are maintained by those supposedly superfluous "intermediaries" and, of course, by low-wage laborers themselves. Companies like TeaTime are not introducing the work of "qualification" or "requalification" to the tea market.[1] That work has been vital to the tea industry from the beginning, and it continues to matter even in the production of the lowest-cost blended tea bags.

Across time and space, between colonial and postcolonial production, plantation and auction house, bureaucratic office and laboratory, experiments with quality have formed the connective tissue of the tea industry. Most such experiments have been carried out in the service not of producing unique, specialized goods and consumptive experiences but in the service of producing reliable, everyday, seemingly interchangeable ones: the "nice cuppa" of British afternoons, the cooling glass of iced tea on the back porch in the Alabama summertime, or the "diplomatic negotiation" of sweetness and bitterness produced in an Iranian grandmother's kitchen.[2] My somewhat counterintuitive suggestion has been that quality is actually most politically salient, and most theoretically compelling, when it is invoked and operationalized in the name of reproducing those reliable, routine, if also comforting and normalizing, affective and sensory states.

Quality is an essential—if ineffable and elusive—component of the market for cheap, mass-market products. Quality is constantly being reproduced and rediscovered in fields, factories, laboratories, tasting rooms, and auction halls. From the colonial period to the present, the pursuit of quality has been the ground and justification for everything from the rollout of new machinery to the passage of labor laws to the funding of chemical research to rural land reform. Laborers, managers, scientists, and brokers put in a great deal of work to coax quality out of bushes; to make quality present in the right combination of molecules, numbers, or words; and to ensure that bodies, materials, and markets exude quality.

Quality is an internally contradictory thing. At some times and in some places, it has connoted singularity, and at other times and in other places, it has connoted standardization. In many instances, quality has appeared, frustratingly to some, to connote both. Quality is one of those concepts for which, as the cultural and literary critic Raymond Williams puts it, "the problem of its meanings seem[s] . . . inextricably bound up with the problems it [is] being used to discuss."[3] Knowing how quality is defined conceptually is important to understanding its role in commodity circulation (and in capitalism more broadly), but as I have tried to suggest in this book, it is equally important to understand how quality is produced: how it is rendered into a workable problem. One implication of this is that quality—like democracy, fairness, freedom, or justice—while easily invoked as a universal good, does not index a uniform set of experiences or values.[4] If we want to understand how quality is produced, I suggest that we must understand it as an experimental undertaking.

In industrial systems, quality is often viewed as a problem of "control." Evidence suggests, however, that industrial managers achieve quality control not by insisting on the rigid repetition of the same series of assembly-line tasks but by experimenting. For example, Alex Blanchette shows how the designers of industrial hog farms in the American Midwest portray those farms as "greenfields," business-speak for uncarved blocks of potential. "The result of this frontier-like agricultural space [is] a series of experiments," from interventions in human resource management to artificial insemination techniques to new uses for the carcasses of pigs themselves.[5] These experiments occur alongside the production of reliably standardized meats, oils, and leathers.

Experimental systems succeed, as Hans-Jörg Rheinberger writes, when they manage to "[elicit] differences without destroying reproductive coherence."[6] An experimental system is held together by two competing ends: the ability of a process to be replicated over and over again and the tendency of that same process to achieve unexpected or surprising results. Like factory or farm complexes, the laboratory experiments described by Rheinberger are highly structured yet open-ended. In India, as the chapters in this book describe, an experimental system has emerged to link an "interrelated set of devices," from teacups to test tubes, "forms of practice and organization," including agricultural experimental stations and brokerage firms, "and conceptual frames," such as glossaries and chemical models.[7] This system aims to achieve replicability on a mass scale, reducing tea's "natural variability" to a short list of chemical constituents, words, and prices. Thanks to changes in climate, the overuse of pesticides, and labor unrest on plantations, however, participants in this system are constantly discovering new dimensions of quality.

It is important to recognize that the question of *who* gets to experiment with quality and, indeed, whose work is "qualified" to count as productive of quality is itself highly contingent on race, gender, and class. The TeaTime CEO's vision of quality was as a more-or-less-than proposition. His company's narrative was dripping with the Michael Pollan-esque notion that by showing consumers what good tea is, right-thinking intermediaries could convince them to make better choices—choices that would be better for tea producing environments and the people working within them.[8] In this view, connoisseurs understand what quality is, and it is connoisseurs—and a proliferation and democratization of connoisseur-style knowledge and appreciation of tea—that will save the industry.

But connoisseurship alone is not enough to ensure the existence and persistence of quality for tea. Drawing on the jargon of techno-innovation common in Silicon Valley, TeaTime's CEO described his company as a "disruptor." In business, "disruption" has come to stand for a kind of radical experimentation, one that intervenes temporally and spatially in the operations of a given market. It connotes an end to history, an acute event, a paradigm shift. One genealogy of the term places its origins in mid-1990s business practices whereby cheaper alternatives disrupted the market share of established companies, but today, disruption has become the stated purpose of almost any techno-fix.[9] Across the popular press, we learn how Silicon Valley is "disrupting" everything from death to city planning to philanthropy. Market takeover is material evidence of disruption. Think Uber over taxis, Netflix over video rental stores.

TeaTime sits alongside other disruptive efforts to join the impulse to "do good" in the world, particularly in the Global South, with the remunerative imperative to "do well" by investors.[10] As Jill Lepore notes, "The rhetoric of disruption—a language of panic, fear, asymmetry, and disorder—calls on the rhetoric of another kind of conflict, in which an upstart refuses to play by the established rules of engagement, and blows things up."[11] TeaTime's talk of disruption is of a piece with other efforts to change the landscape of technology, development, and trade using high-tech tools, but it is also consistent with the longer history of experimentation I have recounted in the preceding chapters. The establishment of brokerage firms in India, the funding of biochemical research in labs and experimental plots in Assam and London, the expansion of warehouses in Calcutta, the recruitment of Indians into brokerage firms, and the extension of tea's monoculture off of the plantation—all were attempts to shake loose an entrenched way of producing and circulating tea with an eye to extracting more capital from tea and the land underneath it as resources. These efforts—each of them experimental in different ways—were all attempts to resolve a pair of contradictions that have posed problems for India's tea industry since its inception.

The first contradiction is the ecological one between perishability and perenniality. As soon as tea leaves are plucked from bushes, they start to decay, as the TeaTime CEO reminded me. Tea is a perishable product, but it is derived from a perennial crop. A single tea bush is not cut down from year to year at harvest time, as with sugarcane or cotton. Instead, a tea bush remains productive for sixty years or more. Unlike perennial crops such as wine and coffee, which are harvested annually, tea is picked nearly weekly, for ten to eleven months a year. The plantation—perhaps the original experiment in producing "quality" tea—was designed to both hedge against perishability and ensure perenniality. As I discussed in chapter 3, Indian tea displaced Chinese tea on the market in the late 1800s. Popular explanations for why this happened laud the technological innovations ushered in by British entrepreneurs: mechanized factories, coal-based production, vertical integration, and so on. As the historian Andrew Liu argues, however, the central market disruption of the Indian plantation—and the reason for its triumph over the Chinese tea production system—was not its mechanization but the practices of labor indenture that preceded that mechanization. These include the conscription of tens of thousands of people and their forced displacement into the new tea-growing regions of India.[12]

This leads to the second, more economic contradiction, between liquidity and fixity. One of tea's material forms is of course liquid. Tea is consumed not as a leaf but as an infusion, and its versatility has made it globally popular. But liquidity also refers to tea's potential convertibility into cash, as well as its potential to move seamlessly from field to market, touched by as few intermediaries as possible. Even as industry actors have pushed to maximize liquidity, they find themselves obligated to establish fixity. By "fixity," I mean the entrenchment of productive infrastructures in particular places. Fixity also refers to the way in which much of what makes crops like tea viable on the market is the willingness of laborers to remain in place, and of capital to make investments that keep them there. The provision of housing and other in-kind benefits over the late nineteenth and early twentieth century established a permanent labor force that was socially and economically fixed to the plantation. After Indian independence, the rise of CTC (another disruptive techno-fix for the market) served to cement the plantation and its labor force even more firmly in place. To put it plainly, plantation labor in the tea industry is not a free, "liquid" market. Rather, jobs and the benefits that go with them are inherited, and people who work on plantations tend to put a great deal of stock in the idea that one of their descendants will also work on a plantation, albeit with an equal degree of reservation. Through fixity, tea production and social reproduction are entangled.

Fixity, then, refers to fixed capital, the machinery of the plantation, but it also refers to the system of auctioning and trading by brokers and buyers in

India that has long kept tea circulating on the market.[13] Despite attempts to sell tea (quickly) on the internet, to digitize the auction, to determine tea's chemical constituents, or to promote small grower production, one element remains fixed: the plantation. The plantation is a tentacular socioecological form—one that ramifies far beyond the fields and the factory.

Herein lies the central finding of this book, which has taken us from London to Kolkata to Assam to the Dooars to Siliguri and through auction houses, factories, and laboratories: the plantation has endured well beyond its colonial origins in large part because quality has also endured as a subject of experimentation. Ideas about what tea is supposed to look, taste, and feel like—ratified by the embodied experimentation of tasters, the chemical experimentation of laboratory scientists, and the economic experimentation of so-called land reformers in the Dooars—are critical to the plantation's persistence. Attempts to alter or improve the industry by speeding up tea's circulation or trying to move production outside of the plantation's boundaries all grossly oversimplify the role of quality in shaping India's lives and landscapes. The idea of quality continues to be rematerialized in the hardware and software of the tea industry, and in the laboring bodies of tea workers.

It seems worth thinking about what the human and environmental consequences of all this are. Amid the endurance of plantation monocultures, workers and environments have become exhausted. As I write, the extension of monoculture means that there is less food being grown, that soils are being pushed to their limits, that pesticides are being used in greater quantities, that trees are being felled and water resources tapped. In other words, the planetary changes we now associate with the Anthropocene are being ramped up, even amid the effort to reform and "modernize" the global tea industry.

Quality is the means by which resources are projected into the future. Think of "clean coal" or the conversion of brownfields into community gardens growing local, sustainable produce. Yet quality is also materialized in the pasts of resources. Next to the reclaimed brownfield, you might find a former factory reborn as a block of luxury lofts where heritage pork and artisanal cheese are being served on a table made of salvaged timber. Experiments with quality do not always lead to destruction, but they do not easily lead to liberation either. My hope is that the story of quality tea might help orient us to the complex and uncertain ways that meanings and objects make one another, and how each step toward augmentation, improvement, or valorization is undergirded by layers of qualities past.

NOTES

NOTE ON ARCHIVAL SOURCES

Manuscripts from the British Library's Indian Tea Association, London office archive (Mss Eur F174), are identified by specific file numbers preceded by "BL" (British Library).

Other British Library files are also identified by "BL" preceding the text.

Archival sources preceded by "LMA" are located at the London Metropolitan Archives.

Indian Tea Association, Calcutta office, annual bulletins are cited as "ITA Calcutta Annual Bulletin, [YEAR]."

INTRODUCTION

1. "In modern bureaucratized economies," Jane Guyer (2004, 83) explains, quality is often seen as a matter of ranking goods on "interval scales" "by formal institutions such as expert panels, trade associations, and competitions."

2. See Guthman 2014; Meneley 2007; Goodman 2003; Roseberry 1996. The market for relatively expensive (or ethically sourced) food and drink tells us much about quality. As the historian of science Steven Shapin (2016) notes, for example, quality in the wine market is enumerated in the "scores" that attempt to capture the relationship between a wine's flavor and its price. But wine's quality is also captured in what Shapin, using a term also common among tea brokers, calls "organoleptic" evaluation, which uses specific words or metaphors ("roasted lilacs," "sweaty saddles") that are intended to convey the sensory experience produced by wine (see also Manning 2012; Silverstein 2006).

3. Guyer 2004, 83.

4. Other well-known examples of such mass-market goods are South Pacific "cheap meat" (Gewertz and Errington 2010), Brazilian coffee (Reichman 2018), and American tobacco (Benson 2012).

5. As Callon, Méadel, and Rabeharisoa (2002, 200) write, "The good . . . as a configuration likely to vary in a continuous process of qualification-requalification, must be considered as an economic variable in the same way that prices are."

6. Hébert 2010, 555.

7. Callon, Méadel, and Rabeharisoa 2002, 201.

8. This is especially true of commodities produced from plants and animals. Assumptions about the cheapness or sameness of such commodities mask the fact that their material makeup and their value must be constantly composed through the violent extraction of human and nonhuman labor (Moore 2015; Patel and Moore 2017). For further discussion of the "composition" of value, see Guyer 2016.

9. The market for green tea from East Asia is not dominated by plantations, and the domestic consumption of tea in China drives production in ways that are different from those in India and other former British colonies. See Hung 2015; Zhang 2013.

10. In 2001, Calcutta was renamed "Kolkata" in line with the Bengali pronunciation. I use "Calcutta" to refer to the city before 2001 and "Kolkata" to refer to it after the name change.

11. Tea is, of course, far from the only commonplace, everyday item that comes to consumers in blended form. Often, when I talk to students and colleagues about the blending of tea, they point out that food staples like coffee, wine, milk, and Scotch whiskey are also blended. This is true, and in fact, the work of blending goes well beyond the world of food. Blending is also essential in generic drug development (Hayden 2007; Banerjee 2017), industrial chemistry (Spackman 2018b), municipal water provision (Spackman and Burlingame 2018), cigarette manufacture (Benson 2012), and even the making of perfume (Latour 2004). Blending is about achieving standardization and consistency amid an inherent variability in raw material.

12. Callon, Méadel, and Rabeharisoa (2002, 200) see this dyad as masking a more complex network of relations revolving around qualification and requalification. As Theodore Bestor (2004, 128) argues with respect to fish markets in Tokyo, "Trends of supply and demand . . . encompass the whole gamut of cultural, social, political, technological, and environmental contexts that make up food culture in the broad sense."

13. See Chatterjee 2001; Besky 2014a.

14. Karen Barad, following the work of Leela Fernandes (1997) on Kolkata jute mills, suggests that low-tech industrial settings are apt sites for understanding the "intra-active" relationship between materials and working bodies (Barad 2007, 227–30; cf. Abrahamsson et al. 2015). For more on "fixity" in tea production, see Besky 2017a. It has become nearly axiomatic in social studies of capitalism that what people come to find meaningful or special in the things they consume can never be disarticulated from their class, race, gender, or ethnicity. This crucial observation has been elaborated in Sarah Ives's (2017) study of the racial symbolism of rooibos tea in

South Africa; in Paige West's (2012) multisited look at the circulation of images of indigeneity and primitivity in Papua New Guinean coffee; and in Deborah Gewertz and Frederick Errington's (2010) examination of the market for fatty meat in Australia, New Zealand, and the Pacific islands. Historians and social scientists have traced how colonial practices of racial, gendered, and ethnic division persist in the organization of biomedicine, ecology, and engineering, as well as in visual art, architecture, and mass media (see, e.g., Bear 2007, 2015; Hecht 2012; Kale 2014).

15. Murphy 2013, 104.

16. An auction center for teas produced in Ceylon (Sri Lanka) opened in Colombo in 1883 and for East African teas in Mombasa in 1956. In addition, the Dutch East India Company and later the Dutch colonial government ran tea auctions in Amsterdam and Batavia (Jakarta) beginning in the eighteenth century. There is still a tea auction in Jakarta today. In India, five additional auction centers were set up after independence: Cochin [Kochi] (1943), Coonoor (1963), Guwahati (1970), Siliguri (1976), and Coimbatore (1981). The Tea Board of India also set up auction centers in Amritsar and Jalpaiguri, but both were closed. There was an attempt by the Tea Board of India to run a tea auction center in Singapore, but this was also unsuccessful.

17. Rappaport 2017; Liu 2015.

18. See Lutgendorf 2012 for discussion of the postindependence popularization of chai in India.

19. Mintz 1960, 1985; see also Besky 2014a; Daniel, Bernstein, and Brass 1992; Chatterjee 2001; Sharma 2011; Stoler 1985; Bass 2012; Jegathesan 2019; Willford 2014.

20. Arnold 2005; Chatterjee 2001; Daniel, Bernstein, and Brass 1992; Dey 2018; Drayton 2000; Sharma 2011.

21. Chamney 1930, 43–45; Baildon 1882, 30–34; McGowan 1860; Ukers 1935a, 297–308; Walsh 1892, 57–58; see also Ball 1848.

22. See Besky 2008, 2014a, 2014b, 2015.

23. During the nineteenth and early twentieth century, many tea plantation owners in Northeast India forcibly conscripted laborers; see Chatterjee 2001; Griffiths 1967; Sharma 2011. In Darjeeling, by contrast, workers were not forcibly conscripted. Instead, owners recruited them, mostly from Nepal, with some monetary compensation, but the bulk of their incentive was nonmonetary, including housing in what were called "labor lines" (see Besky 2014a).

24. Hybridization came with the inception of the plantation system. Jayeeta Sharma (2011) describes how under the ideological rubric "improvement," British planters sought to "civilize" the indigenous Assam jaat with Chinese botanical stock so that the plant would be more readily available for large-scale production. I discuss hybridization further in chapter 4.

25. Lutgendorf 2012; Bhadra 2005.

26. This has also been a concern in cultural studies of capitalism and commodities, beginning with the work of philosophers associated with the Frankfurt School in early twentieth-century Germany (see, e.g., Horkheimer and Adorno [1944] 1972;

Benjamin 1968). Such concerns continue to animate studies of mass culture in anthropology, particularly insofar as questions of singularity and commensurability overlap with questions of colonial order and difference (Appadurai 1996; Bhabha 1984; see also Guyer 2004).

27. See Spackman and Burlingame 2018 on water; Wahlberg 2018 on sperm banking and population; Adams 2017 and Murphy 2017 on quality of life metrics; Ferry 2013, 2016 and Calvão 2013 on minerals and metals; Hayden 2007 and Banerjee 2017 on pharmaceuticals.

28. Dabashi 2017.

29. Durkheim [1912] 1995. See also Mazzarella 2017.

30. Dabashi 2017.

31. See Appadurai 1986.

32. Mazzarella 2017.

33. Dabashi 2017.

34. Dabashi 2017.

35. Paxson 2012.

36. Weiss 2016.

37. Callon, Millo, and Muniesa 2007; Callon, Méadel, and Rabeharisoa 2002; Hébert 2014; MacKenzie 2006; LiPuma and Lee 2004; Zaloom 2006; Preda 2006; Leins 2018.

38. Mintz 1985; see also Marx [1867] 1967; Nash 1979; Taussig 1980.

39. Appadurai 1986; Clifford 1997; Marcus and Myers 1995; Steiner 1994; Hansen 2000.

40. Marcus 2005; see also Kopytoff 1986. Food studies scholars working within this framework have traced the circulation of things from coffee to curry to cocktails. See, e.g., Roseberry 1996; Ray and Srinivas 2012; Bowen 2015. My own previous work examined how Darjeeling tea, some of the most expensive tea in the world, gains and maintains its "distinction" on the global market. I argued that Darjeeling has gained its distinction among consumers as "the Champagne of teas" thanks to a history of dispossession wrought by colonial labor recruitment practices at the point of production (Besky 2014a, 2017a). I consider this book a continuation of that inquiry into the relationship between agriculture and inequality, but my approach to quality here differs in some significant respects.

41. Bestor 2004, 129; emphasis in original. I thank an anonymous reviewer for directing me to this passage. Fred Myers (2001, 6) distinguishes between qualitative and quantitative value, suggesting that the tension between them plays a formative role in structuring social action (see also Besky 2014a, 16).

42. Here, I draw on an observation by Sebastian Abrahamsson, Filippo Bertoni, Annemarie Mol, and Rebecca Ibáñez, who write about the material power of foods. They point out that Omega-3s from fish oils are not an independently active substance but "matter in relation" (Abrahamsson et al. 2015, 13). Fish oil's efficacy as a health food is not innate; rather, it is "done" in a variety of interconnected practices, from exploitative fish harvesting in the Global South to the making and marketing of pills in the Global North to experimental medical trials.

43. Murphy 2013, 104.

44. Murphy 2013. See also Nading 2017.

45. Callon, Méadel, and Rabeharisoa 2002, 212.

46. Shapin 2012, 179. Shapin calls such devices "intersubjectivity engines." Callon, Méadel, and Rabeharisoa (2002, 212) refer to them as "distributed cognition devices." See also Berenstein 2018.

47. I follow science and technology studies scholars who see experiments as entailing an "interrelated set of devices, forms of practice and organization, and conceptual frames that facilitate the making of new objects" (Jensen and Morita 2015, 83). The experimental making of new objects is perhaps even more interesting when, as in mass markets, that which is "new" to the maker must appear to the consumer as stable, familiar, and standard.

48. Callon, Méadel, and Rabeharisoa 2002, 212.

49. In any experimental system, every time a subject seems to become stabilized technologies for working on it tend to change. In other words, at the moment of stabilization, the technology becomes the subject of the experiment. See Rheinberger 1994.

CHAPTER ONE. THE WORK OF TASTE

1. See Chatterjee 2012, chap. 1.

2. "Writers" were a group of entrepreneurial emissaries working semiautonomously on behalf of the company. They went across India, looked for sources of goods, and tried to make deals, "writing" to would-be financiers to convince them to invest.

3. In 2013, in a politically controversial decision, Chief Minister of West Bengal Mamata Banerjee moved much of the secretariat across the Hooghly River.

4. R. N. Mukherjee was the Indian industrialist whose company built the most iconic monument to British imperial control in India, the Victoria Memorial, in the early 1900s.

5. A note on pseudonyms: I have not changed the names of brokerage firms, but all of the people who work in them have been given pseudonyms. Further, many of the buying companies—and all of the buyers—have been given pseudonyms. Buying companies generally are not given pseudonyms if they are rendered as only buying tea at auction (sales are public information), but they are given them if personal information is somehow conveyed in the text.

6. There are four auction categories: orthodox, CTC, CTC dust, and Darjeeling. Tastings are also organized into these categories.

7. The challenge of variability is not unique to tea brokers. Bestor (2004, 128) highlights a similar characteristic of Tokyo fish brokerage.

8. Heath and Meneley 2007, 594.

9. Callon, Méadel, and Rabeharisoa 2002, 212.

10. Shapin 2012, 177; see also Hennion 2007.

11. Bourdieu 1984.

12. S. Priyadershini 2012.

13. Bourdieu 1984.

14. See, e.g., Barad 2007; Mol 2002. The linguistic anthropologist Lily Chumley (2013, 172) has developed a similar set of ideas about evaluation, noting in her study of Chinese art schools that the assessment of students' work was simultaneously "quantifying" ("organized around a concept of standard") and "rhematizing" ("organized around a concept of personhood"). In Chumley's telling, a "disjuncture" between these regimes "can be a source of considerable anxiety for people moving from one regime to another" (cf. Gal 2005).

15. Barad 2007.

16. Shapin 2012, 177.

17. Mol 2009, 278.

18. Mol 2009, 278.

19. Bourdieu 1984; see also Latour 2004.

20. See Barad 2007, 230; Murphy 2013.

21. The study of brokers allows for an interplay in anthropological analysis between the internal organization of communities and the integration of those communities into larger systems. Eric Wolf (1956, 1075) describes brokers as people who "act as buffers between groups, maintaining the tensions which provide the dynamic of their actions."

22. The quality and condition of tea chests and warehouses have been a matter of concern since the inception of the industry. The Indian Tea Association archives were full of references to these issues. If the wood of tea chests is not properly cured or if it gets too wet, this can lead to "minty" or "cheesy" teas. The expansion of an auctioning infrastructure in India after independence required ensuring suitable warehousing space and conditions—conditions that preserved both the tea chests and the tea held inside them.

23. Shapin (2016, 440) identifies a related distinction between "taste" and "flavor": "In common vernacular, and in some expert practice, and from the distant past to the present, the notion of 'taste' tends to fold together olfactory and gustatory experiences. In more rigorous terms of technical art, the term 'flavor' is meant to encompass both olfaction and gustation, the total sensory experience of consuming … through all pertinent sensory channels—smell and taste, of course, but also chemical and temperature senses, the tactile sense and vision—and, though this is only occasionally spelled out, the role of memory, the emotions, prior beliefs, and expectations." What these rigorous technical definitions exclude is price, something that is an explicit and unavoidable part of the evaluation of tea.

24. BL Mss Eur F174/904: Cover letter from the ITA on the revised glossary (1935); see also ITA Calcutta Annual Bulletin for 1934, ix.

25. Harler 1932, 78, found in BL Mss Eur F174/904: "Glossary of Tea Tasters' Terms"; Shapin (2016) describes a similar story in his profile of Maynard Amerine, an enologist at the University of California, Davis, in the mid-twentieth century who helped devise a set of methods for the "sensory evaluation" of wine.

26. Harler 1932, 78–79. Anthropological studies of such lexicons have shown how they link agriculture, technoscience, and aesthetics "in one field" (Meneley 2007, 684; Silverstein 2006; Shankar and Cavanaugh 2012).

27. BL Mss Eur F174/904: Cover letter from the ITA on the revised glossary (1935).

28. See Ukers 1935a, 167–70, for Harler's term of service and information about the officers of the ITA Scientific Department.

29. See BL Mss Eur F174/904 for the draft revisions of the glossary from the 1930s. CTTA (ca. 2008) is the most updated version of the glossary.

30. Adrienne Lehrer's (2009) influential work overviews the social lives of wine words. Popular media, including from within the wine industry, have criticized male dominance within the communities of both wine making and sommeliers (see Denig 2016). Economists have also written extensively about the relationships between wine and value (see, e.g., Combris, Lecocq, and Visser 1997), including in the *Journal of Wine Economics*.

31. "Wine talk" has such a "performative potency" that, as Michael Silverstein (2006, 493) notes, everyday consumers come to confuse the linguistic descriptors "with the [wine] itself." In this sense, wine terms have become linguistic commodities in their own right (there are numerous best-selling books about how to learn and use wine words) (Shapin 2016; Heller 2010; Duchêne and Heller 2012). The Wine Aroma Wheel devised by Ann Noble at the University of California, Davis, is now commonly used by amateur wine enthusiasts. Noble's work was undertaken in conjunction with the American Society for Viticulture's Committee on Sensory Evaluation. According to Shapin (2016, 450), the wheel was originally "oriented to groups that were part of the wine industry, rather than to consumers, and the intention was to produce descriptive terms that were 'analytic and free of hedonic or value-judgment connotations'—that is, in their usage, objective. The hoped-for virtue of such a language was its capacity to facilitate reliable communication among winemakers, marketers, researchers, and writers, a means to eventually put in place international 'reference standards.'"

32. This mode of tying quality to words is now a central component of what Callon, Méadel, and Rabeharisoa (2002) call the "economy of qualities." As Mol (2009, 278) suggests, "Talking provides everyone with linguistic repertoires that help to refine their ability to differentiate between tastes."

33. "Tea Tasters Terms" (Serial No. 69/2) produced by Tocklai/TRA. Original July 1953, with revisions in December 1967. Xeroxed material found in ITA Calcutta archive. Much like the *oinoglossic* ('wine talk') register" described by Silverstein, words such as *chesty, biscuity,* and *bakey* connect tastes, smells, and looks to events in the field and the factory (2006, 484; emphasis in original). According to Silverstein (2006, 493), "At every culturally recognizable node in the trajectory from production to consumption . . . special lexical registers . . . conceptually define the object of discourse, frequently with a view back or forward to other nodes in the chain of sites."

34. Harkness 2015, 583; see also Peirce [1903] 1998.

35. Chumley and Harkness 2013, 3. As Harkness (2015, 574–75) puts it, "Attention to qualia enables anthropologists to consider ethnographically what is continuous semiotically across and within practice."

36. Munn 1986.

37. Williams [1976] 2015.

38. Callon, Millo, and Muniesa 2007. In his work on the semiotics of brands, the linguistic anthropologist Constantine Nakassis (2012) describes citational practices such as those that link *stewy, earthy, flat,* and *flaky* as acts that "performatively" constitute both the market and its participants (see also MacKenzie 2006; Hébert 2014).

39. Shapin 2016, 450.

40. Here I draw on Sawyer and Agrawal's (2000) idea of "environmental orientalism," a framework for understanding the racialization of environments. For more on racialization in plantation agriculture, see Stoler 2002; Jegathesan 2019; and Daniel 2008.

41. Besky 2014a; Chatterjee 2001; Sharma 2011.

42. For more on these algorithms, see Besky 2017b.

43. Fernandes 1997; Barad 2007, 228.

44. As Gewertz and Errington (2010, 44) explain in their profile of independent meat traders in Australia and New Zealand, "A background in the meat industry is useful. A background in business more generally may also be useful. And many have worked in export firms. But what really counts is having a trading spirit and being a quick learner—being able to make the most of opportunities in a business with 'a steep learning curve.'"

CHAPTER TWO. THE AUCTION AND THE ARCHIVE

1. See Twining 1785; Committee of Tea Dealers 1785; Forrest 1973; Ibbetson 1910, chap. 8; Harler 1956, 230–31.

2. ["A Tea Dealer"] 1826, 108; emphasis in the original.

3. From 1834 to 1937 the public auctions were held at the London Commercial Sale Rooms on Mincing Lane. In 1937 Plantation House at Mincing Lane and Fenchurch Street opened. The London auctions moved from Plantation House to Sir John Lyon House after auction centers were set up across India (as well as in East Africa and Singapore). In 1990, now even smaller, the London tea auction moved to the London Chamber of Commerce. See Harler 1956, 231; Forrest 1973, chap. 7, on the London tea auctions.

4. On tea plantation work in India and Sri Lanka, see Sharma 2011; Chatterjee 2001; Jegathesan 2019; Daniel 2008; Bass 2012.

5. See Besky 2014a.

6. See Debnath 2011; Das Gupta 1992; Chatterjee 2001 on the history of the Dooars and the Jalpaiguri district of West Bengal.

7. Rappaport 2017, chaps. 5 and 6; see also Buckingham 1910, 13.

8. Ukers 1935a, 44.

9. Besky 2017a; see also Brenner 1998; Collins 2002; Harvey 2001.

10. Larkin 2013, 329; Carse 2014.

11. I am drawing here on Julia Elyachar's (2010) notion of a "social infrastructure of communicative channels." Elyachar describes women's everyday behind-the-scenes communication and movement through Cairo as constituting an infrastructure that is as important to economic life as roads and bridges.

12. Polanyi 2001. Communicative conventions help brokers navigate what Bestor (2004, 51), borrowing from Clifford Geertz, calls "the market's 'grooved channels' . . . that lead them again and again through familiar settings to regular partners in accustomed arenas of trade."

13. Auction catalogs from the mid- to late 1800s take a similar form, whether for indigo, as seen in the Nilhat House archive, or London Commercial Sale Rooms catalogs for coffee, cinnamon, cloves, and semolina, housed in the London Metropolitan Archive (LMA/4294/02).

14. See Kumar 2012 and Ali 2018 on indigo; Banaji 2013 and Farooqui 1998 on opium.

15. See Aldous 2017; Roy 2014; Bag 2015. See also Jones 1992 on a history of agency houses in Calcutta.

16. J. Thomas 1976, 8.

17. J. Thomas 1976, 9.

18. J. Thomas 1976, 11.

19. The Calcutta auctions were first organized by the Calcutta Tea Brokers' Association and after 1887 by the newly organized Calcutta Tea Traders Association (CTTA).

20. J. Thomas 1976, 2. Auction centers were later set up in Colombo (1883), Kochi (1943), and Nairobi (1956); the latter was subsequently moved to Mombasa, where the East Africa auctions are currently held.

21. Buerkle 1998.

22. Reid 1998.

23. I join other anthropologists in highlighting the resilience of sociality and meaning in trading practices amid neoliberalization and financialization (Bestor 2004; Gewertz and Errington 2010; Cross and Heslop 2019; Zaloom 2006).

24. Bestor 2004, 181–82.

25. Buerkle 1998.

26. Mazzarella 2017. Christina Grasseni (2003, 261), writing about the intersection of food localism and the quality control demands of a globalizing market among dairy traders in northern Italy, suggests that "commodification reaches into personal identity in complex, fluid, and dynamic ways, seeping into the everyday practice of our daily routines, by means that include self-representation."

27. Rules on where and how buyers could participate in Indian tea auctions have since been relaxed. See chap. 6.

28. Zaloom 2006, 111.

29. In interviews with me, buyers, brokers, and the officials at the CTTA all stressed the significance of warehousing in the tea brokering landscape. The quality

and space of warehousing infrastructure has long been a concern to people in the industry. In fact, one major concern with regard to expanding the Calcutta auction in the 1950s after independence was the warehouse infrastructure. See BL Mss Eur F174/1251: "Tea Auctions Committee Working Papers"; and BL Mss Eur F174/2107: "Report on the Tea Auctions Committee."

30. The Tea Act, passed in 1953, established the Tea Board of India (initially called the Central Tea Board) and charged the new office with regulatory control of India's plantations and tea auctions. For the auctions, it outlined some basic rules of conduct. The Tea Act was modified by the Tea Marketing Control Order of 1984, which mandated that 70 percent of tea produced on every plantation should be sold at auction. There were, however, still loopholes. For example, "packet tea" was not included in the total output of a plantation. The 1984 act was replaced by the Tea Marketing and Control Order of 2003, which loosened these regulations. After a backlash against that loosening, they were again tightened by a 2016 amendment (see chap. 6). Recent amendments have also allowed for the expansion of smallholder tea production, described in chap. 5.

31. Bestor (2004, 178) describes a similar kind of internal etiquette enforcement in Japanese fish auctions.

32. See Season 18, episode 10.

33. Bestor 2004, 179–80.

34. Callon, Méadel, and Rabeharisoa. 2002; Mazzarella 2006.

35. See MacKenzie 2006; Callon, Millo, and Muniesa 2007; Preda 2006; LiPuma and Lee 2004.

36. The interplay between written communicative genres and modes of conversation or nonverbal registers has been noted in several anthropological studies of language and the market. What Jillian Cavanaugh (2016, 692) calls "linguistic labor" "is ... essential to contemporary capitalist production[,] ... entangling worker-selves in particular social as well as economic relationships." See also Cavanaugh and Shankar 2014; Carr 2010.

37. See Anand 2017; Kale 2014; Carse 2014.

CHAPTER THREE. THE PROBLEM WITH BLENDING

1. BL Mss Eur F174/2074: Percival Griffiths Papers, "A Note on the Origin and Growth of Packet Tea," unpublished manuscript ca. mid-1930s written by Gervas Huxley. Hereafter Huxley n.d.

2. Buckingham 1910, 4, 13.

3. Rappaport 2017, chap. 5.

4. This interplay between desire and marketing, measurement and production, is central to how Callon, Méadel, and Rabeharisoa (2002) discuss the work of "qualification" in late capitalism.

5. Rabinbach 1992.

6. Bauch 2017, 15. See also Cronon 1990.

7. Biltekoff 2013; DuPuis 2015; Freidberg 2010; Nestle 2003; Scrinis 2013; Zeide 2018.

8. As Kyla Tompkins (2009, 54) notes in her analysis of dietetic movements centered on the consumption of bread in antebellum America, "The continuing materialization of the body, through the performative and physiological functions of eating, [was] metonymic of the continually expanding material borders" of the United States. For the (white) British public, consumption of plantation-grown tea, with its distinct flavor, color, and texture, was metonymic in this way. The advent of empire-grown tea presented what the postcolonial studies scholar Parama Roy (2010, 9) calls an "alimentary challenge" to the eating bodies of the colonial metropole.

9. Besky 2014a; Sharma 2011; Chatterjee 2001.

10. BL Mss Eur F174/1407: *A New Essay upon Tea* (1936). The file includes a copy of the pamphlet and correspondence about its production.

11. The outcome of the ITA's two-pronged effort, to distinguish Indian tea on the international market and to establish its safety, was what Michelle Murphy 2006 calls a "regime of perceptibility" that remains central to the operation of the global tea market.

12. Elsewhere, science and technology studies scholars have examined the role of such rematerialization, in analyses of the health effects of MSG (Tracy 2018), the microbial liveliness of fermented or raw foods (Spackman 2018a; Paxson 2012), the potability of water (Spackman and Burlingame 2018), and the potency of generic drugs (Hayden 2007; Banerjee 2017). In Murphy's (2006, 15) formulation of "materialization," "matter" must be understood "not in terms of a prior thingness but rather in terms of the process of history, concrete social and technical arrangements and the effects of power."

13. The story of how tannins shaped and were shaped by normative understandings of taste and value is indicative of a kind of process that scholars of science, technology, and capital have documented elsewhere: in the determination of acceptable levels of chemical exposure in homes, factory farms, and offices (Liboiron, Tironi, and Calvillo 2018; Murphy 2006; Nash 2007; Shapiro 2015); the rise of the calorie as the measure of food's nutritional impact (Biltekoff 2013; Guthman 2011); and the purification of Caribbean sugar through automation (Singerman 2017). Recent engagements in anthropology, science studies, and critical theory with "chemosociality" strongly associate anxieties about chemical toxicity with the conditions of late twentieth- and early twenty-first-century industrial production (Shapiro and Kirksey 2017). Substances from lead to antibiotic-resistant bacteria to polychlorinated biphenyls (PCBs) are frequently depicted as by-products of negligent production practices, either by large corporations in the Global North or emerging economic powers, including China and India (Murphy 2013; Landecker 2016; Fortun 2001; Chen 2012). The story of tea blending and tea tannins, however, reveals a deeper history of chemosociality, in which fears about toxicity and industrial production were tied to broader popular and scientific interest in the digestive system as a site for the making and unmaking of health.

14. Chamney 1930, 43–45; Ukers 1935a, 297–308; Walsh 1892, 57–58; see also Ball 1848.

15. Chamney 1930, 43–45; Baildon 1882, 30–34; McGowan 1860.

16. Arnold 2005; Chatterjee 2001; Daniel, Bernstein, and Brass 1992; Drayton 2000; Sharma 2011.

17. See Brockway 1979; Bonneuil 2000; Maat 2013.

18. *The Art of Tea Blending* 1893, 44; emphasis added.

19. Rappaport 2017, chap. 4; Liu 2015.

20. *Tea and Tea Blending* 1894, 131–32. Tea was popularly referred to as either "China tea" or "Indian tea." China tea was associated with lighter tastes, aromas, and flavors as opposed to the malty punch of Indian teas. See also Sharma 2010 on planters' engagement with Assam jaat and China jaat of tea in Assam.

21. *Tea and Tea Blending* 1894, 133–34.

22. *The Art of Tea Blending* 1893, 5–6.

23. Huxley n.d.; see also Ukers 1935b, 13; Rappaport 2017, 120–21.

24. Huxley n.d; BL Mss Eur F197/913: *Reports of the Imperial Economic Committee, Eighteenth Report: Tea* (1931).

25. Huxley n.d. Other writers within the industry referred to alleged methods Chinese producers used to make tea more visually appealing for shipment to the United Kingdom (Money 1884; Baildon 1882, 20–34; Walsh 1892, 134–45).

26. Rappaport 2017, 164–66. Such arguments, as Rappaport's archival materials and my own contemporary ethnographic work have shown, are misleading. Work in tea plantation fields and factories was, and remains, a matter of close visceral contact between human bodies, tea leaves, machines, oils, coal, soot, and smoke (see Besky 2014a, 2017b).

27. See LMA/4364/01/002: "Horniman's Tea Advertisements."

28. *Tea and Tea Blending* 1894, 139–40.

29. *Lancet* 1893, 48. At the same time, M. K. Bamber, a scientist based in Assam with the Horticultural Society, was conducting experiments on the chemical makeup of tea, looking at the relationships between production and chemical constituency. See ITA 1894 [for 1893]; Bamber 1893.

30. Lancet 1893, 48.

31. Lancet 1893, 48. Theine and caffeine were eventually recognized as the same substance.

32. The phrase "the cup that cheers but does not inebriate" to describe tea is attributed to the poet William Cowper ([1785] 1899). It was then used widely in writing on tea. See Gray 1903, ix; Reade 1884, 36.

33. Lancet 1893, 48.

34. Lancet 1893, 49. This and other experiments showed that Indian tea was higher in all three constituents, but it was caffeine, as Sir James Buckingham wrote in *A Few Facts about Indian Tea*, "to which the stimulating and sustaining power of tea is chiefly due" (Buckingham 1910, 18). See Buckingham 1910, 18–21, for a review of early scientific work on tannins and caffeine, including at the ITA's experimental station at Tocklai.

35. Lancet 1893, 49.

36. Lancet 1893, 49.

37. Lancet 1903, 838.

38. Lancet 1908, 325.

39. Lancet 1908, 325.

40. Letter from MacLeod in the *Lancet,* August 8, 1908, 421.

41. Letter from MacLeod in the *Lancet,* August 8, 1908, 421.

42. Letter from MacLeod in the *Lancet,* August 8, 1908, 421. Congou and Souchong are grades of tea that described both China and Indian teas at the time, before the postindependence introduction of the grading system that I discuss in chaps. 1 and 2.

43. Rappaport 2017, 166.

44. BL Mss Eur F174/912: "Revised Draft as amended after consultation with solicitor, Merchandise Marks Act. In the matter of an application by Indian Tea Association, London, The South Indian Association of London, and the Ceylon Association in London" (1928). Hereafter Revised draft from producer organizations (1928).

45. Revised draft from producer organizations (1928).

46. Revised draft from producer organizations (1928).

47. Revised draft from producer organizations (1928). See additional documents in BL Mss Eur F174/912: "Note on the Dutch Menace to the Indian Tea Industry" and "Draft memorandum regarding the increasing use of foreign teas in the United Kingdom."

48. Board of Trade 1929, included in BL Mss Eur F174/1904: "Mr. Fraser's File."

49. Revised draft from producer organizations (1928).

50. Revised draft from producer organizations (1928).

51. BL Mss Eur F174/1094: "Statement on Behalf of the British Tea Industry in Java and Sumatra."

52. BL Mss Eur F174/1094: "Joint Parliamentary Committee of the Cooperative Congress: Precis of Evidence to be submitted to the Standing Committee under the Merchandise Marks Act against the proposal for the Marking of Imported tea."

53. See Rappaport 2017, 240–42, for a discussion of how parties to the Board of Trade hearing debated the role of the idea of "Empire" in consumer preferences.

54. BL Mss Eur F174/1094: "Notes for Counsel in support of Case for the applicants and criticism of cases for the opposition." See also BL Mss Eur F174/912 and BL Mss Eur F174/1094: "Statement of Opposition of the Tea Buyers Association."

55. BL Mss Eur F174/1094: "Notes for Counsel in support of Case for the applicants and criticism of cases for the opposition." See also BL Mss Eur F174/912.

56. One can find echoes of these arguments in present-day debates over the integrity of fair trade, Geographical Indication (GI), and other product markers—many of them applied to tea and other crops of empire. See Besky 2014a; Reichman 2018; West 2012.

57. Callon, Méadel, and Rabeharisoa 2002; Guyer 2004.

58. BL Mss Eur F174/1094: "Statement of Opposition of the Tea Buyers Association."

59. BL Mss Eur F174/1094: "Statement of Opposition of the Tea Buyers Association."

60. Callon, Méadel, and Rabeharisoa 2002; Callon, Millo, and Muniesa 2007.

61. As *The Art of Tea Blending* describes, "The reason is that most Indian teas have a sharp acrid taste, not to be found in the teas of China. This acrid taste tea-drinkers rarely like, unless it is tempered by the softer and milder flavors of some China variety. Indians, should however, be used freely. No China tea possesses such sharp piquancy, such great strength, and such pronounced yet delicate flavor. " *The Art of Tea Blending* 1893, 43; see also Walsh 1892, 175–83.

62. Lancet 1911a, 44. See also BL Mss Eur F174/1405 on tannins. The ITA circulated this article amongst themselves for decades after its publication.

63. BL Mss Eur F174/1902: Day 2 of hearings, p. 196.

64. BL Mss Eur F174/1902: Day 2 of hearings, p. 197.

65. BL Mss Eur F174/1902: Day 2 of hearings, p. 197.

66. BL Mss Eur F174/1902: Day 2 of hearings, p. 198.

67. BL Mss Eur F174/1902: Day 2 of hearings, p. 198.

68. Board of Trade 1929, 6–7. This report was compiled in March shortly after the proceedings and gives an overview of the arguments and resolution.

69. Rappaport 2017, 244–45.

70. BL Mss Eur F174/854: Leaflet distributed by the Indian Tea Association of London, the Ceylon Association in London, and the South Indian Association in London. Emphasis in original.

71. See Money 1884; Baildon 1882; Hauser 1890, 6.

72. BL Mss Eur F174/854: "A Plea for Empire Tea."

73. BL Mss Eur F174/854: Letter dated May 20, 1931, from Mrs. A. L. (Henry) Bayly to ITA London.

74. BL Mss Eur F174/854: Letter dated May 21, 1931, to Mrs. A. L. Bayly from ITA London.

75. BL Mss Eur F174/1405: G. H. Harden, 1931, *Treatise from a Medical Point of View on Various Facts Relating to Tea,* p. 5. File also includes ITA responses to Harden and claims about tanninless teas. Hereafter Harden 1931.

76. Harden 1931, 7.

77. Harden 1931, 11.

78. Harden 1931, 11.

79. Harden 1931, 14.

80. Bauch 2017.

81. Harden 1931, 15.

82. Harden 1931, 17.

83. Bodleian Library, University of Oxford, John Jay Collection: Tea and Coffee 1(88), "Copy of a letter received from a Medical Officer of Health testifying to the Digestive Qualities of The Doctor's China Tea."

84. Bodleian Library, University of Oxford, John Jay Collection: Tea and Coffee 1(88), "Copy of a letter from a lady who was previously entirely unknown to us, showing the health value of the Doctor's China Tea."

85. BL Mss Eur F174/1405. The file includes several newspaper clippings of Doctor's China Tea advertisements. This one is from the *News Chronicle,* June 10, 1932.

86. BL Mss Eur F174/1405.

87. See BL Mss Eur F174/1405.

88. BL Mss Eur F174/1405: Draft letter addressed to Harden from ITA, dated July 1931.

89. BL Mss Eur F174/1405: Draft letter addressed to Harden from ITA, dated July 1931.

90. BL Mss Eur F174/1405: Letter dated October 23, 1931, to ITA London from Coward, Chance, & Co. (ITA's lawyers).

91. Industrial science was not unique to the tea industry. Colonial industrialists set up similar agricultural experimental stations for rubber, coffee, sugar, and an array of other crops. Agricultural experimental stations aimed to expand the reach of colonial crops and to maximize their market output.

92. For more on depression-era crop controls, see Rappaport 2017, 244; Dey 2018.

93. As the ITA had written in its preparations for the merchandise marking order case, "It is not the practice to restrict production although after the disastrous year of 1920 the necessity for such action was forced on growers by the pressure of economic conditions. This applied to Java as well and India and China. There has been, on the decontrol by Government, an excessive stock of common teas, of which the market could only absorb a limited quantity. In practice therefore instead of producing a large quantity of 'coarse' tea which could only be sold at a loss finer plucking was adopted resulting in a smaller crop which could be sold at a profit" (BL Mss Eur F174/1094: "Notes for Counsel in support of Case for the applicants and criticism of cases for the opposition"). A modified version of this document also appears in BL Mss Eur F174/912.

94. BL Mss Eur F174/1405.

95. Bauch 2017.

96. Mss Eur F174/1405: Letter from P. H. Carpenter to the ITA, Calcutta re: Doctor's China Tea, dated January 2, 1932.

97. Mss Eur F174/1405: Letter from P. H. Carpenter to the ITA, Calcutta re: Doctor's China Tea, dated January 2, 1932.

98. BL Mss Eur F174/1405: Draft copy of "The Influence of Tea on Digestion." See also Harler 1964.

99. BL Mss Eur F174/1405. Letter from W. H. Pease to the Indian Tea Cess Committee Secretary, dated January 27, 1933. File also includes a draft version of this letter titled "Tea Tannin."

100. BL Mss Eur F174/1405: Letter from W. H. Pease to the Indian Tea Cess Committee Secretary, dated January 27, 1933; emphasis added.

101. Later that year, on April 7, 1933, another experimental proposal was floated, this time at a meeting of the American and Foreign Markets Sub-Committee. Committee members suggested first finding scientists to evaluate the digestive tea claims in an experimental investigation, but this was not supported by most of the members as they believed that nothing would come of proving what they already knew. Then another suggestion was made: "that the insidious Digestive Tea propaganda might be better countered by advertising that 'All Empire Tea is Digestive Tea'" (BL Mss Eur F174/1407: "Extract from minutes of meeting of American and Foreign Markets Sub-Committee held on 7 April 1933").

102. BL Mss Eur F174/1405: Letter from the Editor of the *Lancet* to the ITA, dated December 14, 1933.

103. BL Mss Eur F174/1405: Letter from ITA Secretary to the Editor of the *Lancet*, dated December 19, 1933.

104. BL Mss Eur F174/1405: Letter from the Editor of the *Lancet* to the ITA, dated December 22, 1933.

105. *A New Essay upon Tea* 1936, 5.

106. *A New Essay upon Tea* 1936, 19.

107. *A New Essay upon Tea* 1936, 23–24.

108. *A New Essay upon Tea* 1936, 25.

109. BL Mss Eur F174/1407. File includes correspondence between Dr. Bach's lawyers (Charles Barker & Sons) and the ITA's lawyers (Coward and Chance) between June 1935 and July 1935.

110. *A New Essay upon Tea* 1936, 27.

111. *A New Essay upon Tea* 1936, 29.

112. *A New Essay upon Tea* 1936, 31.

113. *A New Essay upon Tea* 1936, 32.

114. *A New Essay upon Tea* 1936, 33; Lancet 1936b, 387–88.

115. *A New Essay upon Tea* 1936, 37.

116. Buckingham (1910) discusses the use of milk to counteract tannins as well.

117. Lancet 1936a, 1534.

118. Mintz 1985.

119. Murphy (2006) calls such terms of judgment a "regime of perceptibility."

120. Andrews 1939, 7–8.

121. "PG Tips: A Manchester Brew," BBC Local Manchester, March 8, 2005, www.bbc.co.uk/manchester/content/articles/2005/03/01/pg_tips_75th_anniversary_feature.shtml.

CHAPTER FOUR. THE SCIENCE OF QUALITY

1. The ITA appointed its first scientific officer, Harold Mann, in 1900. He conducted research out of the Indian Museum in Calcutta. It became apparent that scientific research required a closer engagement with tea growing. The ITA set up

the Heelanka Experimental Station (1904–11), then shifted research to larger facilities at Tocklai in 1911.

2. Hazarika and Talukdar 2001, 48.

3. Brown 2015; Cross 2015; Neveling 2014; Lezaun and Montgomery 2015.

4. A note on sources: The material on which I draw in this chapter comes primarily from papers and records available in the Indian Tea Association archives in Kolkata, as well as ITA materials now held in the British Library and the Engledow papers at the University of Cambridge. Access to Tocklai itself was restricted. Though historical sources from within the subcontinent were less abundant, I also draw on Tea Board of India records from the early years after Indian independence.

5. See also Besky 2017a.

6. The Tea Board's official history, *From Imperial Product to National Drink* (Bhadra 2005), suggests such a clean break, relying mostly on visual representations in advertising, film, and popular media that normalized tea consumption among Indians.

7. Prakash 1992, 172; quoted in Seth 2009, 377. See also Anderson 2002.

8. Bray 2008, 320. See also Heath and Meneley 2007.

9. Bray 2008, 321. See also Latour 1993.

10. All of this implies another tense divide: the one between sensibility and objectivity. Shapin (2016) explores this tension in the history of enology, the science of wine and wine flavor.

11. See www.tocklai.org/activities/tea-chemistry/.

12. Shapin's (2016) account of the work of Maynard Amerine and the effort to objectively account for the taste of wine notes that "flavor" tends to be the preferred technical term for the array of olfactory and gustatory experiences that obtain in encounters with food. For this reason, the work of Amerine and others is described as "flavor chemistry."

13. See Griffiths (1967, 423–40) on early scientific research through the ITA. Of particular significance is M. Kelway Bamber's early work on the chemistry of tea, which began in 1891. See Bamber 1893; ITA Calcutta Annual Bulletin for 1893, pp. 90–97. Harold Mann also conducted research on quality. The ITA issued Mann's report, "The Factors which Determine the Quality of Tea," to members in 1907 (BL Mss Eur F174/1515).

14. Harler 1932, 78. Emphasis in original.

15. The first International Tea Agreement lasted from 1933 to 1938; the second began in 1938 and was in effect into World War II. Both agreements curbed production. The second agreement even promoted replantation. These production controls doubled as price controls for Indian, Ceylon, and Dutch Indonesian tea producers. The Indian government credited these agreements with permitting the industry to survive the war years; see "The Report of the Government of India's Ad Hoc Committee on Tea" (1950), 8–13.

16. Harler 1932, 89. See BL Mss Eur F174/904: "Tea Tasters' Glossary."

17. Harler 1932, 78.

18. BL Mss Eur F174/913: *Reports of the Imperial Economic Committee, Eighteenth Report: Tea* (1931).

19. Members were Frank Engledow, leader; James Insch, who represented "commercial members" (i.e., plantation administration and upper management); and J. M. Kilburn, who represented planters. Engledow did extensive work across the British Empire as an agricultural and development adviser. His work was carried out in what Heike Jons (2016, 94) calls a "post-Victorian" mode of knowledge production, an ambivalent combination of belief in the humanitarian value of scientific planning and an abiding belief in the innate superiority of white European science.

20. BL Mss Eur F174/1413: "Correspondence on the 1935–36 Commission of Enquiry."

21. BL Mss Eur F174/1416: "Indian Tea Association Report of the Commission of Enquiry on the Scientific Department, 1935–1936" (1936), p. 58.

22. See Lutgendorf 2012; Bhadra 2005; Rappaport 2017 on tea consumption in India. The Indian Tea Cess Committee (1903) became the Indian Tea Market Expansion Board in 1937.

23. BL Mss Eur F174/1413: Letter from Engledow to Pease, dated May 25, 1935. See also BL Mss Eur F174/1416: 1936 Report, p. 13.

24. See BL Mss Eur F174/1414: Correspondence on the 1935–36 Commission of Enquiry. This file includes the questionnaire answers from dozens of respondents.

25. BL Mss Eur F174/1416: 1936 Report, pp. 10–11.

26. BL Mss Eur F174/1416: 1936 Report, pp. 12–13.

27. BL Mss Eur F174/1414.

28. BL Mss Eur F174/1414: Notes of discussion at a meeting of the General Committee held on Wednesday, October 2, 1935.

29. BL Mss Eur F174/1414: Notes on General Committee meeting held on Wednesday, October 2, 1935.

30. BL Mss Eur F174/1416: 1936 Report, p. 14.

31. BL Mss Eur F174/1416: 1936 Report, p. 58.

32. BL Mss Eur F174/1416: 1936 Report, p. 59.

33. BL Mss Eur F174/1416: 1936 Report, pp. 60–61.

34. BL Mss Eur F174/1416: 1936 Report, p. 61.

35. BL Mss Eur F174/1416: 1936 Report, pp. 61–62.

36. BL Mss Eur F174/1416: 1936 Report, pp. 62–63.

37. BL Mss Eur F174/1416: 1936 Report, p. 68.

38. BL Mss Eur F174/1416: 1936 Report, p. 85.

39. BL Mss Eur F174/1416: 1936 Report, p. 62.

40. BL Mss Eur F174/1416: 1936 Report, pp. 65–69.

41. BL Mss Eur F174/1317: "The Chemistry of Tea Quality." Foreword by Leslie Lampitt to "A Summary of the Investigation 1939–1943" by A. E. Bradfield. The London Advisory Commission was formed at the suggestion of the 1936 Commission of Enquiry.

42. BL Mss Eur F174/1317: Letter from ITA London, dated February 10, 1939.

43. BL Mss Eur F174/1317: Note from ITA London, dated June 1, 1939.

44. See early reports on Bradfield's work in BL Mss Eur F174/1317. The first report was published in May 1940.

45. BL Mss Eur F174/1317: "The Chemistry of Tea Quality." Foreword by Leslie Lampitt to "A Summary of the Investigation 1939–1943" by A. E. Bradfield.

46. BL Mss Eur F174/1317: A. E. Bradfield, "Summary of the Investigation 1939–1943," dated June 1943.

47. BL Mss Eur F174/1317: A. E. Bradfield, "Summary of the Investigation 1939–1943," dated June 1943.

48. BL Ms Eur F174/1322: Minutes of the March 17, 1948, LAC meeting.

49. See Mss Eur F174/1248, 1249, and 1250: "Resumption of London Tea Auctions" [1947–52].

50. BL Mss Eur F174/1249: "Resumption of London Tea Auctions."

51. BL Mss Eur F174/1248. See also BL IOR/L/E/8/7528: Letter from L. Harrison (Eastern House, New Delhi) to J. Thompson (Trade and Transport Department, Commonwealth Relations Office, London), dated June 27, 1949.

52. See ITA Calcutta Annual Bulletins for this period.

53. William Mazzarella (2017, 10) uses the term "settlement" "to suggest the tension between the appearance of a negotiated, reasonable compromise and the violence of the settler whose stability of residence depends on the displacement and disavowal of the one that his presence silences." In his use of the term, Mazzarella refers to the compromises and silences that create disciplinary knowledge, for example, the settlements that create illusive divisions between "primitive" and "modern" or between "art" and "magic."

54. See Besky 2014a.

55. "The Report of the Government of India's Ad Hoc Committee on Tea" (1950). This report described a "decline in the volume of exports, particular to hard currency areas" in Europe.

56. Besky 2014a, 2017a.

57. BL IOR/L/E/8/7528: "Press Release: Central Tea Board Inauguration at Calcutta on August 1," dated July 21, 1949.

58. The Tea Board of India was formed by the Tea Act (No. 29 of 1953).

59. "Report of the Ad Hoc Committee on Tea, 1950," p. 6. See also Lutgendorf 2012.

60. "Report of the Ad Hoc Committee on Tea, 1950," p. 10.

61. See "Report of the Ad Hoc Committee on Tea, 1950."

62. BL Mss Eur F174/798: "Notes on the Scheme for Development of Tea Propaganda in India" (1955), p. 10.

63. GOI, "Report of the Plantations Inquiry Commission, 1956," p. 23.

64. GOI, "Report of the Plantations Inquiry Commission, 1956," p. 247.

65. GOI, "Report of the Plantations Inquiry Commission, 1956," p. 244.

66. "Report of the Ad Hoc Committee on Tea, 1950," p. 44.

67. GOI, "Report of the Plantations Inquiry Commission, 1956," p. 235.

68. GOI, "Report of the Plantations Inquiry Commission, 1956," p. 235; emphasis added.

69. BL Mss Eur F174/1437: "Indian Tea Association Report of the Commission of Enquiry on the Scientific Department, 1953–1954" (1954), pp. 62–63.

70. BL Mss Eur F174/1437: 1954 Report, p. 16.

71. BL Mss Eur F174/1437: 1954 Report, p. 55.

72. BL Mss Eur F174/1437: 1954 Report, p. 16.

73. BL Mss Eur F174/1323: June 13, 1951, LAC meeting at Trocadero Restaurant. Roberts started his career as a biochemist at Tocklai in 1937 but worked elsewhere during the war and was rehired by Tocklai in 1946; see BL Mss Eur F174/1320: Letter dated April 16, 1946, from E. A. H. Roberts to ITA London in which he states that he wants to resume work with them on "tea research to be done at home."

74. BL Mss Eur F174/1428: "Correspondence and papers concerning the Scientific Dept's investigation into the chemistry of made tea" (1964).

75. BL Mss Eur F174/1423: "Correspondence and papers concerning the Scientific Dept's investigation into the chemistry of made tea" (1959).

76. BL Mss Eur F174/1325: "Note on the Progress of Work of Made Tea by L. H. Lampitt." Roberts was also designing research to examine low and high polymers.

77. BL Mss Eur F174/1325: LAC Scientific Panel Meeting, November 27, 1952.

78. BL Mss Eur F174/1325: "Note on the Progress of Work of Made Tea by L. H. Lampitt."

79. BL Mss Eur F174/1348: "Studies of the liquor characters of manufactured teas," November 29, 1954.

80. BL Mss Eur F174/1349: "Notes on a short talk given by E.A.H. Roberts on the estimation of theaflavins and thearubigins in made tea," dated September 19, 1957.

81. BL Mss Eur F174/1349: "Notes on a short talk given by E.A.H. Roberts on the estimation of theaflavins and thearubigins in made tea," dated September 19, 1957.

82. BL Mss Eur F174/1349: "Memorandum to note about Dr. Roberts' work."

83. BL Mss Eur F174/1349: "Memorandum to note about Dr. Roberts' work."

84. BL Mss Eur F174/1349: "Investigations into the chemistry of made tea," dated June 6, 1957.

85. BL Mss Eur F174/1324: "Tocklai Experimental Tea Samples," dated March 11, 1952. See also BL Mss Eur F174/1348: "Engineering Department," dated November 30, 1954.

86. BL Mss Eur F174/1324: "Tocklai Experimental Tea Samples," dated March 11, 1952.

87. BL Mss Eur F174/1327: Letter from Livermore to Nicholls (ITA), dated February 5, 1954.

88. BL Mss Eur F174/1324: Letter from Engledow to Rainey, dated March 3, 1952.

89. BL Mss Eur F174/1389: "ITA Scientific Department Papers/Correspondences" (1958–59).

90. BL Mss Eur F174/1351: LAC Circulars (1958).

91. BL Mss Eur F174/1349: Engineering department report for August 1957.

92. BL Mss Eur F174/1348.

93. BL Mss Eur F174/1332: "Talk with Mr. Chatterji on Friday, October 17, 1958." Filed with "LAC Correspondences" (1958).

94. BL Mss Eur F174/1450: Tocklai files, 1959–60.

95. BL Mss Eur F174/1441: Letter from Robert to Rainey, dated June 1, 1960.

96. BL Mss Eur F174/1423: Letter from Roberts to Mardon, dated October 13, 1959.

97. BL Mss Eur F174/1441: "Instant Tea"; Letter from Verende to Bell, dated August 11, 1958. The Government of India enacted increasingly stringent regulations on the repatriation of money to the United Kingdom that was made in India, culminating in the Foreign Exchange Regulation Act (1973). The ITA was making money on Indian plantations and funneling into the London laboratory, which they claimed was an extension of the plantations in India.

98. BL Mss Eur F174/1451: Notes from ITA committee meeting, March 1961.

99. BL Mss Eur F174/1380: *Tea Looks Forward* (1951). Written by Tull and presenting an overview of mechanization work at Tocklai from 1949 to 1951. See also BL Mss Eur F174/1381: *Tea Progresses*, a follow-up to *Tea Looks Forward* published in 1955; and BL Mss Eur F174/1382, which contains additional unpublished material for a book on "tea's achievements" in engineering work at Tocklai (1960).

100. BL Mss Eur F174/1380. The Plantations Labour Act of 1951 ensured that workers received some basic benefits from plantation owners, including housing, food rations, and medical facilities; see Besky 2014a, 2017a.

101. BL Mss Eur F174/1380.

102. BL Mss Eur F174/1437: 1954 Report, p. 68.

103. See chap. 3. See also Nijhawan 2017; Rappaport 2017.

104. Lutgendorf 2012, 19.

105. BL Mss Eur F174/798: "Notes on the Scheme for Development of Tea Propaganda in India" (1955), p. 20.

106. BL Mss Eur F174/798: "Notes on the Scheme for Development of Tea Propaganda in India" (1955), p. 20.

107. BL Mss Eur F174/798: "Notes on the Scheme for Development of Tea Propaganda in India" (1955), p. 1.

108. University of Cambridge Johnson Papers: "Amgoorie Tea Estates, Ltd: The History of the McKercher CTC Machine," written by F. G. Johnson, dated August 23, 1956.

109. University of Cambridge Johnson Papers: "Amgoorie Tea Estates, Ltd: The History of the McKercher CTC Machine," written by F. G. Johnson, dated August 23, 1956.

110. BL Mss Eur F174/1424: Tea Chemistry [1960]; and 1390: Speech delivered by Mr. H. Ferguson, director of Tocklai and the Assam Branch of the ITA General meeting, 1959.

111. Lutgendorf 2012, 22. According to Lutgendorf, the Indian redesign of the CTC machine was liberally pirated.

112. Lutgendorf 2012, 22.

113. See Besky 2014a.

1. See Lutgendorf 2012.
2. Forum for the Future 2014, 5.
3. Forum for the Future 2013.
4. Povinelli 2011, 191.
5. Mintz 1979.
6. McGowan 1860.
7. McGowan 1860; Baildon 1882, 30–34; Chamney 1930, 43–45.
8. Debnath 2010, 138. See also Das Gupta 1992 on the history of the Dooars and the Jalpaiguri district.
9. The following passages from *Tea Cultivation* (1865) appear on pp. 20–23.
10. *Tea Cultivation* 1865, 21.
11. *Tea Cultivation* 1865, 5; emphasis in original.
12. Tsing 2015, 5.
13. Tsing 2015.
14. Besky 2017a.
15. See Besky 2014a.
16. Moore 2016, 89–90.
17. Povinelli 2011, 31–32.
18. Povinelli 2011, 32.
19. In recent years, some tea companies, such as Hindustan Unilever, have sold their plantations, claiming that it is cheaper to buy tea than to produce it. Tata, supported by the International Finance Corporation, devised a "stakeholder model" that would give workers part ownership of some plantations. This model faced fierce opposition from plantation workers who did not see the move to employee ownership as beneficial (see Besky 2017b; Rosenblum and Sukthankar 2014).
20. See, e.g., Shaktan 2016, n.d.; Pandey 2014; Chauduri 2015; Bera 2015; Reevell 2014; Chakrabarty 2016.
21. The use of the term "sick" is not unique to this case. From textile mills to tea plantations, "sickness" is a widely used term in India to describe faltering industrial production. See Finkelstein 2019 for an ethnography of ruination and persistence of the mills of Mumbai.
22. Tsing, quoted in Haraway 2015, 159; Tsing 2015.
23. Povinelli 2011; Fennell 2015.
24. Tsing 2015, 5.
25. Tsing 2015, 6.
26. Haraway 2015.
27. Moore 2016.
28. Harvey 2002, 106.
29. The obstacles to complete abandonment are also deeply rooted in the tea industry. The ITA Calcutta Annual Bulletin for 1920 includes the following passage: "For a tea garden is in a less favourable position, when trade prospects are bad, than any ordinary manufacturing concern. A mill or a factory can reduce its staff,

or go on short time, or if need be close down temporarily, and wait for better times. But a tea garden must carry on, and the extent to which it can restrict its operations or reduce its working costs is necessarily small. To close down altogether means the abandonment of the capital sunk in the enterprise; and tea garden labour is so costly to recruit that any material reduction in the labour strength represents a partial loss of capital" (p. 3). Thanks to Andrew Liu for alerting me to this reference.

30. Besky 2017a.

31. This is still how many cooperative tea growing arrangements work in North Bengal and Assam. This is problematic for fair trade and cooperative movements (see Besky 2015; for a discussion of small farmers in Darjeeling, see Sen 2017).

32. Hannan 2014, 62.

33. Sankrityayana 2014, 46.

34. Sankrityayana 2014, 53.

35. Stoler 2008.

36. Povinelli 2011, 191. See also Collins 2017 for a discussion of post-2008 movements in the United States to remake the economy through critiques and engagements with the concept and meaning of value.

CHAPTER SIX. THE QUALITY OF MARKETS

1. The process I describe in this chapter is similar to Caitlin Zaloom's (2006) account of how digital trading in the Chicago and London financial spheres was introduced to rationalize pit trading, with its hand gestures and aggressive hyper-masculine posturing. The shift from outcry to digital tea auctioning, however, is also different. While Zaloom's brokers contemplated a move from outcry to digital trading in already financialized commodities, the Indian tea brokers with whom I worked were trading a commodity that was in the process of being converted, through a combination of applied economic theory and state intervention, into a commodity open to speculation.

2. Akerlof 1970; Combris, Lecocq, and Visser 1997; for more on wine quality and markets, see Shapin 2016.

3. See Yano 2009.

4. One can think here of classic work on rural development in pastoral societies (e.g., Ferguson 1991); "high modernist" state planning (e.g., Scott 1999); postsocialist transformations in Eastern Europe (e.g., Burawoy and Verdery 1999; Lampland 2016); and even the rise of fair trade agriculture (e.g., Lyon and Moberg 2010).

5. Mazzarella 2006, 476.

6. Gupta 1995; Mazzarella 2006; Hull 2012; Mathur 2015.

7. Elyachar (2012) discusses such secrets in the context of neoliberalizing Egypt, but the economic and social value of secret knowledge, and its relationship to forms of labor, has been discussed elsewhere by anthropologists. See, e.g., Herzfeld 2004 on artisans and Jones 2011 on magicians.

8. See Simmel 1950.

9. Sethi 2018; Herring 2015; Stone 2007; Sunder Rajan 2006, 2012. See also Kloppenburg 1988.

10. Elyachar (2005, 49) and Murphy (2017, 80) have spoken of experiments in economic development in this way.

11. Callon and Muniesa 2005, 1246.

12. A. F. Ferguson 2002, 2.4.03; and see chap. 2.

13. Bestor 2004, 178.

14. This was also true of Tokyo fish markets during the time of Bestor's (2004) ethnographic study.

15. See Smith 1989. See also Krishnamurthy 2012 on wheat auctions and trading in India.

16. Guyer 2009, 203. This observation is rooted in Marx's (1976) notion of the commodity fetish and Karl Polanyi's subsequent analysis of "fictitious commodities" (Polanyi 2001).

17. Guyer 2009, 203–5.

18. Elyachar 2010, 452. See also Bestor 2004, 178, 180.

19. Steiner 1992, 635; emphasis mine.

20. In her description of the shift from pit to digital trading in Chicago and London, by contrast, Zaloom (2006, 136) notes that the market was on the mind of traders. In the transition there, which bears some resemblance to my case study, the market became not something traders worked *with* but something they reacted *to* (see also Searle 2016 and Kar 2018 on financial transitions in India).

21. A. F. Ferguson 2002, 2.3.79; emphasis in original.

22. Cohn 1996, 8. See also Arnold 2005; Drayton 2000.

23. Appadurai 1996, 117.

24. Chatterjee 2001; Besky 2014b.

25. "Report of the Ad Hoc Committee on Tea, 1950," p. 119; emphasis mine.

26. "Report of the Ad Hoc Committee on Tea, 1950," p. 123.

27. "Report of the Ad Hoc Committee on Tea, 1950," pp. 122–23.

28. "Report of the Ad Hoc Committee on Tea, 1950," p. 123.

29. Mazzarella 2017.

30. Subjective, nonquantitative ideas about places of production like Darjeeling or Assam have long circulated outside the space of the auction through various marketing projects like GI, but the knowledge that circulated in the auction halls and tasting rooms of Kolkata or Siliguri remained mostly invisible to outsiders (and to state regulators). See Besky 2014a, 2014b on GI for Darjeeling tea.

31. BL Mss Eur F174/1302: "Tea Futures Market Study Group Final Report," March 20, 1972.

32. ITA Calcutta Annual Bulletin for 1981, p. 62.

33. Elyachar 2012, 80.

34. Elyachar 2010, 452.

35. A. F. Ferguson 2002, 2.4.03.

36. A. F. Ferguson 2002, 6.2.22; emphasis in original.

37. A. F. Ferguson 2002, 6.2.25; emphasis in original.

38. A. F. Ferguson 2002, 2.3.79.

39. Sutanuka Ghosal, "Tea Brokers Called to Account," *Economic Times,* April 30, 2009.

40. Ishita Ayan Dutt, "Tea Auctions Need Risk Mitigation: Ferguson," *Business Standard,* June 3, 2009.

41. Jeremy Kahn, "Pounding Gavels, Not Keys, to Sell India's Tea," *New York Times,* April 22, 2008.

42. As she spoke, she continued to refer to the 2002 A. F. Ferguson report, which was now sitting in my lap. This is "the Bible for us," she said, gesturing to the bound paper. "You need to reference this in your study." I asked if I could make a copy. She explained that this was her only copy but that she could email one. With some irony, her attachment failed to send, so she allowed me to take her "Bible" and return it immediately after I had it copied.

43. Cooper 2010, 170.

44. Lakoff 2008; Briggs 2011; Samimian-Darash 2013.

45. Zaloom 2006, 97.

46. Callon and Muniesa 2005, 1246.

47. MacKenzie 2006; Zaloom 2006; cf. Amrute 2016.

48. A. F. Ferguson 2002, 3.2.09–3.2.11.

49. A. F. Ferguson 2002, 4.4.05.

50. See Sunder Rajan 2006.

51. Elyachar 2012, 88–90; Guyer 2009; Amrute 2016.

52. MacKenzie 2006, 13–15; Cronon 1992; Callon 1998.

53. Mazzarella 2006, 476; cf. Gupta 1995; Hull 2012.

54. Dan Bolton, "India's Tea Board Explores Expanding Tea Auction," *World Tea News,* July 5, 2017, https://worldteanews.com/news/indias-tea-board-wants-auction-100-tea-output.

55. On finance, see Zaloom 2006; MacKenzie 2006; Preda 2006; Miyazaki 2013. On scenarios, nature, and numbers, see Lakoff 2008; Samimian-Darash 2013; Edwards 2010.

56. Anand 2017. See also Appel 2012; Larkin 2013.

CONCLUSION

1. Callon, Méadel, and Rabeharisoa 2002.

2. Dabashi 2017.

3. Williams 2015, xxvii.

4. Tsing 2005.

5. Blanchette 2015, 653.

6. Rheinberger 1998, 287–88; quoted in Vine 2018, 407.

7. Jensen and Morita 2015, 83.

8. Guthman 2007.

9. See Schulevitz 2013; Tiku 2018. I am using "disruption" here in the narrow sense in which it appears in North American techno-speak. While there is a robust literature on rupture, disruption, and upending of normativity that derives from a feminist tradition, that is not how disruption is spoken about in the sectors to which I refer here. Importantly, many of the underlying structures and feelings that shape the market are not being unthought in Silicon Valley–style disruption. As I argue here, the opposite is the case. The plantation and its fundamental inequalities—including gender inequalities—persist.

10. See, e.g., Cross 2013. This conjoining of market and ethical goals separates TeaTime from earlier ethical trade schemes such as fair trade and puts it closer to C.K. Prahalad–inspired "bottom of the pyramid economic development" (see Street and Cross 2009). Though fair trade shares TeaTime's emphasis on direct sales and eliminating intermediaries, unlike TeaTime, fair trade organizations like Equal Exchange are less interested in growing as corporate brands.

11. Lepore 2014.

12. Liu 2015.

13. Besky 2017a.

BIBLIOGRAPHY

PRIMARY AND HISTORICAL SOURCES

Andrews, E. A. 1939. "Observations on Tea." Empire Tea Bureau, London.

The Art of Tea Blending: A Handbook for the Tea Trade. Guide to the Merchants, Brokers, Dealers and Consumers, in the Secret of Successful Tea Mixing. 1893. London: W. B. Whittingham & Co.

Bag, Sharmik. 2015. "Russel Exchange Auction House: Everything Is Saleable." *LiveMint,* March 21.

Baildon, Samuel. 1882. *The Tea Industry in India: A Review of Finance and Labor and a Guide for Capitalists.* London: W. H. Allen and Co.

Ball, Samuel. 1848. *An Account of the Cultivation and Manufacture of Tea in China.* London: Longman, Brown, Green, and Longmans.

Bamber, M. Kelway. 1893. *A Textbook on the Chemistry and Agriculture of Tea, including the Growth and Manufacture.* Calcutta: Law Publishing Press.

Bera, Sayantan. 2015. "Crushed and Torn." *Down to Earth,* June 11. www .downtoearth.org.in/coverage/crushed-and-torn-43885.

Bolton, Dan. 2017. "India's Tea Board Explores Expanding Tea Auction." *World Tea News,* July 5. https://worldteanews.com/news/indias-tea-board-wants-auction-100-tea-output.

Buerkle, Tom. 1998. "After 300 Years of Auctions, This Tea Break Is Final." *New York Times,* June 30.

Buckingham, Sir James. 1910. *A Few Facts about Indian Tea.* London: Indian Tea Association.

Calcutta Tea Traders Association (CTTA). ca. 2008. *CTTA Tea Digest.* Calcutta: Self-published. [In author's personal collection.]

Chakrabarty, Ashoke. 2016. "The Dying Tea Gardens of North Bengal." *The Hindu,* Business Line, February 23. www.thehindubusinessline.com/economy/agri-business/the-dying-tea-gardens-of-north-bengal/article8272419.ece.

Chamney, Montfort. 1930. *The Story of the Tea Leaf.* Calcutta: New India Press.

Chaudhuri, Mohuya. 2015. "Tea Gardens in the East Are Brewing Starvation, Malnutrition." *The Wire,* July 30. https://thewire.in/economy/tea-gardens-in-the-east-are-brewing-starvation-malnutrition.

Committee of Tea Dealers. 1785. *A Narrative of the Conduct of the Tea Dealers, During the Sale of Teas at the India House.* London: n.p.

Cowper, William. [1785] 1899. *The Task and Other Poems.* London: Cassel & Cassel Co.

Dutt, Ishita Ayan. 2009. "Tea Auctions Need Risk Mitigation: Ferguson." *Business Standard,* June 3.

Ferguson, A. F., & Co. 2002. "Study on Primary Marketing of Tea in India—Final Report." [Author's personal collection.]

Forum for the Future. 2013. "Tea 2030: 19 Factors Likely to Drive Future Development of Value Chain." www.forumforthefuture.org/media-centre/tea-2030-19-factors-likely-drive-future-development-value-chain. Accessed December 28, 2014.

———. 2014. *The Future of Tea: A Hero Crop for 2030.* London: Forum for the Future.

Ghosal, Sutanuka. 2009. "Tea Brokers Called to Account." *Economic Times,* April 30.

Government of India. 1956. *Report of the Plantation Inquiry Commission.* Delhi: Government of India Press.

———. Ministry of Commerce and Industry. 1950. "The Report of the Government of India's Ad Hoc Committee on Tea." Government of India, Calcutta.

Gray, Arthur. 1903. *The Little Tea Book.* New York: Baker Taylor Co.

Harler, C. R. [1933] 1956. *The Culture and Marketing of Tea.* 2nd ed. Bombay: Oxford University Press.

Hauser, I. L. 1890. *Tea: Its Origin, Cultivation, Manufacture, and Use.* Chicago: Rand McNally & Co.

Hazarika, Mridul, and Mrinal Talukdar. 2001. *Tocklai and Tea . . . as the Road Fades Away.* Self-published by TRA.

Ibbetson, A. 1910. *Tea: From Grower to Consumer.* London: Sir Isaac Pitman & Sons.

J. Thomas & Co. Pvt. Ltd. ca. 1976. *Celebrating 125 Years of Tea Auctions in India: A History.* n.p.: J. Thomas & Co. [Author's personal collection.]

Kahn, Jeremy. 2008. "Pounding Gavels, Not Keys, to Sell India's Tea." *New York Times,* April 22.

Lancet. 1893. "*The Lancet* Analytical Commission on Tannin and Theine in China and Indian Teas." *Lancet,* July 1, 48–49.

———. 1903. "Probable Poisoning by Tannic Acid." *Lancet,* September 19, 838.

———. 1908. "A Controversy about Tea." *Lancet,* August 8, 325.

———. 1911a. "The Chemistry, Physiology, and Aesthetics of a Cup of Tea." *Lancet,* January 7, 44, 46–49.

———. 1911b. "The Chemistry, Physiology, and Aesthetics of a Cup of Tea" [Follow-up study]. *Lancet,* December 2, 1499, 1573–76.

———. 1936a. "Tea." *Lancet,* December 26, 1533–34.

———. 1936b. "Tea and Coffee: A Pharmacological Discussion." *Lancet,* February 15, 387–88.

MacLeod, H. W. G. 1908. "A Controversy about Tea: To the Editor of *The Lancet.*" *Lancet,* August 8, 421.

McGowan, Alexander. 1860. *Tea Planting in the Outer Himalayah.* London: Smith, Elder, and Co.

Money, Edward. 1884. *The Tea Controversy: Indian versus Chinese Teas. Which are Adulterated? Which Are Better?* 2nd ed. London: W. B. Whittingham.

A New Essay on Tea. 1936. London: Empire Tea Bureau.

Pandey, Sanjay. 2014. "India's Starving Tea Garden Workers." *Al Jazeera,* September 5. www.aljazeera.com/indepth/features/2014/09/india-starving-tea-garden-workers-201493123018527103.html.

Reade, Arthur. 1884. *Tea and Tea Drinking.* London: Sampson Low, Marston, Searle & Rivington.

Reevel, Patrick. 2014. "Abandoned Tea Plantation Workers in India Are Stalked by Hunger, Death." *Seattle Times,* October 18. www.seattletimes.com/business/abandoned-tea-plantation-workers-in-india-are-stalked-by-hunger-death/.

Reid, T. R. 1998. "Tea and Sympathy: Traders Lament End of London Auction." *Washington Post,* June 30.

S. Priyadershini 2012. "A Tea Time Story." *The Hindu,* January 28.

Shaktan, Ashutosh. 2016. "The Plight of Tea Plantation Workers of Dooars." *Caravan,* June 23. https://caravanmagazine.in/vantage/plight-tea-plantation-workers-dooars

———. n.d. "Tea, the Ugly Beverage." Lensculture.com. www.lensculture.com/articles/ashutosh-shaktan-tea-the-ugly-beverage

Shulevitz, Judith. 2013. "Don't You Dare Say 'Disruptive.'" *New Republic,* August 15. https://newrepublic.com/article/114125/disruption-silicon-valleys-worst-buzzwor.

Tea and Tea Blending by a Member of the Firm of Lewis & Co. 1894. 4th ed. London: Eden Fisher.

Tea Cultivation. 1865. Calcutta: Military Orphan Press. [Collection of the National Library of India.]

["A Tea Dealer"]. 1826. *Tsiology: A Discourse on Tea, Being an Account of That Exotic; Botanical, Chymical, Commercial, & Medicinal, with Notices of Its Adulteration, the Means of Detection, Tea Making, with a Brief History of the East India Company.* London: Wh. Walker.

Tiku, Nitasha. 2018. "An Alternative History of Silicon Valley Disruption." *Wired,* October 22. www.wired.com/story/alternative-history-of-silicon-valley-disruption/.

Twining, Richard. 1785. *Remarks on the Report of the East India Directors, Respecting the Sale and Prices of Tea.* London: T. Cadell.

Walsh, Joseph. 1892. *Tea, Its History and Mystery.* Philadelphia: Published by the Author.

Abrahamsson, Sebastian, Fillipo Bertoni, Annemarie Mol, and Rebeca Ibáñez Martín. 2015. "Living with Omega-3: New Materialism and Enduring Concerns." *Environment and Planning D: Society and Space* 33 (1): 4–19.

Adams, Vincanne, ed. 2017. *Metrics: What Counts in Global Health.* Durham, NC: Duke University Press.

Akerlof, George. 1970. "The Market for Lemons: Quality Uncertainty and the Market Mechanism." *Quarterly Journal of Economics* 84 (3): 488–500.

Aldous, Michael. 2017. "Rehabilitating the Intermediary: Brokers and Auctioneers in the Nineteenth-Century Anglo-Indian Trade." *Business History* 59 (4): 525–53.

Ali, Tariq Omar. 2018. *A Local History of Global Capital: Jute and Peasant Life in the Bengal Delta.* Princeton, NJ: Princeton University Press.

Amrute, Sareeta. 2016. *Encoding Race, Encoding Class: Indian IT Workers in Berlin.* Durham, NC: Duke University Press.

Anand, Nikhil. 2017. *Hydraulic City: Water and the Infrastructures of Citizenship in Mumbai.* Durham, NC: Duke University Press.

Anderson, Warwick. 2002. "Introduction: Postcolonial Technoscience." *Social Studies of Science* 32 (5–6): 643–58.

Appadurai, Arjun, ed. 1986. *The Social Life of Things: Commodities in Cultural Perspective.* Cambridge: Cambridge University Press.

———. 1996. *Modernity at Large: Cultural Dimensions of Globalization.* Minneapolis: University of Minnesota Press.

Appel, Hannah. 2012. "Offshore Work: Oil, Modularity, and the How of Capitalism in Equatorial Guinea." *American Ethnologist* 39 (4): 692–709.

Arnold, David. 2005. "Agriculture and 'Improvement' in Early Colonial India: A Pre-History of Development." *Journal of Agrarian Change* 5 (4): 505–25.

Banaji, Jarius. 2013. "Seasons of Self-Delusion: Opium, Capitalism, and the Financial Markets." *Historical Materialism* 21 (2): 3–19.

Banerjee, Dwaipayan. 2017. "Markets and Molecules: A Pharmaceutical Primer from the South." *Medical Anthropology* 36 (4): 363–80.

Barad, Karen. 2007. *Meeting the Universe Halfway: Quantum Physics and the Entanglement of Matter and Meaning.* Durham, NC: Duke University Press.

Bass, Daniel. 2012. *Everyday Ethnicity in Sri Lanka: Up-Country Tamil Identity Politics.* New York: Routledge.

Bauch, Nicholas. 2017. *A Geography of Digestion: Biotechnology and the Kellogg Cereal Enterprise.* Oakland: University of California Press.

Bear, Laura. 2007. *Lines of the Nation: Indian Railway Workers, Bureaucracy, and the Intimate Historical Self.* New York: Columbia University Press.

———. 2015. *Navigating Austerity: Currents of Debt along a South Asian River.* Palo Alto, CA: Stanford University Press.

Benjamin, Walter. 1968. *Illuminations: Essays and Reflections.* Trans. H. Zohn. Ed. H. Arendt. New York: Random House.

Benson, Peter. 2012. *Tobacco Capitalism: Growers, Migrant Workers, and the Changing Face of a Global Industry*. Princeton, NJ: Princeton University Press.

Berenstein, Nadia. 2018. "Designing Flavors for Mass Consumption." *Senses and Society* 13 (1): 19–40.

Besky, Sarah. 2008. "Can a Plantation Be Fair? Paradoxes and Possibilities in Fair Trade Darjeeling Tea Certification." *Anthropology of Work Review* 29 (1): 1–9.

———. 2014a. *The Darjeeling Distinction: Labor and Justice on Fair-Trade Tea Plantations in India*. Berkeley: University of California Press.

———. 2014b. "The Labor of *Terroir* and the *Terroir* of Labor: Geographical Indication on Darjeeling Tea Plantations." *Agriculture and Human Values* 31 (1): 83–96.

———. 2015. "Agricultural Justice, Abnormal Justice? Fair Trade's Plantation Problem." *Antipode* 47 (5): 1141–60.

———. 2017a. "Fixity: On the Inheritance and Maintenance of Tea Plantation Houses in Darjeeling, India." *American Ethnologist* 44 (4): 617–31.

———. 2017b. "Tea as 'Hero Crop'? Embodied Algorithms and Industrial Reform in India." *Science as Culture* 26 (1): 11–31.

Bestor, Theodore. 2004. *Tsukiji: The Fishmarket at the Center of the World*. Berkeley: University of California Press.

Bhabha, Homi. 1984. "Of Mimicry and Man: The Ambivalence of Colonial Discourse." *October* 28: 125–33.

Bhadra, Gautam. 2005. *From an Imperial Product to a National Drink: The Culture of Tea Consumption in Modern India*. Kolkata: Centre for Studies in the Social Sciences and Tea Board of India.

Biltekoff, Charlotte. 2013. *Eating Right in America: The Cultural Politics of Food and Health*. Berkeley: University of California Press.

Biltekoff, Charlotte, Jessica Mudry, Aya Kimura, Hannah Landecker, and Julie Guthman. 2014. "Interrogating Moral and Quantification Discourses in Nutritional Knowledge." *Gastronomica* 14 (3): 17–26.

Blanchette, Alex. 2015. "Herding Species: Biosecurity, Posthuman Labor, and the American Industrial Pig." *Cultural Anthropology* 30 (4): 640–69.

Bonneuil, Christophe. 2000. "Science and State Building in Late Colonial and Postcolonial Africa, 1930–1970." *Osiris* 15 (1): 258–81.

Bourdieu, Pierre. 1984. *Distinction: A Social Critique of the Judgment of Taste*. London: Routledge.

Bowen, Sarah. 2015. *Divided Spirits: Tequila, Mezcal, and the Politics of Production*. Berkeley: University of California Press.

Bray, Francesca. 2008. "Science, Technique, Technology: Passages between Matter and Knowledge in Imperial Chinese Agriculture." *British Journal for the History of Science* 41 (3): 319–44.

Brenner, Neil. 1998. "Between Fixity and Motion: Accumulation, Territorial Organization and the Historical Geography of Spatial Scales." *Environment and Planning D* 16 (4): 459–81.

Briggs, Charles. 2011. "Communicating Biosecurity." *Medical Anthropology* 30 (1): 6–29.

Brockway, Lucile. 1979. *Science and Colonial Expansion: The Role of the British Royal Botanic Gardens*. London: Academic Press.

Brown, Hannah. 2015. "Global Health Partnerships, Governance, and Sovereign Responsibility in Western Kenya." *American Ethnologist* 42 (2): 340–55.

Burawoy, Michael, and Katherine Verdery. 1999. *Uncertain Transition: Ethnographies of Change in the Postsocialist World*. New York: Rowman and Littlefield.

Callon, Michel, ed. 1998. *Laws of the Markets*. London: Blackwell.

Callon, Michel, Cécile Méadel, and Vololona Rabeharisoa. 2002. "Economy of Qualities." *Economy and Society* 31 (2): 194–217.

Callon, Michel, Yuval Millo, and Fabian Muniesa, eds. 2007. *Market Devices*. Malden, MA: Blackwell.

Callon, Michel, and Fabian Muniesa. 2005. "Economic Markets as Calculative Collective Devices." *Organizational Studies*. 26 (8): 1229–50.

Calvão, Filipe. 2013. "The Transporter, the Agitator, and the Kamanguista: Qualia and the In/visible Materiality of Diamonds." *Anthropological Theory* 13 (1–2): 119–36.

Carr, E. Summerson. 2010. "Enactments of Expertise." *Annual Review of Anthropology* 39: 17–32.

Carse, Ashley. 2014. *Beyond the Big Ditch: Nature and Culture at the Panama Canal*. Cambridge, MA: MIT Press.

Cavanaugh, Jillian. 2016. "Documenting Subjects: Performativity and Audit Culture in Food Production in Northern Italy." *American Ethnologist* 43 (4): 691–703.

Cavanaugh, Jillian, and Shalini Shankar. 2014. "Producing Authenticity in Global Capitalism: Language, Materiality, and Value." *American Anthropologist* 116 (1): 51–64.

Chatterjee, Partha. 2012. *The Black Hole of Empire: A History of a Global Practice of Power*. Princeton, NJ: Princeton University Press.

Chatterjee, Piya. 2001. *A Time for Tea: Women, Labor, and Post/Colonial Politics on an Indian Plantation*. Durham, NC: Duke University Press.

Chen, Mel. 2012. *Animacies: Biopolitics, Racial Mattering, and Queer Affect*. Durham, NC: Duke University Press.

Chumley, Lily. 2013. "Evaluation Regimes and the Qualia of Quality." *Anthropological Theory* 13 (1–2): 169–83.

Chumley, Lily, and Nicholas Harkness. 2013. "Introduction: Qualia." *Anthropological Theory* 13 (1–2): 3–11.

Clifford, James. 1997. *Routes: Travel and Translation in the Late Twentieth Century*. Cambridge, MA: Harvard University Press.

Cohn, Bernard. 1996. *Colonialism and Its Forms of Knowledge: The British in India*. Princeton, NJ: Princeton University Press.

Collins, Jane. 2002. "Deterritorialization and Workplace Culture." *American Ethnologist* 29 (1): 51–71.

———. 2017. *The Politics of Value: Three Movements to Change How We Think about the Economy.* Chicago: University of Chicago Press.

Combris, Pierre, Sebastien Lecocq, and Michael Visser. 1997. "Estimation of a Hedonic Price Equation for Bordeaux Wine: Does Quality Matter? *The Economic Journal* 107: 390–402.

Cooper, Melinda. 2010. "Turbulent Worlds: Financial Markets and Environmental Crisis." *Theory, Culture & Society* 27 (2–3): 167–90.

Cronon, William. 1992. *Nature's Metropolis: Chicago and the Great West.* New York: Norton.

Cross, Jamie. 2013. "The 100th Object: Solar Lighting Technology and Humanitarian Goods." *Journal of Material Culture* 18 (4): 367–87.

———. 2015. "The Economy of Anticipation: Hope, Infrastructure, and Economic Zones in South India." *Comparative Studies of South Asia, Africa and the Middle East* 35 (3): 424–37.

Cross, Jamie, and Luke Hesslop. 2019. "Anthropology for Sale." *Ethnos* 84 (3): 369–79.

Dabashi, Hamid. 2017. "How British Colonialism Ruined a Perfect Cup of Tea." *Al Jazeera,* September 18. www.aljazeera.com/indepth/opinion/british-colonialism-ruined-perfect-cup-tea-170918113331476.html.

Daniel, E. Valentine. 2008. "The Coolie." *Cultural Anthropology* 23 (2): 254–78.

Daniel, E. Valentine, Harry Bernstein, and Tom Brass, eds. 1992. *Plantations, Proletarians, and Peasants in Colonial Asia.* London: Frank Cass.

Das Gupta, Ranajit. 1992. *Economy, Society, and Politics in Bengal: Jalpaiguri, 1869–1947.* New Delhi: Oxford University Press.

Debnath, Sailen. 2011. *The Dooars in Historical Transition.* Siliguri: NL Publishers.

Denig, Viki. 2016. "Why I Hate Female Sommeliers and So Should You." VinePair, November 28. https://vinepair.com/articles/hate-female-somms/.

Dey, Arnab. 2018. *Tea Environments and Plantation Culture: Imperial Disarray in Eastern India.* Cambridge: Cambridge University Press.

Drayton, Richard. 2000. *Nature's Government: Science, Imperial Britain, and the "Improvement" of the World.* New Haven, CT: Yale University Press.

Duchêne, Alexandre, and Monica Heller. 2012. *Language in Late Capitalism: Pride and Profit.* New York: Routledge.

DuPuis, Melanie. 2015. *Dangerous Digestion: The Politics of American Dietary Advice.* Oakland: University of California Press.

Durkheim, Émile. [1912] 1995. *The Elementary Forms of Religious Life.* New York: Free Press.

Edwards, Paul. 2010. *A Vast Machine: Computer Models, Climate Data, and the Politics of Global Warming.* Cambridge, MA: MIT Press.

Elyachar, Julia. 2005. *Markets of Dispossession: NGOs, Economic Development, and the State in Cairo.* Durham, NC: Duke University Press.

———. 2010. "Phatic Labor, Infrastructure, and the Question of Empowerment in Cairo." *American Ethnologist* 37 (3): 452–64.

———. 2012. "Before (and After) Neoliberalism: Tacit Knowledge, Secrets of the Trade, and the Public Sector in Egypt." *Cultural Anthropology* 27 (1): 76–96.

Farooqui, Amar. 1998. *Smuggling as Subversion: Colonialism, Indian Merchants, and the Politics of Opium, 1790–1843.* New Delhi: New Age International.

Ferguson, James. 1991. *The Anti-Politics Machine: Development, Depoliticization, and Bureaucratic Power in Lesotho.* Minneapolis: University of Minnesota Press.

Fernandes, Leela. 1997. *Producing Workers: The Politics of Gender, Class, and Culture in the Calcutta Jute Mills.* Philadelphia: University of Pennsylvania Press.

Ferry, Elizabeth. 2013. *Minerals, Collecting, and Value across the U.S.-Mexican Border.* Bloomington: University of Indiana Press.

———. 2016. "On Not Being a Sign: Gold's Semiotic Claims." *Signs and Society* 4 (1): 57–79.

Finkelstein, Maura. 2019. *The Archive of Loss: Lively Ruination in Mill Land Mumbai.* Durham, NC: Duke University Press.

Forrest, Denys. 1973. *Tea for the British: The Social and Economic History of a Famous Trade.* London: Chatto & Windus.

Fortun, Kim. 2001. *Advocacy after Bhopal: Environmentalism, Disasters, New Global Orders.* Chicago: University of Chicago Press.

Freidberg, Susanne. 2010. *Fresh: A Perishable History.* Cambridge, MA: Harvard University Press.

Gal, Susan. 2005. "Language Ideologies Compared: Metaphors and Circulations of Public and Private. " *Journal of Linguistic Anthropology* 15 (1): 23–37.

Gewertz, Deborah, and Frederick Errington. 2010. *Cheap Meat: Flap Food Nations in the Pacific Islands.* Berkeley: University of California Press.

Goodman, Michael. 2003. "The Quality 'Turn' and Alternative Food Practices: Reflections and Agenda." *Journal of Rural Studies* 19 (1): 1–7.

Grasseni, Cristina. 2003. "Packaging Skills: Calibrating Cheese to the Global Market." In *Commodifying Everything: Relationships of the Market,* ed. Susan Strasser, 259–88. New York: Routledge.

Griffiths, Percival. 1967. *The History of the Indian Tea Industry.* London: Weidenfeld and Nicolson.

Gupta, Akhil. 1995. "Blurred Boundaries: The Discourse of Corruption, the Culture of Politics, and the Imagined State." *American Ethnologist* 22 (2): 375–402.

Guthman, Julie. 2007. "Can't Stomach It: How Michael Pollan et al. Made Me Want to Eat Cheetos." *Gastronomica: Journal of Critical Food Studies* 7 (3): 75–79.

———. 2011. *Weighing In: Obesity, Food Justice, and the Limits of Capitalism.* Berkeley: University of California Press.

———. 2014. *Agrarian Dreams: The Paradox of Organic Farming in California.* 2nd ed. Berkeley: University of California Press.

Guyer, Jane. 2004. *Marginal Gains: Monetary Transactions in Atlantic Africa.* Chicago: University of Chicago Press.

———. 2009. "Composites, Fictions and Risk: Toward an Ethnography of Price." In *Market and Society: The Great Transformation Today,* ed. Chris Hann and Keith Hart, 203–20. Cambridge: Cambridge University Press.

———. 2016. *Legacies, Logics, Logistics: Essays in the Anthropology of the Platform Economy.* Chicago: University of Chicago Press.

Hannan, Abdul. 2014. "Critical Review of Tea Producing Societies within Tea Industry." In *Poverty, Livelihood Rights and the Small Tea Growers in the Northeast,* ed. J. John, 39–58. New Delhi: Centre for Education and Communication.

Hansen, Karen Tranberg. 2000. *Salaula: The World of Secondhand Clothing and Zambia.* Chicago: University of Chicago Press.

Haraway, Donna. 2015. "Anthropocene, Capitalocene, Plantationocene, Cthulucene: Making Kin." *Environmental Humanities* 6 (1): 159–65.

Harkness, Nicholas. 2015. "The Pragmatics of Qualia in Practice." *Annual Review of Anthropology* 44: 573–89.

Harvey, David. 2001. *Spaces of Capital: Towards a Critical Geography.* New York: Routledge.

Hayden, Cory. 2007. "A Generic Solution? Pharmaceuticals and the Politics of the Similar in Mexico." *Current Anthropology* 48 (4): 475–95.

Heath, Deborah, and Anne Meneley. 2007. "Techne, Technoscience, and the Circulation of Comestible Commodities: An Introduction." *American Anthropologist* 109 (4): 593–602.

Hébert, Karen. 2010. "In Pursuit of Singular Salmon: Paradoxes of Sustainability and the Quality Commodity." *Science as Culture* 19 (4): 553–81.

———. 2014. "The Matter of Market Devices: Economic Transformation in a Southwest Alaska Salmon Fishery." *Geoforum* 53: 21–30.

Hecht, Gabrielle. 2012. *Being Nuclear: Africans in the Global Uranium Trade.* Cambridge, MA: MIT Press.

Heller, Monica. 2010. "The Commodification of Language." *Annual Review of Anthropology* 39: 101–14.

Hennion, Antione. 2007. "Those Things That Hold Us Together: Taste and Sociology." *Cultural Sociology* 1 (1): 97–114.

Herring, Ronald. 2015. "State Science, Risk and Agricultural Biotechnology: Bt Cotton to Bt Brinjal in India." *Journal of Peasant Studies* 42: 159–86.

Herzfeld, Michael. 2004. *The Body Impolitic: Artisans and Artifice in the Global Hierarchy of Value.* Chicago: University of Chicago Press.

Horkheimer, Max, and Theodor Adorno. [1944] 1972. *Dialectic of Enlightenment.* New York: Continuum.

Hull, Matthew. 2012. *Government of Paper: The Materiality of Bureaucracy in Urban Pakistan.* Berkeley: University of California Press.

Hung, Po-Yi. 2015. *Tea Production, Land Use Politics, and Ethnic Minorities: Struggling over Dilemmas in China's Southwest Frontier.* London: Palgrave Macmillan.

Ives, Sarah. *Steeped in Heritage: The Racial Politics of South African Rooibos Tea.* Durham, NC: Duke University Press.

Jegathesan, Mythri. 2019. *Tea and Solidarity: Tamil Women and Work in Postwar Sri Lanka.* Seattle: University of Washington Press.

Jensen, Casper Bruun, and Atsuro Morita. 2015. "Infrastructures as Ontological Experiments." *Engaging Science, Technology, and Society* 1: 81–87.

Jones, Graham. 2011. *Trade of the Tricks: Inside the Magician's Craft.* Berkeley: University of California Press.

Jones, Stephanie. 1992. *Merchants of the Raj: British Managing Agency Houses in Calcutta Yesterday and Today.* London: Basingstoke.

Jons, Heike. 2016. "The University of Cambridge, Academic Expertise and the British Empire, 1885–1962." *Environment and Planning A* 48 (1): 94–114.

Kale, Sunila. 2014. *Electrifying India: Regional Political Economies of Development.* Palo Alto, CA: Stanford University Press.

Kar, Sohini. 2018. *Financializing Poverty: Labor and Risk in Indian Microfinance.* Stanford, CA: Stanford University Press.

Kloppenburg, Jack. 2005. *First the Seed: The Political Ecology of Plant Biotechnology, 1492–2000.* 2nd ed. Madison: University of Wisconsin Press.

Kopytoff, Igor. 1986. "The Cultural Biography of Things: Commoditization as Process." In *The Social Life of Things: Commodities in Cultural Perspective,* ed. Arjun Appadurai, 64–94. Cambridge: Cambridge University Press.

Krishnamurthy, Mekhala. 2012. "States of Wheat: The Changing Dynamics of Public Procurement in Madhya Pradesh." *Economic and Political Weekly* 47 (52): 72–83.

Kumar, Prakash. 2012. *Indigo Plantations and Science in Colonial India.* Cambridge: Cambridge University Press.

Lakoff, Andrew. 2008. "The Generic Biothreat, or, How We Became Unprepared." *Cultural Anthropology* 23 (3): 399–428.

Lampland, Martha. 2016. *The Value of Labor: The Science of Commodification in Hungary, 1920–1956.* Chicago: University of Chicago Press.

Landecker, Hannah. 2016. "Antibiotic Resistance and the Biology of History." *Body and Society* 22 (4): 19–52.

Larkin, Brian. 2013. "The Politics and Poetics of Infrastructure." *Annual Review of Anthropology* 42: 327–43.

Latour, Bruno. 1993. *We Have Never Been Modern.* Cambridge, MA: Harvard University Press.

———. 2004. "How to Talk about the Body? The Normative Dimension of Science Studies." *Body & Society* 10 (2–3): 205–29.

Lehrer, Adrienne. 2009. *Wine and Conversation.* 2nd ed. Oxford: Oxford University Press.

Leins, Stefan. 2018. *Stories of Capitalism: Inside the Role of Financial Analysts.* Chicago: University of Chicago Press.

Lepore, Jill. 2014. "The Disruption Machine: What the Gospel of Innovation Gets Wrong." *New Yorker,* June 23.

Lezaun, Javier, and Catherine Montgomery. 2015. "The Pharmaceutical Commons: Sharing and Exclusion in Global Health Drug Development." *Science, Technology, and Human Values* 40 (1): 3–29.

Liboiron, Max, Manuel Tironi, and Nerea Calvillo. 2018. "Toxic Politics: Acting in a Permanently Polluted World." *Social Studies of Science* 48 (3): 331–49.

LiPuma, Edward, and Benjamin Lee. 2004. *Financial Derivatives and the Globalization of Risk*. Durham, NC: Duke University Press.

Liu, Andrew. 2015. "The Two Tea Countries: Competition, Labor, and Economic Thought in Coastal China and Eastern India, 1834–1942." PhD diss., Columbia University.

Lutgendorf, Philip. 2012. "Making Tea in India: Chai, Capitalism, Culture." *Thesis Eleven* 113 (1): 11–31.

Lyon, Sarah, and Mark Moberg. 2010. *Fair Trade and Social Justice: Global Ethnographies*. New York: New York University Press.

Maat, Harro. 2001. *Science Cultivating Practice: A History of Agricultural Science in the Netherlands and Its Colonies, 1863–1986*. Dordrecht: Kluwer Academic.

MacKenzie, Donald. 2006. *An Engine, Not a Camera: How Financial Models Shape Markets*. Cambridge, MA: MIT Press.

Manning, Paul. 2012. *Semiotics of Food and Drink*. London: Continuum.

Marcus, George. 2005. "Ethnography in/of the World System: The Emergence of Multi-Sited Ethnography." *Annual Review of Anthropology* 24: 95–117.

Marcus, George, and Fred Myers. 1995. *The Traffic in Culture: Refiguring Art and Anthropology*. Berkeley: University of California Press.

Marx, Karl. [1867] 1967. *Capital*. Vol. 1. New York: Penguin.

Mathur, Nayanika. 2015. *Law, Bureaucracy, and the Developmental State in Himalayan India*. Cambridge: Cambridge University Press

Mazzarella, William. 2006. "Internet X-Ray: E-Governance, Transparency, and the Politics of Immediation in India." *Public Culture* 18 (3): 473–505.

———. 2017. *The Mana of Mass Society*. Chicago: University of Chicago Press.

Meneley, Anne. 2007. "Like an Extra Virgin." *American Anthropologist* 109 (4): 678–87.

Mintz, Sidney. 1960. *Worker in the Cane: A Puerto Rican Life History*. New Haven, CT: Yale University Press.

———. 1979. "Time, Sugar, and Sweetness." *Marxist Perspectives* 2: 56–73.

———. 1985. *Sweetness and Power: The Place of Sugar in Modern History*. New York: Penguin Books.

Miyazaki, Hirokazu. 2013. *Arbitraging Japan: Dreams of Capitalism at the End of Finance*. Berkeley: University of California Press.

Mol, Annemarie. 2002. *The Body Multiple: Ontology in Medical Practice*. Durham, NC: Duke University Press.

———. 2009. "Good Taste: The Embodied Normativity of the Consumer-Citizen." *Journal of Cultural Economy* 2 (3): 269–83.

Moore, Jason. 2015. *Capitalism in the Web of Life: Ecology and the Accumulation of Capital*. New York: Verso.

Munn, Nancy. 1986. *The Fame of Gawa: A Symbolic Study of Value Transformation in a Massim Society*. Durham, NC: Duke University Press.

Murphy, Michelle. 2006. *Sick Building Syndrome and the Problem of Uncertainty*. Durham, NC: Duke University Press.

———. 2013. "Chemical Infrastructures of the St Clair River." In *Toxicants, Health, and Regulation since 1945,* ed. Soraya Boudia and Nathalie Jas, 103–15. London: Pickering & Chatto.

———. 2017. *The Economization of Life.* Durham, NC: Duke University Press.

Myers, Fred. 2001. "Introduction: The Empire of Things." In *The Empire of Things: Regimes of Value and Material Culture,* ed. F. Myers, 3–61. Santa Fe, NM: SAR Press.

Nading, Alex. 2017. "Orientation and Crafted Bureaucracy: Finding Dignity in Nicaraguan Food Safety." *American Anthropologist* 119 (3): 478–90.

Nakassis, Constantine. 2012. "Brand, Citationality, and Performativity." *American Anthropologist* 111 (4): 624–38.

Nash, June. 1979. *We Eat the Mines and the Mines Eat Us: Dependency and Exploitation in Bolivian Tin Mines.* New York: Columbia University Press.

Nash, Linda. 2007. *Inescapable Ecologies: A History of Environment, Disease, and Knowledge.* Durham, NC: Duke University Press.

Nestle, Marion. 2003. *Safe Food: The Politics of Food Safety.* Berkeley: University of California Press.

Neveling, Patrick. 2014. "Structural Contingencies and Untimely Coincidences in the Making of Neoliberal India: The Kandla Free Trade Zone, 1967–91." *Contributions to Indian Sociology* 48 (1): 17–43.

Nijhawan, Shobna. 2017. "Nationalizing the Consumption of Tea for the Hindi Reader: The Indian Tea Market Expansion Board's Advertisement Campaign." *Modern Asian Studies* 51 (5): 1229–52.

Patel, Raj, and Jason Moore. 2017. *A History of the World in Seven Cheap Things: A Guide to Capitalism, Nature, and the Future of the Planet.* Oakland: University of California Press.

Paxson, Heather. 2012. *The Life of Cheese: Crafting Food and Value in America.* Berkeley: University of California Press.

Peirce, Charles. [1903] 1998. "Nomenclature and Division of Triadic Relations, as Far as They Are Determined." In *The Essential Peirce, Selected Philosophical Writings: Volume 2 (1893–1913),* ed. Peirce Edition Project, 289–99. Bloomington: Indiana University Press.

Polanyi, Karl. [1944] 2001. *The Great Transformation: The Political and Economic Origins of Our Time.* Boston: Beacon Press.

Povinelli, Elizabeth. 2011. *Economies of Abandonment: Social Belonging and Endurance in Late Liberalism.* Durham, NC: Duke University Press.

Prakash, Gyan. 1992. "Science 'Gone Native' in Colonial India." *Representations* 40: 153–78.

Preda, Alex. 2006. "Socio-Technical Agency in Financial Markets: The Case of the Stock Ticker." *Social Studies of Science* 36 (5): 753–82.

Rabinbach, Anson. 1992. *The Human Motor: Energy, Fatigue, and the Origins of Modernity.* Berkeley: University of California Press.

Rappaport, Erika. 2017. *A Thirst for Empire: How Tea Shaped the Modern World.* Princeton, NJ: Princeton University Press.

Ray, Krishnendu, and Tulasi Srinivas, eds. 2012. *Curried Cultures: Globalization, Food, and South Asia.* Berkeley: University of California Press.

Reichman, Daniel. 2018. "Big Coffee in Brazil: Historical Origins and Implications for Anthropological Political Economy." *Journal of Latin American and Caribbean Anthropology* 23 (2): 241–61.

Rheinberger, Hans-Jörg. 1994. "Experimental Systems: Historiality, Narration, and Deconstruction." *Science in Context* 7 (1): 65–81.

Roseberry, William. 1996. "The Rise of Yuppie Coffees and the Reimagination of Class in the United States." *American Anthropologist* 94 (4): 762–75.

Rosenblum, Peter, and Ashwini Sukthankar. 2014. "*The More Things Change . . .*": *The World Bank, Tata, and Enduring Abuses on India's Tea Plantations.* New York: Columbia Law School Human Rights Institute.

Roy, Parama. 2010. *Alimentary Tracts: Appetites, Aversion, and the Postcolonial.* Durham, NC: Duke University Press.

Roy, Tirthankar. 2014. "Trading Firms in Colonial India." *Business History Review* 88 (Spring): 9–42.

Samimian-Darash, Limor. 2013. "Governing Future Potential Biothreats: Toward an Anthropology of Uncertainty." *Current Anthropology* 54 (1): 1–22.

Sankritayana, Jeta. 2014. "Change in Production Systems with Tea Industry." In *Poverty, Livelihood Rights and the Small Tea Growers in the Northeast,* ed. J. John, 39–58. New Delhi: Centre for Education and Communication.

Sawyer, Suzana and Arun Agrawal. 2000. "Environmental Orientalisms." *Cultural Critique* 45 (Spring): 71–108.

Scott, James. 1999. *Seeing Like a State: How Certain Schemes to Improve the Human Condition Have Failed.* New Haven, CT: Yale University Press.

Scrinis, Gyorgy. 2013. *Nutritionism: The Science and Politics of Dietary Advice.* New York: Columbia University Press.

Searle, Llerena. 2016. *Landscapes of Accumulation: Real Estate and the Neoliberal Imagination in Contemporary India.* Chicago: University of Chicago Press.

Sen, Debarati. 2017. *Everyday Sustainability: Gender Justice and Fair Trade in Darjeeling.* Albany: State University of New York Press.

Seth, Suman. 2009. "Putting Knowledge in Its Place: Science, Colonialism, and the Postcolonial." *Postcolonial Studies* 12 (4): 373–88.

Sethi, Aarti. 2018. "The Life of Debt in Rural India." PhD diss., Columbia University.

Shankar, Shalini, and Jillian Cavanaugh. 2012. "Language and Materiality in Global Capitalism." *Annual Review of Anthropology* 41: 355–69.

Shapin, Steven. 2012. "The Sense of Subjectivity." *Social Studies of Science* 42 (2): 170–84.

———. 2016. "A Taste of Science: Making the Subjective Objective in the California Wine World." *Social Studies of Science* 46 (3): 436–60.

Shapiro, Nicholas. 2015. "Attuning to the Chemosphere: Domestic Formaldehyde, Bodily Reasoning, and the Chemical Sublime." *Cultural Anthropology* 30 (3): 368–93.

Shapiro, Nicholas, and Eben Kirksey. 2017. "Chemo-Ethnography: An Introduction." *Cultural Anthropology* 32 (4): 481–93.

Sharma, Jayeeta. 2011. *Empire's Garden: Assam and the Making of Modern India.* Durham, NC: Duke University Press.

Silverstein, Michael. 2006. "Old Wine, New Ethnographic Lexicography." *Annual Review of Anthropology* 35: 481–96.

Simmel, Georg. 1950. *The Sociology of Georg Simmel.* Ed. K. Wolff. New York: Free Press.

Singerman, David. 2017. "The Limits of Chemical Control in the Caribbean Sugar Factory." *Radical History Review* 127: 39–61.

Smith, Charles. 1989. *Auctions: The Social Construction of Value.* Berkeley: University of California Press.

Spackman, Christy. 2018a. "Formulating Citizenship: The Microbiopolitics of the Malfunctioning Functional Beverage." *Biosocieties* 13 (1): 41–63.

———. 2018b. "Perfumer, Chemist, Machine: Gas Chromatography and the Industrial Search to 'Improve' Flavor." *Senses and Society* 13 (1): 41–59.

Spackman, Christy, and Gary Burlingame. 2018. "Sensory Politics: The Tug-of-War between Potability and Palatability in Municipal Water Production." *Social Studies of Science* 48 (3): 350–71.

Steiner, Christopher. 1992. Review of *Auctions: The Social Construction of Value* by Charles W. Smith. *American Ethnologist* 19 (3): 634–35.

———. 1994. *African Art in Transit.* Cambridge: Cambridge University Press.

Stoler, Ann. 1985. *Capitalism and Confrontation in Sumatra's Plantation Belt, 1870–1979.* New Haven, CT: Yale University Press.

———. 2002. *Carnal Knowledge and Imperial Power: Race and the Intimate in Colonial Rule.* Chicago: University of Chicago Press.

———. 2008. "Imperial Debris: Reflections on Ruins and Ruination." *Cultural Anthropology* 23 (2): 191–219.

Stone, Glenn Davis. 2007. "Agricultural Deskilling and the Spread of Genetically Modified Cotton in Warangal." *Current Anthropology* 48 (1): 67–103.

Street, Alice, and Jamie Cross. 2009. "Anthropology at the Bottom of the Pyramid." *Anthropology Today* 25 (4): 4–9.

Sunder Rajan, Kaushik. 2006. *Biocapital: The Constitution of Postgenomic Life.* Durham, NC: Duke University Press.

———, ed. 2012. *Lively Capital: Biotechnologies, Ethics, and Governance in Global Markets.* Durham, NC: Duke University Press.

Taussig, Michael. 1980. *The Devil and Commodity Fetishism in South America.* Chapel Hill: University of North Carolina Press.

Tompkins, Kyla. 2009. "Sylvester Graham's Imperial Dietetics." *Gastronomica* 9 (1): 50–60.

Tracy, Sarah. 2017. "Delicious Molecules: Big Food Science, the Chemosenses, and Umami." *Senses and Society* 13 (1): 89–107.

Tsing, Anna. 2005. *Friction: An Ethnography of Global Connection.* Princeton, NJ: Princeton University Press.

———. 2015. *The Mushroom at the End of the World: The Possibility of Life in Capitalist Ruins.* Princeton, NJ: Princeton University Press.

Ukers, William. 1935a. *All About Tea.* Vol. 1. New York: Tea and Coffee Trade Journal Company.

———. 1935b. *All About Tea.* Vol. 2. New York: Tea and Coffee Trade Journal Co.

Wahlberg, Ayo. 2018. *Good Quality: The Routinization of Sperm Banking in China.* Oakland: University of California Press.

Weiss, Brad. 2016. *Real Pigs: Shifting Values in the Field of Local Pork.* Durham, NC: Duke University Press.

West, Paige. 2012. *From Modern Production to Imagined Primitive: The Social World of Coffee from Papua New Guinea.* Durham, NC: Duke University Press.

Willford, Andrew. 2014. *Tamils and the Haunting of Justice: History and Recognition in Malaysia's Plantations.* Honolulu: University of Hawaii Press.

Williams, Raymond. [1976] 2015. *Keywords: A Vocabulary of Culture and Society.* Oxford: Oxford University Press.

Wolf, Eric. 1956. "Aspects of Group Relations in a Complex Society." *American Anthropologist* 58 (6): 1065–78.

Yano, Makoto. 2009. "The Foundation of Market Quality Economics." *Japanese Economic Review* 60 (1): 1–32.

Zaloom, Caitlin. 2006. *Out of the Pits: Traders and Technology from New York to London.* Chicago: University of Chicago Press.

Zeide, Anna. 2018. *Canned: The Rise and Fall of Consumer Confidence in the American Food Industry.* Oakland: University of California Press.

Zhang, Jihong. 2013. *Puer Tea: Ancient Caravans and Urban Chic.* Seattle: University of Washington Press.

INDEX

Abrahamsson, Sebastian, 188n42
active role of materials, 12, 30, 72, 188n42, 190n14
Adorno, Theodor, 187n26
agricultural experimental stations, 77, 94, 101, 199n91, 200–201n1
Amazing Race, The, 72
Amerine, Maynard, 190n25, 201n12
Andrews, E.A., 99
Anthropocene era, 137, 183
Appadurai, Arjun, 157
artisanal foods. *See* specialty products
Art of Tea Blending, The, 76, 77, 79, 198n61
Assam teas. *See* Indian teas
auction system, 9; African locations, 193n20; buyer tasting, 66–67; catalogs, 53*fig*, 54, 57, 58–60, 73, 193n13; and colonialism/imperialism, 50–51, 52, 56, 157, 192n3; and communicative infrastructure, 72–73, 155, 158, 162, 194n36; community within, 62, 158–59, 168, 173; as creator of markets, 157; direct sales encroachment on, 169–70, 174, 177, 178; drama in, 67–69; and experimentation, 59, 72; fixity in, 182–83; vs. futures market system, 56–57; London Commercial Sale Rooms, 52, 53–54, 56, 192n3; lot splitting, 69–71, 160, 165; media coverage of, 71–72; origins of, 5, 50–51, 187n16, 192n3; participation rules, 57–58, 193n27; performative nature of, 57, 72, 193n26; postindependence transition, 55–56, 110–11, 158,

190n22, 194n29; regulation of, 64, 65–66, 144, 194n30; Siliguri, 144, 175; as spot market, 156; and storage, 63, 190n22; tea categories for, 25–26, 58, 189n6; and variability, 65, 156, 159, 208n14. *See also* auction system reforms
auction system reforms: futures market conversion, 152, 171, 207n1; and leakage, 174; and markets, 157, 160–61, 169, 208n20; and power of tea brokers, 128–29, 153, 155, 161, 170; and regulation, 161–62, 170; and tasting training, 170–71, 172–73; and Tea Marketing Control Order, 169, 172; and technical expertise, 170. *See also* digital auctions
A.W. Figgis, 118

Bagnall, H.H., 98
Bamber, M.K., 196n29
Banerjee, Mamata, 189n3
Barad, Karen, 30, 41, 186n14
BBD Bagh, 21–22
Benjamin, Walter, 188n26
Bertoni, Filippo, 188n42
Bestor, Theodore, 13, 57, 72, 156, 186n12, 193n12
Bezboruah, Prabhat, 172
bhar, 22–23
"blackness," 34
Blanchette, Alex, 180
blending: and colonialism/imperialism, 74, 76, 78, 79; and cooperative movement, 84; and experimentation, 77, 78, 88;

83, 88–89; as regime of perceptibility, 195n11
indigo cultivation, 55
Indonesia. *See* Dutch East Indies
industrialization, 92. *See also* factory finishing
industrial science. *See* food sciences; tea research
inequality of race, class, and gender: and active role of materials, 30; and cheap tea, 3; and disruption, 210n9; and experimentation, 180; and plantation laborers, 6–7, 41, 77–78, 192n40; and taste descriptors, 37–38. *See also* colonialism/imperialism; racism
Insch, James, 202n19
instant tea, 119–20
International Tea Agreements, 111, 201n15
intersubjectivity engines, 37, 189n46

Java, 110. *See also* Dutch East Indies
Jensen, Casper Bruun, 189n47
J. Lyons and Company, 109
Johnson, F. G., 123–24
Jons, Heike, 202n19
J. Thomas and Company: archive of, 51–52; auction catalogs, 54, 55, 57, 63; and auction process, 60, 64, 67–69, 70–71; boardroom of, 49–51; consultancy work, 173; growth of, 144; hiring process, 28–29, 42–44; tasting process, 23–27, 34–35, 36, 38–39, 45–48; and tea research, 118; training at, 31–34, 42, 44–45

"keep," 34
Kilburn, J. M., 202n19

labor. *See* plantation laborers
Lal Dighi, 21
Lampitt, Leslie, 109, 110
Lancet: and Carpenter/Harler article, 95; and Leeds tea study, 96; and *New Essay*, 98; tea study (1893), 81–83, 91; tea study (1911), 87, 88, 95
laws. *See* regulation
leakage, 174
Leeder, John, 56

Lehrer, Adrienne, 191n30
Lepore, Jill, 181
Lettsom, John Coakley, 96
Lipton, 79
liquidity/fixity divide, 54, 182–83
Liu, Andrew, 181, 182
London Advisory Commission, 109–10, 202n41
London Commercial Sale Rooms, 52, 53–54, 56, 192n3
lot splitting, 69–71, 160, 165
Lutgendorf, Philip, 123, 124, 205n111

machinery. *See* factory finishing
MacKenzie, Donald, 171
MacKenzie Lyall, 55
MacLeod, H. W. G., 83
Mann, Harold, 200n1
Marcus, George, 13
marketing: and colonialism/imperialism, 74–75, 99; and domestic market, 112; and gender, 41; and monocropping, 6; and postindependence transition, 201n6; and racism, 80; and tea chemistry, 104
markets: auction system as creator of, 157; and auction system reforms, 157, 160–61, 169, 208n20; fairness of, 154, 207nn4,7; quality of, 154, 155; role in quality, 3, 12–13, 118, 153–54, 186n5; and taste descriptors, 37, 192n38
Marx, Karl, 208n16
masculinity, 29, 51. *See also* gender
mass-market tea. *See* cheap tea
Mazzarella, William, 11, 154, 158, 171, 203n53
McKercher, William, 123–24
McLeod, Charles, 89
Méadel, Cecile, 3, 15, 186nn5,12, 189n46, 191n32, 194n4
men. *See* gender
Meneley, Anne, 27, 30
Merchandise Mark Act (MMA) (1926) (United Kingdom), 84–85, 87–88, 199n93
Mincing Lane. *See* London Commercial Sale Rooms
Mintz, Sidney, 13, 98, 130
Modi, Narendra, 5

pendence transition, 10, 113–14, 201n6; regulatory powers, 6, 112–13, 144; and Tea Marketing Control Order, 169, 172; and tea research, 113–14; and Tea Research Association, 101. *See also* digital auctions

tea brokers: as arbiters of quality, 8–9; and auction system reforms, 128–29, 153, 155, 161, 170; as buffers, 31, 190n21; class of, 28–29, 36, 44; and colonialism/imperialism, 28–30, 157–58; as financiers, 56, 65, 159–60, 172; gender of, 9, 29, 36, 42, 43; hiring of, 29, 31, 42–44, 192n44; new consultancy roles, 173; Nilhat House environment, 22–23, 49–50, 51–52; and postindependence transition, 157–58; and secrecy, 154–55, 208n30; and standardization, 155; taste descriptors used by, 34–38; tea categories, 25–26, 189n6; training of, 31–33, 32*fig*, 42, 44–45, 170–71, 172–73. *See also* auction system; tasting process

Tea Brokers' Association, 36, 158

Tea Buyers' Association, 84

tea chemistry: and blending, 75, 76, 87–88; and colonialism/imperialism, 75, 76; and flavor vs. taste, 103; and food safety, 75–76; Harden on, 90–92; and racism, 83; and stimulant effects, 81, 196nn32,34; and taste descriptors, 35, 104–5, 191n26; and tea commodity chain, 14. *See also* tea chemistry research

tea chemistry research: Bamber, 196n29; Bradfield experiment, 109–10; Carpenter/Harler article, 94–95; and digestive teas, 200n101; First Engledow Commission recommendation for, 108–9; and grades of tea, 197n42; and instant tea, 119–20; *Lancet* study (1893), 81–83, 91; Leeds study, 96; London Advisory Commission report, 109–10, 202n41; Roberts/Wood, 115–18, 119, 120, 204nn73,76; on stimulant effects, 196n34

tea chests. *See* storage

tea commodity chain, 1–2; and colonialism/imperialism, 188n40; communica-

tive infrastructure in, 54, 72–73, 155, 158, 162, 193nn11–12, 194n36; and Darjeeling distinction, 188n40; direct sales, 169–70, 174, 177, 178; and embodiment, 31; experimentation in, 180; and freshness, 177; interstitial roles in, 2, 15; and plantation system reforms, 128–29; regimes of perceptibility in, 195n11, 200n119; storage, 33, 63, 158, 190n22, 193–94n29; and taste, 31; and taste descriptors, 37–38, 191n33; tea broker role in, 8–9; and tea chemistry, 14

Tea Cultivation, 131–32

Tea Marketing Control Order (TMCO) (India), 64, 65, 169, 172, 194n30

tea plant varieties, 7–8, 100, 187n24

tea research: agricultural experimental stations, 77, 94, 101, 199n91, 200–201n1; Eurocentrism in, 102, 202n19; on factory finishing, 122–23, 124; First Engledow Commission, 105–9, 202n19; IEC report (1931), 88, 105; and postindependence transition, 102–3, 104, 111, 113–14, 119, 120–21, 201n6; Second Engledow Commission, 114–15; and taste descriptors, 36, 104–5; Tea Research Association founding, 100, 104, 121, 124. *See also* tea chemistry research

Tea Research Association (TRA), 36, 100, 104, 121, 124, 140

teauction.com, 152–53, 153*fig*, 155, 161, 168

teawords. *See* taste descriptors

theaflavins, 117

thearubigins, 117

theine, 81, 82

theogallin, 116, 117

TMCO (Tea Marketing Control Order) (India), 64, 65, 169, 172, 194n30

Tocklai Experimental Station, 104, 201n1; clonal tea research, 101; and factory finishing research, 122, 124; First Engledow Commission, 105–9, 202n19; founding of, 101; and postindependence transition, 114, 121; yield research at, 94. *See also* tea chemistry research

Tompkins, Kyla, 195n8

TRA (Tea Research Association), 36, 100, 104, 121, 124, 140

trade liberalization, 170

Treatise from a Medical Point of View on Various Facts Relating to Tea (Harden), 90–92, 93

Tsing, Anna, 133, 134, 137

Tull, D. W., 122

Typhoo, 90, 96

valuation tastings, 45–48, 46*fig*

variability, 3–4; and auction system, 65, 156, 159, 208n14; and blending, 3–4; and experimentation, 180; and plantation system, 23, 26–27; and taste descriptors, 34, 35; and tasting process, 25–26, 189n7

warehouses. *See* storage

Weiss, Brad, 12

Williams, Raymond, 37, 179

wine, taste descriptors for, 36, 190n25, 191nn30–31, 201n12

Wolf, Eric, 190n21

women. *See* gender

World War II, 110, 111, 148, 201n15

yield, 17–18, 94, 100, 106

Zaloom, Caitlin, 207n1, 208n20

Founded in 1893,
UNIVERSITY OF CALIFORNIA PRESS
publishes bold, progressive books and journals
on topics in the arts, humanities, social sciences,
and natural sciences—with a focus on social
justice issues—that inspire thought and action
among readers worldwide.

The UC PRESS FOUNDATION
raises funds to uphold the press's vital role
as an independent, nonprofit publisher, and
receives philanthropic support from a wide
range of individuals and institutions—and from
committed readers like you. To learn more, visit
ucpress.edu/supportus.

www.ingramcontent.com/pod-product-compliance
Lightning Source LLC
Chambersburg PA
CBHW020855270326
41928CB00006B/720